Hey la mama! huh! huh! huh! huh! "

"Hey la mamm

they sang the lion dance; Then

a tell they put her down and everyone

shyly, shook hands. The boys saying

mensahib," and M'cola and the porters all

"mazuri, mama."

afterwards

"Don't worry." Pop said. "You shoot it. M

didn't shoot it?"

you didn't."

"You know I feel as though I did shoot

kill anyone who said you didn't."

"I don't believe I'd be able to stand it if I

had shot it. I'd be too

"Good old

"I believe you did

Ernest Hemingway

GREEN HILLS
OF AFRICA

THE HEMINGWAY LIBRARY EDITION

Foreword by PATRICK HEMINGWAY

Edited with an Introduction by SEÁN HEMINGWAY

Decorations by EDWARD SHENTON

SCRIBNER

New York   London   Toronto   Sydney   New Delhi

SCRIBNER
An Imprint of Simon & Schuster, Inc.
1230 Avenue of the Americas
New York, NY 10020

This Scribner hardcover edition July 2015

SCRIBNER and design are registered trademarks of The Gale Group, Inc.,
used under license by Simon & Schuster, Inc., the publisher of this work.

For information about special discounts for bulk purchases,
please contact Simon & Schuster Special Sales at 1-866-506-1949
or business@simonandschuster.com.

The Simon & Schuster Speakers Bureau can bring authors to your live event.
For more information or to book an event, contact the Simon & Schuster Speakers
Bureau at 1-866-248-3049 or visit our website at www.simonspeakers.com.

Interior design by Brooke Zimmer

Manufactured in the United States of America

1   3   5   7   9   10   8   6   4   2

Library of Congress Cataloging-in-Publication Data is available.

ISBN 978-1-4767-8755-8
ISBN 978-1-4767-8761-9 (ebook)

Endpaper images are pages 51–52 of the handwritten holograph manuscript
of *Green Hills of Africa*. Ernest Hemingway Papers, 1925–1966,
Accession #6250, etc., Clifton Waller Barrett Library of American Literature,
Albert and Shirley Small Special Collections Library, University of Virginia,
Charlottesville, VA. Images courtesy of the University of Virginia Library.

to Philip, to Charles, and to Sully

CONTENTS

FOREWORD

G*reen Hills of Africa*, like Gaul, is divided into parts, specifically four pursuits, of which the last is pursuit as happiness. The American reader will recognize this rearrangement of Jefferson's elegant phrase.

Pursuit as happiness, "isn't it pretty to think so" that ends *The Sun Also Rises*, and a one and only life were the three things my father felt he had to believe. For the rest, he had only to so understand reality as to make up stories readers would feel were real, using short sentences or, if necessary, ones as long as any ever penned by Henry James.

In a trip my parents took me with them to New York in 1935 riding down Fifth Avenue in an open-top bus with my father when I was still just learning to read we got off at the Scribner bookstore for Papa to look at a handsome display of green and black books that now I know was *Green Hills of Africa*. Papa was happy. As I remember, we didn't go in the building, just looked in the window.

Another day in that trip to New York, Papa took me to see the African Hall at the American Museum of Natural History. The African Hall was not yet open to the public and Papa talked with Louis Jonas about his finishing the elephant group started by Carl Akeley and interrupted by his untimely death from fever in the Congo while collecting gorilla specimens for the Hall in what is now Virunga National Park.

Our third excursion was by train north of the city to the Jonas Brothers taxidermy firm to check on the trophy mounts they were doing for my father.

Later the arrival in Key West of Papa's trophy mounts of buffalo, lion, greater kudu, and other antelope tastefully distributed by my mother throughout every room in the house (in the bedroom I shared with my younger brother Gregory it was a wildebeest) made East Africa my promised land. But then, who of us hasn't had a promised land, caught up with happiness, the constant nymph, and run with her swiftly through the green birch forest of Arden only to trip and fall and watch her disappear into the trees without a backward glance? So light a candle, love the light, and face the darkness when the candle fails.

Patrick Hemingway

INTRODUCTION

A WISE MAN ONCE WROTE that hunting is "the old religion."[1] He used the word *religion* in the sense of the Latin term *religio*, meaning to bind people together through repeated rituals. Hunting big game, one of mankind's oldest pursuits, appears in our earliest artistic expressions—the magnificent cave paintings in France and Spain and the petroglyphs of southern and eastern Africa. Hunting was a key activity in ancient societies. It was more than simply a means of sustenance or, as in later times, a way to procure a trophy for display. Take the central place of the American bison in the lives of the first peoples of North America—particularly the Plains Indian tribes who exploited every part of the animal for many uses, from food, clothing, and shelter to tools, medicine, and cultural rituals. On a recent trip to Montana, I stood on the edge of a buffalo jump and looked out across the vast plain that stretched so far that I could see the curvature of the earth. I tried to envision the plain teeming with buffalo, once the most populous large mammal on the planet, and the great hunts that brought down those massive woolly creatures with nothing but the simplest weapons and human ingenuity. It is a sight now left only to the imagination.

Twentieth-century African big-game trophy hunting was practiced for the most part by a small group of some of the wealthiest people in the world; but it carried on, if distantly, the tradition of the royal lion hunts of the ancient Persian and Macedonian kings, which were heralded in art and song as signs of the kings' strength, bravery, and achievement. For Ernest Hemingway, hunting dangerous game in Africa was a personal test of courage, and hunting was for him one of life's great pleasures. No small part of the achievement of *Green Hills of Africa* is the way that Hemingway's writing brings alive for the reader the experience of being part of a motorcar safari on the Serengeti Plains in the 1930s and what it was like to hunt at that time in the Edenic paradise of the Great Rift Valley in East Africa. On one level, *Green Hills of Africa* belongs to a tradition of African hunting safari writing, along with such works as Frederick Selous's *A Hunter's Wanderings in Africa* (1881) and Theodore Roosevelt's *African Game Trails* (1910).[2] However, it is also a departure from these earlier works, since Hemingway wrote it as a novel that combined the act of hunting on safari with the author's thoughts on literature and writing. *Green Hills of Africa* did much to shape the impression of Africa in the minds of its readers, especially those in America and Europe.

Going on an African safari was a major undertaking in the 1930s. Hemingway had probably dreamed of hunting in Africa ever since Teddy Roosevelt returned from his African safari in 1910. His own plans finally materialized in 1930 when Gus Pfeiffer, the wealthy uncle of Hemingway's wife Pauline (see Figure 1), offered to underwrite the exorbitant cost of such an endeavor.[3] The journey started in Key West on August 4, 1933, when Ernest and Pauline Hemingway and their sons Jack and Patrick, along with Pauline's sister, Jinny, boarded a steamer to Havana, Cuba, a country in the midst of a violent revolution. In *Green Hills of Africa*, Hemingway alludes to the coup that ousted Cuban president Gerardo Machado y Morales (an early draft of the scene appears in Appendix IV of this edition).[4] Ernest and Pauline left Havana on August 7 to begin their weeklong transatlantic crossing aboard the *Riena de la Pacifica*, bound for Madrid.[5] Ernest remained in Madrid until late October, preparing for the African expedition, writing, and acquiring new, custom-made leather hunting boots. Pauline, Jinny, and the children went on to Paris, where Pauline made her own preparations for the trip—purchasing a grand traveling jacket, new pajamas, and, among other items, bathrobes for her and Ernest.[6] In Spain, Hemingway took the opportunity to hunt partridge and wild boar to break in his boots before rejoining Pauline. Charles Thompson (Karl in *Green Hills of Africa*), their friend and neighbor from Key West, flew to Paris to join them in November. Shortly before setting out for Africa on November 22, Ernest and Pauline dined with James and Nora Joyce in Paris. Joyce envied them for their impending African adventure and wondered to Hemingway if his own writing was not too suburban. Even Nora exclaimed that perhaps her husband could do with "a spot of that lion hunting."[7]

In planning for the penultimate leg of the journey aboard the SS *General Metzinger* from the port of Marseille, France, to Mombasa, Kenya, Hemingway made a list of their twenty-one pieces of luggage: seven suitcases (three for Charles and four for Ernest and Pauline), five gun cases, one tackle box, one rod case, one gun-cleaning-rod case, one camera case, one trunk, one hatbox, one duffel bag, one shell box, and one zipper bag.[8] Charles and Ernest each brought .30-06 Springfield rifles (see Figure 6) modified by Griffin and Howe, and Pauline brought her Mannlicher-Schönauer 6.5mm rifle (see Figure 5). Ernest had decided that if they should need a double-barreled .470 rifle for large, dangerous game, they could rent one from the safari outfit. For bird shooting he brought his Winchester 12 gauge shotgun and Pauline's Darme 28 gauge double-barreled shotgun.[9]

While cruising the Red Sea aboard the *Metzinger*, Hemingway wrote to his five-year-old son, Patrick, that the weather had been cold and rainy on the Mediterranean Sea and then hot in Egypt, and that they saw camels in the desert while passing through the Suez Canal. He compared the landscape, dotted with palm trees and Australian pines, to that of Key West.[10] On December 8, 1933, Ernest, Pauline, and Charles Thompson arrived in Mombasa, where they spent the night at the Palace Hotel.[11] The next morning they boarded a Kenya-Uganda Railways train for a 330-mile overnight journey to Nairobi. At the New Stanley Hotel in Nairobi, Hemingway finalized the safari arrangements with Tanganyika Guides and secured the services of Philip Percival, who had served as Teddy Roosevelt's professional hunter and hosted many other prominent and wealthy American clients such as George Eastman and Alfred Vanderbilt (grandson of Cornelius).[12] As Percival was not available until December 20, Tanganyika Guides provided some local hunting excursions for antelope and birds on the Kapiti Plain, where Ernest shot a kongoni, a subspecies of hartebeest (see his safari notes of December 15 in Appendix II). Finally, on December 20, nearly a month after they had left Paris, the Hemingways, Charles Thompson, and Philip Percival set out from Percival's farm for the Tanganyika border.

The Great Rift Valley of East Africa, formed at the end of the Cretaceous period after the demise of the dinosaurs, is a complex, unique environment that provides a diverse landscape for plants and animals.[13] As Hemingway notes in his second Tanganyika Letter (see Appendix III), the Serengeti in the 1930s was the premier hunting ground for lions. In the first two weeks they saw eighty-three lions (see Figures 2–4), which was not unusual, and was an indication that at the top of the food chain the ecosystem was working smoothly. As there was an abundance of game, their quota of trophies (see Appendix II and Figure 14 for Hemingway's final list of the haul) did not unfavorably impact the sustainability of wildlife. However, this special environment was already threatened by human encroachment, as Hemingway alludes in *Green Hills of Africa* when Philip Percival suggests that Ernest could always sell a rhinoceros horn if he wanted to do so. It is, indeed, tragic that over the past decades rhinoceroses have been driven out of Tanzania—and, for that matter, can hardly be found in the wild anywhere in Africa. They have been annihilated through systematic poaching with automatic weapons. It is feared that the elephant is on a similar trajectory.[14] Many of the places that my grandfather hunted are now national parks and world heritage sites where visitors may only observe—not hunt—wildlife.

The supplementary material included in this new edition of *Green Hills of Africa* begins with the safari journal (see Figure 12) kept by my grandmother, Pauline Pfeiffer Hemingway, and published here in its entirety for the first time. My uncle Patrick remembers that my grandfather asked my grandmother to keep the journal, which he used as a reference when he wrote *Green Hills of Africa*. Ernest Hemingway had an exceptionally fine memory, and, as Philip Percival later remarked, he did not generally take notes during the safari.[15] Some of the very few notes that he did make were jotted down in the endpapers of a bird book that he had bought in Nairobi (see Figure 13). A transcription of these notes is included in Appendix II of this edition. In addition to the counts of game sightings and animals shot, there is a remarkable description of lions on a zebra kill that reads like a National Geographic documentary on African wildlife. It includes my grandfather's acutely observed description of the tender interaction between lioness and lion.

Pauline's journal records the day-to-day activities of the safari, especially the game pursued and killed. Pauline studied writing at the University of Missouri and received her undergraduate degree in journalism. Before marrying, she was a professional freelance writer and wrote for *Vogue* magazine in Paris and *Vanity Fair*. Her viewpoint is quite different from Ernest's, and her journal adds a fresh perspective and a wealth of additional information recorded on the day each event occurred. How enchanting is her description of sitting on the edge of the Ngorongoro Crater on Christmas Eve and looking out for the first time at the thousands of animals grazing below in a rainy mist. Elsewhere she whimsically likens Mount Kilimanjaro to the Cheshire Cat in *Alice's Adventures in Wonderland* when she describes the way its looming mass appears and disappears on the horizon.

Pauline originally planned to be on safari for only one month (see Appendix II, Ernest Hemingway's introductory letter) and to spend the remaining time abroad with friends while Ernest continued to hunt for another month with Charles.[16] Her primary interest in the safari was sharing the experience with her husband, not securing animal trophies (see Figure 14). Having hunted with Ernest in Montana and Wyoming, she was well aware of the skills and stamina that such an activity required. In her journal, she writes honestly of her difficulties with shooting big game, but maintains a sense of humor about it. She describes her "characteristic good shot, just a l-i-t-t-l-e high, or low or right or left." Pauline also vividly recounts shooting (and missing) her first lion, featured in *Green Hills* as P.O.M.'s lion, and later describes with evident satisfaction the time she successfully shot another, which is not mentioned in Hemingway's novel.

Pauline's journal provides details of the safari that Hemingway chose to leave out of *Green Hills of Africa* and confirms others, such as his fear of snakes. She observes how Ernest missed his mark many times at the beginning of the safari, and she records Philip Percival's comment that everyone misses when they first come out on safari. Early on, she describes an embarrassing moment when Ernest leaves his loaded rifle uncocked on the hood of the car while out hunting. It fell off the hood and landed stock first, discharging and nearly killing him, leaving them both shaken. This real-life scenario sparked the idea for the accidental shooting in Hemingway's short story "The Short Happy Life of Francis Macomber." Pauline also records in detail the progress of Ernest's dysentery, which had a significant impact on the safari but is only alluded to in the book.[17] She writes that his condition got so bad that he had to be flown to Arusha and that it worsened as they waited for the pilot, Fatty Pearson, who finally arrived and flew Hemingway to safety.[18] The episode, as recounted by Pauline, was the real-life inspiration for a similar scene in "The Snows of Kilimanjaro." No doubt Hemingway did not want to dwell on the hazards and uncomfortable aspects of dysentery in his book, fearing it would not sustain the reader's interest. Instead, he wrote briefly and comically about the debilitating effects of the disease in his first Tanganyika Letter for the then newly established *Esquire* magazine, which is included in Appendix III of this edition.

Like the observant, nimble *Vogue* writer she was, Pauline notes in her journal that her nail polish fades within a few hours from the extreme heat and the bright African sunlight. She candidly admits that she does not enjoy the long, dusty rides in the motor vehicles and, after several weeks in the bush as the only female in the group, writes of her dark mood. Growing up very close to her sister, Jinny, she most likely was missing female companionship and was understandably tired of prolonged travel in a remote land. My grandmother was a private person, and is the least understood of Hemingway's wives. Even in her journal, she chooses not to share deeply personal reflections. Gender stereotyping and a lack of knowledge about her nature has led some scholars to characterize Pauline's time on the safari as unhappy and ill-fitted to her chic Parisian lifestyle. They see her as merely playing the role of dutiful wife, misinterpreting Hemingway's comical moniker P.O.M.—"Poor Old Mama"—in *Green Hills of Africa*, which was intended as the counterpart to "Poor Old Papa."[19] On the contrary, my grandmother wrote to her mother-in-law in January 1934 describing how she and Ernest had never had a more perfect time together.[20] She notes that he looks marvelous after having lost so much weight from the dysentery, and that his physique is as hard as nails from all of the hunting.[21] While on the mend in his bed at the New Stanley Hotel in Nairobi, Ernest wrote to his editor, Maxwell Perkins, that Pauline was thrilled with the country.[22] My uncle Patrick and my father, Gregory, shared the impression of the safari as a happy period in my grandparents' married life. They grew up listening to stories of that remarkable adventure and lived with the multitude of African hunting trophies displayed in their home in Key West and afterward at the Finca Vigía in Cuba.[23] Both sons would later go to East Africa to see it for themselves and hunt. Patrick, who also learned how to hunt African big game from Philip Percival, was a successful professional hunter in Tanganyika for many years.[24]

A romantic vision of *Green Hills of Africa* as the pursuit of happiness was passed down to my generation. My father, wanting to share the beauty of East Africa with us, took our family on safari when I was only seven years old, and my parents hunted with my uncle Patrick in Tanzania. As a young man I went on photographic safaris in South Africa, Botswana, and Zimbabwe, and later visited Madagascar, parts of North Africa, and, again, East Africa with my wife. The most vivid and life-changing experience for me was the summer I spent as an apprentice photographic safari guide with Norman Carr in the South Luangwa Valley in Zambia. There, on the southern end of the Great Rift, I lived in the bush for three months and got to know the rhythms of the African wild. Encountering a leopard sitting high in a fig tree with its big yellow eyes shaded from the sun and its tail twitching on alert, walking through Mopane woodlands and sighting a flock of Lilian's lovebirds chattering in a bush that shimmered electric green from their constant movement, and looking an elephant in the eye on a moonlit night are just three of a thousand indelible experiences. Coming to know Africa's amazing natural beauty and delicate, complex web of life have stayed with me as some of the most memorable times of my life. In much the same way, my grandfather describes feeling at one with the land in the last part of his safari in *Green Hills of Africa* when he is hunting alone with his native guide.

When Ernest Hemingway returned to America in April 1934, he stopped first in New York. He told his friend Guy Hickock, in an interview for the *Brooklyn Daily Eagle* (see Figure 15), that he was not going to write a book about Africa for a long time until he could learn more.[25] He proved himself wrong, however, by beginning to write about the safari as soon as he returned to Key West (see Figure 16). At first he thought it would be a short story, but by the end of April he had written fifty pages, thirty of which he discarded.[26] At that point he became determined to write an absolutely true book covering a month's worth of action to see if it could compete with a work of fiction. He realized that he would need all of the skills at his command in order to write it well, and—as he wrote on the back of a manuscript page—if he failed, then he may "simply write good prose and that is worth doing" (see Appendix IV). In May 1934 he wrote to his friend Waldo Peirce that he had completed sixty pages of such a book, and only one month later he had 137 pages.[27] Hemingway worked steadily in Key West, writing in the mornings at the family home on Whitehead Street. Afternoons were spent fishing on his new boat, the *Pilar*. In July 1934 he set off for Havana, where he worked on the book at the Hotel Ambos Mundos in the mornings and fished in the afternoons. By August 14 he had 23,000 words.[28] He continued to work through September, and by October 3 he had some 50,000 words. The first draft, consisting of 491 pages, was finished in Key West on November 16, 1934.

Pauline's day-to-day account in her journal reveals how much Hemingway reshaped the events of the safari into a narrative that does not follow a strictly chronological order. One of the most interesting characters in *Green Hills of Africa* is the Austrian gentleman whose broken-down truck spoils Hemingway's kudu hunt in the opening scene. It was a remarkable coincidence—truth is stranger than fiction—that he had read Hemingway's poetry (still my grandfather's least-known writing) in *Der Querschnitt*, a relatively obscure German avant-garde art magazine. Their literary discussions make for fascinating reading, though some reviewers have questioned the veracity of this encounter and wondered whether the man's conversations with Hemingway were a product of the author's imagination. Pauline's journal, however, confirms his existence—the Austrian gentleman, called Kandisky in the novel, is identified as Hans Koritschoner. In the book, Kandisky tells the safari party that he is fascinated with the natives, particularly with their language and music. He sings for them an African song and performs a traditional tribal dance. In fact, Koritschoner went on to become an important anthropologist of the old school in Tanganyika, publishing many articles and books on local songs, lore, magic, medicine, and tribal customs.[29] His writings show that he was a man of great sensitivity and intelligence. He also had a considerable collection of tribal art.[30] Kandisky's remarks about the value of having a daughter resonated with both Ernest and Pauline, who hoped to have one of their own. Koritschoner later reflected on his chance meeting with the Hemingways and stated that the events recorded in *Green Hills of Africa*—notably the breaking down of his lorry and his knowledge of Hemingway the poet from *Der Querschnitt*—were true, but that the conversation did not take place exactly as quoted. They had had many amusing and interesting conversations over the course of the three days the Hemingways hosted him as their guest.[31]

In total, four working drafts of *Green Hills of Africa* are preserved. The first complete handwritten draft manuscript establishes the essential framework followed by the final version, though Hemingway made many edits to it before he had it typed by his secretary, Jane Armstrong.[32] The original text is one long narrative without chapter or section breaks, which came later. Mainly, Hemingway cut sections from the first draft, especially personal references and references to individuals that anchored the safari in his own experience. In this way, he made the book a timeless experience for the reader, one that the reader could relate to. For example, his conversation with Kandisky in the first draft includes a long list of things that Hemingway likes, which he first shortened and then cut entirely. The cut sections are included in Appendix IV of this edition. Also included in Appendix IV is an alternate draft of the opening of chapter eleven, which contains an amusing defense of social drinking set beneath a brilliantly starry sky in the bush (see Figure 17).

Hemingway continued to make edits to each following draft right up to the time the manuscript was typeset. In many places he revised passages in order to improve them, or added material that does not appear in the first draft. A characteristic example occurs at the end of the novel, when the characters are having lunch by the Dead Sea and Hemingway observes grebes on the water (see Figure 18). He revised the scene in the next draft, adding: "There were many grebes, making spreading wakes in the water as they swam and I was counting them and wondering why they never were mentioned in the Bible. I decided those people were not naturalists."

The handwritten first-draft manuscript was untitled, but between pages ninety-nine and one hundred, during the rhino hunt in hill country, Hemingway wrote two potential titles for the book: "The Highlands of Africa" and "Hunters Are Brothers." "The Highlands of Africa" became Hemingway's working title, which his editor, Maxwell Perkins, tried to convince him to modify to "In the Highlands of Africa" so that readers would not think it simply a travel book.[33] Unlike for many of Hemingway's other books, no lengthy list of alternate titles exists, and it is not clear that he ever wrote one. A third title, written by hand on the first page of the setting copy and then crossed out, is "Africa Is Cold" (see Figure 19). Above this, also handwritten, is nearly the final title that Hemingway settled on: "The Green Hills of Africa." In the last preserved carbon typescript annotated by Hemingway, the title page reads "Green Hills of Africa." His emphasis on the country itself in the title is notable. Clearly not swayed by Perkins's advice, Hemingway chose to call attention to the land, which he knew was good country where he could be happy. It is only with mankind's care and stewardship of the land that wildlife will survive; otherwise, as Hemingway somberly observes at the end of the book, all countries will eventually end up looking like the desolate, barren stretches of windswept Mongolia.

Hemingway sent the revised typescript to Perkins in February 1935. It was decided that they would publish it first in seven parts in *Scribner's Magazine*, along with illustrations by the staff illustrator, Edward Shenton.[34] Shenton's art was so successful that Hemingway and Perkins decided to use a selection of them for the book itself. Although my grandfather generally did not care for illustrated editions of his writings, he was pleased with Shenton's work.[35] This new Hemingway Library Edition of *Green Hills of Africa* also includes a number of black-and-white photographs taken on the safari (see Figures 2–11), especially those of Ernest and Pauline with their trophies.

Chapter breaks and the division into parts came in the setting draft. At that time, Hemingway had divided the book into three sections: "Pursuit and Conversation," "Pursuit Remembered," and "Pursuit as Happiness." In the later carbon typescript, he changed the divisions into four parts, adding, by hand, "Pursuit and Failure" before "Pursuit as Happiness" (see Figure 20). The introductory note about how the book is a true account meant to rival a work of the imagination first appears in this last annotated carbon typescript.

In his acceptance speech for the Nobel Prize in Literature on December 10, 1954, Ernest Hemingway said:

> For a true writer each book should be a new beginning where he tries again for something that is beyond attainment. He should always try for something that has never been done or that others have tried and failed. Then sometimes, with great luck, he will succeed.

With *Green Hills of Africa*, Hemingway was attempting something new by striving to create, using the techniques of fiction writing, a work of nonfiction that would rival a work of fiction. When he finished the manuscript in November 1934, he wrote to Maxwell Perkins that he thought it was his best work yet.[36] It was new and different, but it received only a lukewarm reception from the critics.[37] Sales were moderate even as it became a cherished work among those interested in hunting and photographic safaris in East Africa.[38] While more scholarly attention has been paid to it in recent years, scholars and critics have tended to overlook *Green Hills of Africa* as a minor work in Hemingway's oeuvre.[39] Most rank his later African short stories—"The Short Happy Life of Francis Macomber" and "The Snows of Kilimanjaro"—as better than *Green Hills of Africa*. In many ways they *are* better stories, crafted from the brilliant and well-informed imagination of an exceptional writer. But this is not the point. What is extraordinary about *Green Hills of Africa* is that it was not invented; rather, it is an eloquent and evocative firsthand account of the writer's actual experiences hunting in East Africa. As this edition shows, a great deal of craft went into its creation. It is a book of lasting value about a very special time and place on earth.

Seán Hemingway

AUTHOR'S NOTE

Unlike many novels, none of the characters or incidents in this book is imaginary. Any one not finding sufficient love interest is at liberty, while reading it, to insert whatever love interest he or she may have at the time. The writer has attempted to write an absolutely true book to see whether the shape of a country and the pattern of a month's action can, if truly presented, compete with a work of the imagination.

GREEN HILLS OF AFRICA

PART I

PURSUIT AND CONVERSATION

CHAPTER

WE WERE SITTING in the blind that Wanderobo hunters had built of twigs and branches at the edge of the salt-lick when we heard the truck coming. At first it was far away and no one could tell what the noise was. Then it was stopped and we hoped it had been nothing or perhaps only the wind. Then it moved slowly nearer, unmistakable now, louder and louder until, agonizing in a clank of loud irregular explosions, it passed close behind us to go on up the road. The theatrical one of the two trackers stood up.

"It is finished," he said.

I put my hand to my mouth and motioned him down.

"It is finished," he said again and spread his arms wide. I had never liked him and I liked him less now.

"After," I whispered. M'Cola shook his head. I looked at his bald black skull and he turned his face a little so that I saw the thin Chinese hairs at the corners of his mouth.

"No good," he said. "*Hapana m'uzuri.*"

"Wait a little," I told him. He bent his head down again so that it would not show above the dead branches and we sat there

ONE

in the dust of the hole until it was too dark to see the front sight on my rifle; but nothing more came. The theatrical tracker was impatient and restless. A little before the last of the light was gone he whispered to M'Cola that it was now too dark to shoot.

"Shut up, you," M'Cola told him. "The Bwana can shoot after you cannot see."

The other tracker, the educated one, gave another demonstration of his education by scratching his name, Abdullah, on the black skin of his leg with a sharp twig. I watched without admiration and M'Cola looked at the word without a shadow of expression on his face. After a while the tracker scratched it out.

Finally I made a last sight against what was left of the light and saw it was no use, even with the large aperture.

M'Cola was watching.

"No good," I said.

"Yes," he agreed, in Swahili. "Go to camp?"

"Yes."

We stood up and made our way out of the blind and out through the trees, walking on the sandy loam, feeling our way between trees and under branches, back to the road. A mile along the road was the car. As we came alongside, Kamau, the driver, put the lights on.

The truck had spoiled it. That afternoon we had left the car up the road and approached the salt-lick very carefully. There had been a little rain, the day before, though not enough to flood the lick, which was simply an opening in the trees with a patch of earth worn into deep circles and grooved at the edges with hollows where the animals had licked the dirt for salt, and we had seen long, heart-shaped, fresh tracks of four greater kudu bulls that had been on the salt the night before, as well as many newly pressed tracks of lesser kudu. There was also a rhino who, from the tracks and the kicked-up mound of strawy dung, came there each night. The blind had been built at close arrow-shot of the lick and sitting, leaning back, knees high, heads low, in a hollow half full of ashes and dust, watching through the dried leaves and thin branches I had seen a lesser kudu bull come out of the brush to the edge of the opening where the salt was and stand there, heavy-necked, gray, and handsome, the horns spiralled against the sun while I sighted on his chest and then refused the shot, wanting not to frighten the greater kudu that should surely come at dusk. But before we ever heard the truck the bull had heard it and run off into the trees and everything else that had been moving, in the bush on the flats, or coming down from the small hills through the trees, coming toward the salt, had halted at that exploding, clanking sound. They would come, later, in the dark; but then it would be too late.

So now, going along the sandy track of the road in the car, the lights picking out the eyes of night birds that squatted close on the sand until the bulk of the car was on them and they rose in soft panic; passing the fires of the travellers that all moved to the westward by day along this road, abandoning the famine country that was ahead of us; me sitting, the butt of my rifle on my foot, the barrel in the crook of my left arm, a flask of whiskey between my knees, pouring the whiskey into a tin cup and passing it over my shoulder in the dark for M'Cola to pour water into it from the canteen, drinking this, the first one of the day, the finest one there is, and looking at the thick bush we passed in the dark, feeling the cool wind of the night and smelling the good smell of Africa, I was altogether happy.

Then ahead we saw a big fire and as we came up and passed, I made out a truck beside the road. I told Kamau to stop and go back and as we backed into the firelight there was a short, bandy-legged man with a Tyroler hat, leather shorts, and an open shirt standing before an un-hooded engine in a crowd of natives.

"Can we help?" I asked him.

"No," he said. "Unless you are a mechanic. It has taken a dislike to me. All engines dislike me."

"Do you think it could be the timer? It sounded as though it might be a timing knock when you went past us."

"I think it is much worse than that. It sounds to be something very bad."

"If you can get to our camp we have a mechanic."

"How far is it?"

"About twenty miles."

"In the morning I will try it. Now I am afraid to make it go farther with that noise of death inside. It is trying to die because it dislikes me. Well, I dislike it too. But if I die it would not annoy it."

"Will you have a drink?" I held out the flask. "Hemingway is my name."

"Kandisky," he said and bowed. "Hemingway is a name I have heard. Where? Where have I heard it? Oh, yes. The *Dichter*. You know Hemingway the poet?"

"Where did you read him?"

"In the *Querschnitt*."

"That is me," I said, very pleased. The *Querschnitt* was a German magazine I had written some rather obscene poems for, and published a long story in, years before I could sell anything in America.

"This is very strange," the man in the Tyroler hat said. "Tell me, what do you think of Ringelnatz?"

"He is splendid."

"So. You like Ringelnatz. Good. What do you think of Heinrich Mann?"

"He is no good."

"You believe it?"

"All I know is that I cannot read him."

"He is no good at all. I see we have things in common. What are you doing here?"

"Shooting."

"Not ivory, I hope."

"No. For kudu."

"Why should any man shoot a kudu? You, an intelligent man, a poet, to shoot kudu."

"I haven't shot any yet," I said. "But we've been hunting them hard now for ten days. We would have got one tonight if it hadn't been for your lorry."

"That poor lorry. But you should hunt for a year. At the end of that time you have shot everything and you are sorry for it. To hunt for one special animal is nonsense. Why do you do it?"

"I like to do it."

"Of course, if you *like* to do it. Tell me, what do you really think of Rilke?"

"I have read only the one thing."

"Which?"

"The Cornet."

"You liked it?"

"Yes."

"I have no patience with it. It is snobbery. Valéry, yes. I see the point of Valéry; although there is much snobbery too. Well at least you do not kill elephants."

"I'd kill a big enough one."

"How big?"

"A seventy pounder. Maybe smaller."

"I see there are things we do not agree on. But it is a pleasure to meet one of the great old *Querschnitt* group. Tell me what is Joyce like? I have not the money to buy it. Sinclair Lewis is nothing. I bought it. No. No. Tell me tomorrow. You do not mind if I am camped near? You are with friends? You have a white hunter?"

"With my wife. We would be delighted. Yes, a white hunter."

"Why is he not out with you?"

"He believes you should hunt kudu alone."

"It is better not to hunt them at all. What is he? English?"

"Yes."

"Bloody English?"

"No. Very nice. You will like him."

"You must go. I must not keep you. Perhaps I will see you tomorrow. It was very strange that we should meet."

"Yes," I said. "Have them look at the truck tomorrow. Anything we can do."

"Good night," he said. "Good trip."

"Good night," I said. We started off and I saw him walking toward the fire waving an arm at the natives. I had not asked him why he had twenty up-country natives with him, nor where he was going. Looking back, I had asked him nothing. I do not like to ask questions, and where I was brought up it was not polite. But here we had not seen a white man for two weeks, not since we had left Babati to go south, and then to run into one on this road where you met only an occasional Indian trader and the steady migration of the natives out of the famine country, to have him look like a caricature of Benchley in Tyrolean costume, to have him know your name, to call you a poet, to have read the *Querschnitt*, to be an admirer of Joachim Ringelnatz and to want to talk about Rilke, was too fantastic to deal with. So, just then, to crown this fantasy, the lights of the car showed three tall, conical, mounds of something smoking in the road ahead. I motioned to Kamau to stop, and putting on the brakes we skidded just short of them. They were from two to three feet high and when I touched one it was quite warm.

"*Tembo*," M'Cola said.

It was dung from elephants that had just crossed the road, and in the cold of the evening you could see it steaming. In a little while we were in camp.

Next morning I was up and gone to another salt-lick before daylight. There was a kudu bull on the lick when we approached through the trees and he gave a loud bark, like a dog's but higher in pitch and sharply throaty, and was gone, making no noise at first, then crashing in the brush when he was well away; and we never saw him. This lick had an impossible approach. Trees grew around its open area so that it was as though the game were in the blind and you had to come to them across the open. The only way to make it would have been for one man to go alone and crawl and then it would be impossible to get any sort of a close shot through the interlacing trees until you were within twenty yards. Of course once you were inside the protecting trees, and in the blind, you were wonderfully placed, for anything that came to the salt had to come out in the open twenty-five yards from any cover. But though we stayed until eleven o'clock nothing came. We smoothed the dust of the lick carefully with our feet so that any new tracks would show when we came back again and walked the two miles to the road. Being hunted, the game had learned to come only at night and leave before daylight. One bull had stayed and our spooking him that morning would make it even more difficult now.

This was the tenth day we had been hunting greater kudu and I had not seen a mature bull yet. We had only three days more because the rains were moving north each day from Rhodesia and unless we were prepared to stay where we were through the rains we must be out as far as Handeni before they came. We had set the seventeenth of February as the last safe date to leave. Every morning now it took the heavy, wooled sky an hour or so longer to clear and you could feel the rains coming, as they moved steadily north, as surely as though you watched them on a chart.

Now it is pleasant to hunt something that you want very much over a long period of time, being outwitted, out-manœuvred, and failing at the end of each day, but having the hunt and knowing every time you are out that, sooner or later, your luck will change and that you will get the chance that you are seeking. But it is not pleasant to have a time limit by which you must get your kudu or perhaps never get it, nor even see one.

It is not the way hunting should be. It is too much like those boys who used to be sent to Paris with two years in which to make good as writers or painters after which, if they had not made good, they could go home and into their fathers' business. The way to hunt is for as long as you live against as long as there is such and such an animal; just as the way to paint is as long as there is you and colors and canvas, and to write as long as you can live and there is pencil and paper or ink or any machine to do it with, or anything you care to write about, and you feel a fool, and you are a fool, to do it any other way. But here we were, now, caught by time, by the season, and by the running out of our money, so that what should have been as much fun to do each day whether you killed or not was being forced into that most exciting perversion of life; the necessity of accomplishing something in less time than should truly be allowed for its doing. So, coming in at noon, up since two hours before daylight, with only three days left, I was starting to be nervous about it, and there, at the table under the dining tent fly, talking away, was Kandisky of the Tyroler pants. I had forgotten all about him.

"Hello. Hello," he said. "No success? Nothing doing? Where is the kudu?"

"He coughed once and went away," I said. "Hello, girl."

She smiled. She was worried too. The two of them had been listening since daylight for a shot. Listening all the time, even when our guest had arrived; listening while writing letters, listening while reading, listening when Kandisky came back and talked.

"You did not shoot him?"

"No. Nor see him." I saw that Pop was worried too, and a little nervous. There had evidently been considerable talking going on.

"Have a beer, Colonel," he said to me.

"We spooked one," I reported. "No chance of a shot. There were plenty of tracks. Nothing more came. The wind was blowing around. Ask the boys about it."

"As I was telling Colonel Phillips," Kandisky began, shifting his leather-breeched behind and crossing one heavy-calved, well-haired, bare leg over the other, "you must not stay here too long. You must realize the rains are coming. There is one stretch of twelve miles beyond here you can never get through if it rains. It is impossible."

"So he's been telling me," Pop said. "I'm a Mister, by the way. We use these military titles as nicknames. No offense if you're a Colonel yourself." Then to me, "Damn these salt-licks. If you'd leave them alone you'd get one."

"They ball it all up," I agreed. "You're so sure of a shot sooner or later on the lick."

"Hunt the hills too."

"I'll hunt them, Pop."

"What is killing a kudu, anyway?" Kandisky asked. "You should not take it so seriously. It is nothing. In a year you kill twenty."

"Best not say anything about that to the game department, though," Pop said.

"You misunderstand," Kandisky said. "I mean in a year a man could. Of course no man would wish to."

"Absolutely," Pop said. "If he lived in kudu country, he could. They're the commonest big antelope in this bush country. It's just that when you want to see them you don't."

"I kill nothing, you understand," Kandisky told us. "Why are you not more interested in the natives?"

"We are," my wife assured him.

"They are really interesting. Listen—" Kandisky said, and he spoke on to her.

"The hell of it is," I said to Pop, "when I'm in the hills I'm sure the bastards are down there on the salt. The cows are in the hills but I don't believe the bulls are with them now. Then you get there in the evening and there are the tracks. They *have* been on the lousy salt. I think they come any time."

"Probably they do."

"I'm sure we get different bulls there. They probably only come to the salt every couple of days. Some are certainly spooked because Karl shot that one. If he'd only killed it clean instead of following it through the whole damn countryside. Christ, if he'd only kill any damn thing clean. Other new ones will come in. All we have to do is to wait them out, though. Of course they can't all know about it. But he's spooked this country to hell."

"He gets so very excited," Pop said. "But he's a good lad. He made a beautiful shot on that leopard, you know. You don't want them killed any cleaner than that. Let it quiet down again."

"Sure. I don't mean anything when I curse him."

"What about staying in the blind all day?"

"The damned wind started to go round in a circle. It blew our scent every bloody direction. No bloody use to sit there broadcasting it. If the damn wind would hold. Abdullah took an ash can today."

"I saw him starting off with it."

"There wasn't a bit of wind when we stalked the salt and

there was just light to shoot. He tried the wind with the ashes all the way. I went alone with Abdullah and left the others behind and we went quietly. I had on these crêpe-soled boots and it's soft cotton dirt. The bastard spooked at fifty yards."

"Did you ever see their ears?"'

"Did I ever see their ears? If I can see the bastard's ears, the skinner can work on him."

"They're bastards," Pop said. "I hate this salt-lick business. They're not as smart as we think. The trouble is you're working on them where they are smart. They've been shot at there ever since there's been salt."

"That's what makes it fun," I said. "I'd be glad to do it for a month. I like to hunt sitting on my tail. No sweat. No nothing. Sit there and catch flies and feed them to the ant lions in the dust. I like it. But what about the time?"

"That's it. The bloody time."

"So," Kandisky was saying to my wife. "That is what you should see. The big ngomas. The big native dance festivals. The real ones."

"Listen," I said to Pop. "The other lick, the one I was at last night, is fool-proof except for being near that *bloody* road."

"The trackers say it is really the property of the lesser kudu. It's a long way too. It's eighty miles there and back."

"I know. But there were four *big* bull tracks. It's certain. If it wasn't for that truck last night. What about staying there tonight? Then I'd get the night and the early morning and give this lick a rest. There's a big rhino there too. Big track, anyway."

"Good," Pop said. "Shoot the damn rhino too." He hated to have anything killed except what we were after, no killing on the side, no ornamental killing, no killing to kill, only when you wanted it more than you wanted not to kill it, only when getting it was necessary to his being first in his trade, and I saw he was offering up the rhino to please me.

"I won't kill him unless he's good," I promised.

"Shoot the bastard," Pop said, making a gift of him.

"Ah, Pop," I said.

"Shoot him," said Pop. "You'll enjoy it, being by yourself. You can sell the horn if you don't want it. You've still one on your license."

"So," said Kandisky. "You have arrested a plan of campaign? You have decided on how to outwit the poor animals?"

"Yes," I said. "How is the truck?"

"That lorry is finished," the Austrian said. "In a way I am glad. It was too much of a symbol. It was all that remained of my shamba. Now everything is gone and it is much simpler."

"What is a shamba?" asked P. O. M., my wife. "I've been hearing about them for months. I'm afraid to ask about those words every one uses."

"A plantation," he said. "It is all gone except that lorry. With the lorry I carry laborers to the shamba of an Indian. It is a very rich Indian who raises sisal. I am a manager for this Indian. An Indian can make a profit from a sisal shamba."

"From anything," Pop said.

"Yes. Where we fail, where we would starve, he makes money. This Indian is very intelligent, however. He values me. I represent European organization. I come now from organizing recruitment of the natives. This takes time. It is impressive. I have been away from my family for three months. The organization is organized. You do it in a week as easily, but it is not so impressive."

"And your wife?" asked mine.

"She waits at my house, the house of the manager, with my daughter."

"Does she love you very much?" my wife asked.

"She must, or she would be gone long ago."

"How old is the daughter?"

"She is thirteen now."

"It must be very nice to have a daughter."

"You cannot know how nice it is. It is like a second wife. My wife knows now all I think, all I say, all I believe, all I can do, all that I cannot do and cannot be. I know also about my wife—completely. But now there is always someone you do not know, who does not know you, who loves you in ignorance and is strange to you both. Some one very attractive that is yours and not yours and that makes the conversation more—how shall I say? Yes, it is like—what do you call—having here with you—with the two of you—yes there— It is the Heinz Tomato Ketchup on the daily food."

"That's very good," I said.

"We have books," he said. "I cannot buy new books now but we can always talk. Ideas and conversation are very interesting. We discuss all things. Everything. We have a very interesting mental life. Formerly, with the shamba, we had the *Querschnitt*. That gave you a feeling of belonging, of being made a part of, to a very brilliant group of people. The people one would see if one saw whom one wished to see. You know all of those people? You must know them."

"Some of them," I said. "Some in Paris. Some in Berlin."

I did not wish to destroy anything this man had, and so I did not go into those brilliant people in detail.

"They're marvellous," I said, lying.

"I envy you to know them," he said. "And tell me, who is the greatest writer in America?"

"My husband," said my wife.

"No. I do not mean for you to speak from family pride. I mean who really? Certainly not Upton Sinclair. Certainly not Sinclair Lewis. Who is your Thomas Mann? Who is your Valéry?"

"We do not have great writers," I said. "Something happens to our good writers at a certain age. I can explain but it is quite long and may bore you."

"Please explain," he said. "This is what I enjoy. This is the best part of life. The life of the mind. This is not killing kudu."

"You haven't heard it yet," I said.

"Ah, but I can see it coming. You must take more beer to loosen your tongue."

"It's loose," I told him. "It's always too bloody loose. But *you* don't drink anything."

"No, I never drink. It is not good for the mind. It is unnecessary. But tell me. Please tell me."

"Well," I said, "we have had, in America, skillful writers. Poe is a skillful writer. It is skillful, marvellously constructed, and it is dead. We have had writers of rhetoric who had the good fortune to find a little, in a chronicle of another man and from voyaging, of how things, actual things, can be, whales for instance, and this knowledge is wrapped in the rhetoric like plums in a pudding. Occasionally it is there, alone, unwrapped in pudding, and it is good. This is Melville. But the people who praise it, praise it for the rhetoric which is not important. They put a mystery in which is not there."

"Yes," he said. "I see. But it is the mind working, its ability to work, which makes the rhetoric. Rhetoric is the blue sparks from the dynamo."

"Sometimes. And sometimes it is only blue sparks and what is the dynamo driving?"

"So. Go on."

"I've forgotten."

"No. Go on. Do not pretend to be stupid."

"Did you ever get up before daylight——"

"Every morning," he said. "Go on."

"All right. There were others who wrote like exiled English colonials from an England of which they were never a part to a newer England that they were making. Very good men with the small, dried, and excellent wisdom of Unitarians; men of letters; Quakers with a sense of humor."

"Who were these?"

"Emerson, Hawthorne, Whittier, and Company. All our early classics who did not know that a new classic does not bear any resemblance to the classics that have preceded it. It can steal from anything that it is better than, anything that is not a classic, all classics do that. Some writers are only born to help another writer to write one sentence. But it cannot derive from or resemble a previous classic. Also all these men were gentlemen, or wished to be. They were all very respectable. They did not use the words that people always have used in speech, the words that survive in language. Nor would you gather that they had bodies. They had minds, yes. Nice, dry, clean minds. This is all very dull, I would not state it except that you ask for it."

"Go on."

"There is one at that time that is supposed to be really good, Thoreau. I cannot tell you about it because I have not yet been able to read it. But that means nothing because I cannot read other naturalists unless they are being extremely accurate and not literary. Naturalists should all work alone and some one else should correlate their findings for them. Writers should work alone. They should see each other only after their work is done, and not too often then. Otherwise they become like writers in New York. All angleworms in a bottle, trying to derive knowledge and nourishment from their own contact and from the bottle. Sometimes the bottle is shaped art, sometimes economics, sometimes economic-religion. But once they are in the bottle they stay there. They are lonesome outside of the bottle. They do not want to be lonesome. They are afraid to be alone in their beliefs and no woman would love any of them enough so that they could kill their lonesomeness in that woman, or pool it with hers, or make something with her that makes the rest unimportant."

"But what about Thoreau?"

"You'll have to read him. Maybe I'll be able to later. I can do nearly everything later."

"Better have some more beer, Papa."

"All right."

"What about the good writers?"

"The good writers are Henry James, Stephen Crane, and Mark Twain. That's not the order they're good in. There is no order for good writers."

"Mark Twain is a humorist. The others I do not know."

"All modern American literature comes from one book by Mark Twain called *Huckleberry Finn*. If you read it you must stop where the Nigger Jim is stolen from the boys. That is the real end. The rest is just cheating. But it's the best book we've had. All American writing comes from that. There was nothing before. There has been nothing as good since."

"What about the others?"

"Crane wrote two fine stories. *The Open Boat* and *The Blue Hotel*. The last one is the best."

"And what happened to him?"

"He died. That's simple. He was dying from the start."

"But the other two?"

"They both lived to be old men but they did not get any wiser as they got older. I don't know what they really wanted. You see we make our writers into something very strange."

"I do not understand."

"We destroy them in many ways. First, economically. They

make money. It is only by hazard that a writer makes money although good books always make money eventually. Then our writers when they have made some money increase their standard of living and they are caught. They have to write to keep up their establishments, their wives, and so on, and they write slop. It is slop not on purpose but because it is hurried. Because they write when there is nothing to say or no water in the well. Because they are ambitious. Then, once they have betrayed themselves, they justify it and you get more slop. Or else they read the critics. If they believe the critics when they say they are great then they must believe them when they say they are rotten and they lose confidence. At present we have two good writers who cannot write because they have lost confidence through reading critics. If they wrote, sometimes it would be good and sometimes not so good and sometimes it would be quite bad, but the good would get out. But they have read the critics and they must write masterpieces. The masterpieces the critics said they wrote. They weren't masterpieces, of course. They were just quite good books. So now they cannot write at all. The critics have made them impotent."

"Who are these writers?"

"Their names would mean nothing to you and by now they may have written, become frightened, and be impotent again."

"But what is it that happens to American writers? Be definite."

"I was not here in the old days so I cannot tell you about them, but now there are various things. At a certain age the men writers change into Old Mother Hubbard. The women writers become Joan of Arc without the fighting. They become leaders. It doesn't matter who they lead. If they do not have followers they invent them. It is useless for those selected as followers to protest. They are accused of disloyalty. Oh, hell. There are too many things that happen to them. That is one thing. The others try to save their souls with what they write. That is an easy way out. Others are ruined by the first money, the first praise, the first attack, the first time they find they cannot write, or the first time they cannot do anything else, or else they get frightened and join organizations that do their thinking for them. Or they do not know what they want. Henry James wanted to make money. He never did, of course."

"And you?"

"I am interested in other things. I have a good life but I must write because if I do not write a certain amount I do not enjoy the rest of my life."

"And what do you want?"

"To write as well as I can and learn as I go along. At the same time I have my life which I enjoy and which is a damned good life."

"Hunting kudu?"

"Yes. Hunting kudu and many other things."

"What other things?"

"Plenty of other things."

"And you know what you want?"

"Yes."

"You really like to do this, what you do now, this silliness of kudu?"

"Just as much as I like to be in the Prado."

"One is not better than the other?"

"One is as necessary as the other. There are other things, too."

"Naturally. There must be. But this sort of thing means some-thing to you, really?"

"Truly."

"And you know what you want?"

"Absolutely, and I get it all the time."

"But it takes money."

"I could always make money and besides I have been very lucky."

"Then you are happy?"

"Except when I think of other people."

"Then you think of other people?"

"Oh, yes."

"But you do nothing for them?"

"No."

"Nothing?"

"Maybe a little."

"Do you think your writing is worth doing—as an end in itself?"

"Oh, yes."

"You are sure?"

"Very sure."

"That must be very pleasant."

"It is," I said. "It is the one altogether pleasant thing about it."

"This is getting awfully serious," my wife said.

"It's a damned serious subject."

"You see, he is really serious about something," Kandisky said. "I knew he must be serious on something besides kudu."

"The reason every one now tries to avoid it, to deny that it is important, to make it seem vain to try to do it, is because it is so difficult. Too many factors must combine to make it possible."

"What is this now?"

"The kind of writing that can be done. How far prose can be carried if any one is serious enough and has luck. There is a fourth and fifth dimension that can be gotten."

"You believe it?"

"I know it."

"And if a writer can get this?"

"Then nothing else matters. It is more important than anything he can do. The chances are, of course, that he will fail. But there is a chance that he succeeds."

"But that is poetry you are talking about."

"No. It is much more difficult than poetry. It is a prose that has never been written. But it can be written, without tricks and without cheating. With nothing that will go bad afterwards."

"And why has it not been written?"

"Because there are too many factors. First, there must be talent, much talent. Talent such as Kipling had. Then there must be discipline. The discipline of Flaubert. Then there must be the conception of what it can be and an absolute conscience as unchanging as the standard meter in Paris, to prevent faking. Then the writer must be intelligent and disinterested and above all he must survive. Try to get all these in one person and have him come through all the influences that press on a writer. The hardest thing, because time is so short, is for him to survive and get his work done. But I would like us to have such a writer and to read what he would write. What do you say? Should we talk about something else?"

"It is interesting what you say. Naturally I do not agree with everything."

"Naturally."

"What about a gimlet?" Pop asked. "Don't you think a gimlet might help?"

"Tell me first what are the things, the actual, concrete things that harm a writer?"

I was tired of the conversation which was becoming an interview. So I would make it an interview and finish it. The necessity to put a thousand intangibles into a sentence, now, before lunch, was too bloody.

"Politics, women, drink, money, ambition. And the lack of politics, women, drink, money and ambition," I said profoundly.

"He's getting much too easy now," Pop said.

"But drink. I do not understand about that. That has always seemed silly to me. I understand it as a weakness."

"It is a way of ending a day. It has great benefits. Don't you ever want to change your ideas?"

"Let's have one," Pop said. "M'Wendi!"

Pop never drank before lunch except as a mistake and I knew he was trying to help me out.

"Let's all have a gimlet," I said.

"I never drink," Kandisky said. "I will go to the lorry and fetch some fresh butter for lunch. It is fresh from Kandoa, un-salted. Very good. Tonight we will have a special dish of Viennese dessert. My cook has learned to make it very well."

He went off and my wife said: "You were getting awfully profound. What was that about all these women?"

"What women?"

"When you were talking about women."

"The hell with them," I said. "Those are the ones you get involved with when you're drunk."

"So that's what you do."

"No."

"I don't get involved with people when I'm drunk."

"Come, come," said Pop. "We're none of us ever drunk. My God, that man can talk."

"He didn't have a chance to talk after B'wana M'Kumba started."

"I did have verbal dysentery," I said.

"What about his lorry? Can we tow it in without ruining ours?"

"I think so," Pop said. "When ours comes back from Handeni."

At lunch under the green fly of the dining tent, in the shade of a big tree, the wind blowing, the fresh butter much admired, Grant's gazelle chops, mashed potatoes, green corn, and then mixed fruit for dessert, Kandisky told us why the East Indians were taking the country over.

"You see, during the war they sent the Indian troops to fight here. To keep them out of India because they feared another mutiny. They promised the Aga Khan that because they fought in Africa, Indians could come freely to settle and for business afterwards. They cannot break that promise and now the Indians have taken the country over from the Europeans. They live on nothing and they send all the money back to India. When they have made enough to go home they leave, bringing out their poor relations to take over from them and continue to exploit the country."

Pop said nothing. He would not argue with a guest at table.

"It is the Aga Khan," Kandisky said. "You are an American. You know nothing of these combinations."

"Were you with Von Lettöw?" Pop asked him.

"From the start," Kandisky said. "Until the end."

"He was a great fighter," Pop said. "I have great admiration for him."

"You fought?" Kandisky asked.

"Yes."

"I do not care for Lettöw," Kandisky said. "He fought, yes. No one ever better. When we wanted quinine he would order it captured. All supplies the same. But afterwards he cared nothing for his men. After the war I am in Germany. I go to see about indemnification for my property. 'You are an Austrian,' they say. 'You must go through Austrian channels.' So I go to Austria. 'But why did you fight?' they ask me. 'You cannot hold us responsible. Suppose you go to fight in China. That is your own affair. We cannot do anything for you.'

" 'But I went as a patriot,' I say, very foolishly. 'I fight where I can because I am an Austrian and I know my duty.' 'Yes,' they say. 'That is very beautiful. But you cannot hold us responsible for your noble sentiments! So they passed me from one to the other and nothing. Still I love the country very much. I have lost everything here but I have more than anyone has in Europe. To me it is always interesting. The natives and the language. I have many books of notes on them. Then too, in reality, I am a king here. It is very pleasant. Waking in the morning I extend one foot and the boy places the sock on it. When I am ready I extend the other foot and he adjusts the other sock. I step from under the mosquito bar into my drawers which are held for me. Don't you think that is very marvellous?"

"It's marvellous."

"When you come back another time we must take a safari to study the natives. And shoot nothing, or only to eat. Look, I will show you a dance and sing a song."

Crouched, elbows lifting and falling, knees humping, he shuffled around the table, singing. Undoubtedly it was very fine.

"That is only one of a thousand," he said. "Now I must go for a time. You will be sleeping."

"There's no hurry. Stay around."

"No. Surely you will be sleeping. I also. I will take the butter to keep it cool."

"We'll see you at supper," Pop said.

"Now you must sleep. Good-bye."

After he was gone, Pop said: "I wouldn't believe all that about the Aga Khan, you know."

"It sounded pretty good."

"Of course he feels badly," Pop said. "Who wouldn't. Von Lettöw was a hell of a man."

"He's very intelligent," my wife said. "He talks wonderfully about the natives. But he's bitter about American women."

"So am I," said Pop. "He's a good man. You better get some shut-eye. You'll need to start about three-thirty."

"Have them call me."

Molo raised the back of the tent, propping it with sticks, so the wind blew through and I went to sleep reading, the wind coming in cool and fresh under the heated canvas.

When I woke it was time to go. There were rain clouds in the sky and it was very hot. They had packed some tinned fruit, a five-pound piece of roast meat, bread, tea, a tea pot, and some tinned milk in a whiskey box with four bottles of beer. There was a canvas water bag and a ground cloth to use as a tent. M'Cola was taking the big gun out to the car.

"There's no hurry about getting back," Pop said. "We'll look for you when we see you."

"All right."

"We'll send the truck to haul that sportsman into Handeni. He's sending his men ahead walking."

"You're sure the truck can stand it? Don't do it because he's a friend of mine."

"Have to get him out. The truck will be in tonight."

"The Memsahib's still asleep," I said. "Maybe she can get out for a walk and shoot some guineas."

"I'm here," she said. "Don't worry about us. *Oh,* I hope you get them."

"Don't send out to look for us along the road until day after tomorrow," I said. "If there's a good chance we'll stay."

"Good luck."

"Good luck, sweet. Good-bye, Mr. J. P."

CHAPTER

WE WERE OUT FROM under the shade of camp and along the sandy river of a road, driving into the western sun, the bush thick to the edge of the sand, solid as a thicket, the little hills rising above it, and all along the road we passed groups of people making their way to the westward. Some were naked except for a greasy cloth knotted over one shoulder, and carried bows and sealed quivers of arrows. Others carried spears. The wealthy carried umbrellas and wore draped white cloth and their women walked behind them, with their pots and pans. Bundles and loads of skins were scattered along ahead on the heads of other natives. All were travelling away from the famine. And in the heat, my feet out over the side of the car to keep them away from the heat of the engine, hat low over the eyes against the sun, watching the road, the people, and all clearings in the bush for game, we drove to the westward.

Once we saw three lesser kudu cows in an open place of broken bush. Gray, big bellied, long necked, small headed, and with big ears, they moved quickly into the woods and were gone. We left the car and tracked them but there was no bull track.

TWO

A little beyond there a flock of guineas quick-legged across the road running steady-headed with the motion of trotters. As I jumped from the car and sprinted after them they rocketed up, their legs tucked close beneath them, heavy-bodied, short wings drumming, cackling, to go over the trees ahead. I dropped two that thumped hard when they fell and as they lay, wings beating, Abdullah cut their heads off so they would be legal eating. He put them in the car where M'Cola sat laughing; his old man's healthy laugh, his making-fun-of-me laugh, his bird-shooting laugh that dated from a streak of raging misses one time that had delighted him. Now when I killed, it was a joke as when we shot a hyena; the funniest joke of all. He laughed always to see the birds tumble and when I missed he roared and shook his head again and again.

"Ask him what the hell he's laughing about?" I asked Pop once.

"At B'wana," M'Cola said, and shook his head, "at the little birds."

"He thinks you're funny," Pop said.

"Goddam it. I am funny. But the hell with him."

"He thinks you're very funny," Pop said. "Now the Memsahib and I would never laugh."

"Shoot them yourself."

"No, you're the bird shot. The self-confessed bird shot," she said.

So bird shooting became this marvellous joke. If I killed, the joke was on the birds and M'Cola would shake his head and laugh and make his hands go round and round to show how the bird turned over in the air. And if I missed, I was the clown of the piece and he would look at me and shake with laughing. Only the hyenas were funnier.

Highly humorous was the hyena obscenely loping, full belly dragging, at daylight on the plain, who, shot from the stern, skittered on into speed to tumble end over end. Mirth provoking was the hyena that stopped out of range by an alkali lake to look back and, hit in the chest, went over on his back, his four feet and his full belly in the air. Nothing could be more jolly than the hyena coming suddenly wedge-headed and stinking out of high grass by a *donga,* hit at ten yards, who raced his tail in three narrowing, scampering circles until he died.

It was funny to M'Cola to see a hyena shot at close range. There was that comic slap of the bullet and the hyena's agitated surprise to find death inside of him. It was funnier to see a hyena shot at a great distance, in the heat shimmer of the plain, to see him go over backwards, to see him start that frantic circle, to see that electric speed that meant that he was racing the little nickelled death inside him. But the great joke of all, the thing M'Cola waved his hands across his face about, and turned away and shook his head and laughed, ashamed even of the hyena; the pinnacle of hyenic humor, was the hyena, the classic hyena, that hit too far back while running, would circle madly, snapping and tearing at himself until he pulled his own intestines out, and then stood there, jerking them out and eating them with relish.

"*Fisi,*" M'Cola would say and shake his head in delighted sorrow at there being such an awful beast. *Fisi,* the hyena, hermaphroditic, self-eating devourer of the dead, trailer of calving cows, ham-stringer, potential biter-off of your face at night while you slept, sad yowler, camp-follower, stinking, foul, with jaws that crack the bones the lion leaves, belly dragging, loping away on the brown plain, looking back, mongrel dog-smart in the face; whack from the little Mannlicher and then the horrid circle starting. "*Fisi,*" M'Cola laughed, ashamed of him, shaking his bald black head. "*Fisi.* Eats himself. *Fisi.*"

The hyena was a dirty joke but bird shooting was a clean joke. My whiskey was a clean joke. There were many variations of that joke. Some we come to later. The Mohammedans and all religions were a joke. A joke on all the people who had them. Charo, the other gun bearer, was short, very serious and highly religious. All Ramadan he never swallowed his saliva until sunset and when the sun was almost down I'd see him watching nervously. He had a bottle with him of some sort of tea and he would finger it and watch the sun and I would see M'Cola watching him and pretending not to see. This was not outrightly funny to him. This was something that he could not laugh about openly but that he felt superior to and wondered at the silliness of it. The Mohammedan religion was very fashionable and all the higher social grades among the boys were Mohammedans. It was something that gave caste, something to believe in, something fashionable and god-giving to suffer a little for each year, something that made you superior to other people, something that gave you more complicated habits of eating, something that I understood and M'Cola did not understand, nor care about, and he watched Charo watch for the sun to set with that blank look on his face that it put on about all things that he was not a part of. Charo was deadly thirsty and truly devout and the sun set very slowly. I looked at it, red over the trees, nudged him and he grinned. M'Cola offered me the water bottle solemnly. I shook my head and Charo grinned again. M'Cola looked blank. Then the sun was down and Charo had the bottle tilted up, his Adam's apple rising and falling greedily and M'Cola looking at him and then looking away.

In the early days, before we became good friends, he did not trust me at all. When anything came up he went into this blankness. I liked Charo much better then. We understood each other on the question of religion and Charo admired my shooting and always shook hands and smiled when we had killed anything particularly good. This was flattering and pleasing. M'Cola looked on all this early shooting as a series of lucky accidents. We were supposed to shoot. We had not yet shot anything that amounted to anything and he was not really my gun bearer. He was Mr. Jackson Phillips' gun bearer and he had been loaned to me. I meant nothing to him. He did not like me nor dislike me. He was politely contemptuous of Karl. Who he liked was Mama.

The evening we killed the first lion it was dark when we came in sight of camp. The killing of the lion had been confused and unsatisfactory. It was agreed beforehand that P. O. M. should have the first shot but since it was the first lion any of us had ever shot at, and it was very late in the day, really too late to take the lion on, once he was hit we were to make a dogfight of it and any one was free to get him. This was a good plan as it was nearly sundown and if the lion got into cover, wounded, it would be too dark to do anything about it without a mess. I remember seeing the lion looking yellow and heavy-headed and enormous against a scrubby-looking tree in a patch of orchard bush and P. O. M. kneeling to shoot and wanting to tell her to sit down and make sure of him. Then there was the short-barrelled explosion of the Mannlicher and the lion was going to the left on a run, a strange, heavy-shouldered, foot-swinging, cat run. I hit him with the Springfield and he went down and spun over and I shot again, too quickly, and threw a cloud of dirt over him. But there he was, stretched out, on his belly, and, with the sun just over the top of the trees, and the grass very green, we walked up on him like a posse, or a gang of Black and Tans, guns ready and cocked, not knowing whether he was stunned or dead. When we were close M'Cola threw a stone at him. It hit him in the flank and from the way it hit you could tell he was a dead animal. I was sure P. O. M. had hit him but there was only one bullet hole, well back, just below the spine and ranging forward to come to the surface under the skin of the chest. You could feel the bullet under the skin and M'Cola made a slit and cut it out. It was a 220-grain solid bullet from the Springfield and it had raked him, going through lungs and heart.

I was so surprised by the way he had rolled over dead from the shot after we had been prepared for a charge, for heroics, and for drama, that I felt more let down than pleased. It was our first lion and we were very ignorant and this was not what we had paid to see. Charo and M'Cola both shook P. O. M.'s hand and then Charo came over and shook hands with me.

"Good shot, B'wana," he said in Swahili. "*Piga m'uzuri.*"

"Did you shoot, Karl?" I asked.

"No. I was just going to when you shot."

"You didn't shoot him, Pop?"

"No. You'd have heard it." He opened the breech and took out the two big .450 No. 2's.

"I'm sure I missed him," P. O. M. said.

"I was sure you hit him. I still think you hit him," I said.

"Mama hit," M'Cola said.

"Where?" Charo asked.

"Hit," said M'Cola. "Hit."

"You rolled him over," Pop said to me. "God, he went over like a rabbit."

"I couldn't believe it."

"Mama *piga,*" M'Cola said. "*Piga Simba.*"

As we saw the camp fire in the dark ahead of us, coming in that night, M'Cola suddenly commenced to shout a stream of high-pitched, rapid, singing words in Wakamba ending in the word "*Simba.*" Some one at the camp shouted back one word.

"Mama!" M'Cola shouted. Then another long stream. Then "Mama! Mama!"

Through the dark came all the porters, the cook, the skinner, the boys, and the headman.

"Mama!" M'Cola shouted. "*Mama piga Simba.*"

The boys came dancing, crowding, and beating time and chanting something from down in their chests that started like a cough and sounded like "*Hey la Mama! Hay la Mama! Hey la Mama!*"

The rolling-eyed skinner picked P. O. M. up, the big cook and the boys held her, and the others pressing forward to lift, and if not to lift to touch and hold, they danced and sang through the dark, around the fire and to our tent.

"*Hey la Mama! huh! huh! huh! Hay la Mama! huh! huh! huh!*" they sang the lion dance with that deep, lion asthmatic cough in it. Then at the tent they put her down and every one, very shyly, shook hands, the boys saying "*m'uzuri, Memsahib*," and M'Cola and the porters all saying "*m'uzuri,* Mama" with much feeling in the accenting of the word "Mama."

Afterwards in the chairs in front of the fire, sitting with the drinks, Pop said, "You shot it. M'Cola would kill any one who said you didn't."

"You know, I feel as though I did shoot it," P. O. M. said. "I don't believe I'd be able to stand it if I really had shot it. I'd be too proud. Isn't triumph marvellous?"

"Good old Mama," Karl said.

"I believe you did shoot him," I said.

"Oh, let's not go into that," P. O. M. said. "I feel so wonderful about just being supposed to have killed him. You know people never used to carry me on their shoulders much at home."

"No one knows how to behave in America," Pop said. "Most uncivilized."

"We'll carry you in Key West," Karl said. "Poor old Mama."

"Let's not talk about it," P. O. M. said. "I like it too much. Shouldn't I maybe distribute largess?"

"They didn't do it for that," Pop said. "But it is all right to give something to celebrate."

"Oh, I want to give them all a great deal of money," P. O. M. said. "Isn't triumph simply marvellous?"

"Good old Mama," I said. "You killed him."

"No I didn't. Don't lie to me. Just let me enjoy my triumph."

Anyway M'Cola did not trust me for a long time. Until P. O. M.'s license ran out, she was his favorite and we were simply a lot of people who interfered and kept Mama from shooting things. Once her license was out and she was no longer shooting, she dropped back into non-combatant status with him and as we began to hunt kudu and Pop stayed in camp and sent us out alone with the trackers, Karl with Charo and M'Cola and I together, M'Cola dropped Pop visibly in his estimation. It was only temporary of course. He was Pop's man and I believe his working estimations were only from day to day and required an unbroken series of events to have any meaning. But something had happened between us.

GREEN HILLS OF AFRICA

PART II

Pursuit Remembered

CHAPTER

I T DATED BACK TO the time of Droopy, after I had come back
from being ill in Nairobi and we had gone on a foot safari to
hunt rhino in the forest. Droopy was a real savage with lids to his
eyes that nearly covered them, handsome, with a great deal of style,
a fine hunter and a beautiful tracker. He was about thirty-five, I
should think, and wore only a piece of cloth, knotted over one
shoulder, and a fez that some hunter had given him.

He always carried a spear. M'Cola wore an old U. S. Army
khaki tunic, complete with buttons, that had originally been
brought out for Droopy who had been away somewhere and had
missed getting it. Twice Pop had brought it out for Droopy and
finally M'Cola had said, "Give it to me."

Pop had let him have it and M'Cola had worn it ever since. It,
a pair of shorts, his fuzzy wool curler's cap, and a knitted army
sweater he wore when washing the tunic, were the only garments
I ever saw on the old man until he took my bird-shooting coat.
For shoes he used sandals cut from old motor-car tires. He had
slim, handsome legs with well-turned ankles on the style of Babe
Ruth's and I remember how surprised I was the first time I saw

THREE

him with the tunic off and noticed how old his upper body was. It had that aged look you see in photographs of Jeffries and Sharkey posing thirty years after, the ugly, old-man biceps and the fallen pectoral muscles.

"How old is M'Cola?" I asked Pop.

"He must be over fifty," Pop said. "He's got a grown-up family in the native reserve."

"How are his kids?"

"No good, worthless. He can't handle them. We tried one as a porter. But he was no good."

M'Cola was not jealous of Droopy. He simply knew that Droop was a better man than he was. More of a hunter, a faster and a cleaner tracker, and a great stylist in everything he did. He admired Droopy in the same way we did and being out with him, it made him realize that he was wearing Droopy's tunic and that he had been a porter before he became a gun bearer and suddenly he ceased being an old timer and we were hunting together; he and I hunting together and Droopy in command of the show.

That had been a fine hunt. The afternoon of the day we came

into the country we walked about four miles from camp along a deep rhino trail that graded through the grassy hills with their abandoned orchard-looking trees, as smoothly and evenly as though an engineer had planned it. The trail was a foot deep in the ground and smoothly worn and we left it where it slanted down through a divide in the hills like a dry irrigation ditch and climbed, sweating, the small, steep hill on the right to sit there with our backs against the hilltop and glass the country. It was a green, pleasant country, with hills below the forest that grew thick on the side of a mountain, and it was cut by the valleys of several watercourses that came down out of the thick timber on the mountain. Fingers of the forest came down onto the heads of some of the slopes and it was there, at the forest edge, that we watched for rhino to come out. If you looked away from the forest and the mountain side you could follow the watercourses and the hilly slope of the land down until the land flattened and the grass was brown and burned and, away, across a long sweep of country, was the brown Rift Valley and the shine of Lake Manyara.

We all lay there on the hillside and watched the country carefully for rhino. Droopy was on the other side of the hilltop, squatted on his heels, looking, and M'Cola sat below us. There was a cool breeze from the east and it blew the grass in waves on the hillsides. There were many large white clouds and the tall trees of the forest on the mountain side grew so closely and were so foliaged that it looked as though you could walk on their tops. Behind this mountain there was a gap and then another mountain and the far mountain was dark blue with forest in the distance.

Until five o'clock we did not see anything. Then, without the glasses, I saw something moving over the shoulder of one of the valleys toward a strip of the timber. In the glasses it was a rhino, showing very clear and minute at the distance, red-colored in the sun, moving with a quick waterbug-like motion across the hill. Then there were three more of them that came out of the forest, dark in the shadow, and two that fought, tinily, in the glasses, pushing head-on, fighting in front of a clump of bushes while we watched them and the light failed. It was too dark to get down the hill, across the valley and up the narrow slope of mountain side to them in time for a shot. So we went back to the camp, down the hill in the dark, edging down on our shoes and then feeling the trail smooth under foot, walking along that deep trail, that wound through the dark hills, until we saw the firelight in the trees.

We were excited that night because we had seen the three rhino and early the next morning while we were eating breakfast before starting out, Droopy came in to report a herd of buffalo he had found feeding at the edge of the forest not two miles from camp. We went there, still tasting coffee and kippers in the early morning heart-pounding of excitement, and the native Droopy had left watching them pointed where they had crossed a deep gulch and gone into an open patch of forest. He said there were two big bulls in a herd of a dozen or more. We followed them in, moving very quietly on the game trails, pushing the vines aside and seeing the tracks and the quantities of fresh dung, but though we went on into the forest where it was too thick to shoot and made a wide circle, we did not see or hear them. Once we heard the tick birds and saw them flying, but that was all. There were numbers of rhino trails there in the woods and many strawy piles of dung, but we saw nothing but the green wood-pigeons and some monkeys, and when we came out we were wet to our waists from the dew and the sun was quite high. The day was very hot, now before the wind had gotten up, and we knew whatever rhino and buffalo had been out would have gone back deep into the forest to rest out of the heat.

The others started back to camp with Pop and M'Cola. There was no meat in camp and I wanted to hunt back in a circle with Droopy to see if we could kill a piece. I was beginning to feel strong again after the dysentery and it was a pleasure to walk in the easy rolling country, simply to walk, and to be able to hunt, not knowing what we might see and free to shoot for the meat we needed. Then, too, I liked Droopy and liked to watch him walk. He strode very loosely and with a slight lift, and I liked to watch him and to feel the grass under my soft-soled shoes and the pleasant weight of the rifle, held just back of the muzzle, the barrel resting on my shoulder, and the sun hot enough to sweat you well as it burned the dew from the grass; with the breeze starting and the country like an abandoned New England orchard to walk through. I knew that I was shooting well again and I wanted to make a shot to impress Droopy.

From the top of one rise we saw two kongoni showing yellow on a hillside about a mile away and I motioned to Droop that we would go after them. We started down and in a ravine jumped a waterbuck bull and two cows. Waterbuck was the one animal we might get that I knew was worthless as meat and I had shot a better head than this one carried. I had the sights on the buck as he tore away, remembered about the worthless meat, and having the head, and did not shoot.

"No shoot kuro?" Droopy asked in Swahili. "*Doumi sana*. A good bull."

I tried to tell him that I had a better one and that it was no good to eat.

He grinned.

"*Piga kongoni m'uzuri.*"

"Piga" was a fine word. It sounded exactly as the command to fire should sound or the announcement of a hit. "M'uzuri," meaning good, well, better, had sounded too much like the name of a state for a long time and walking I used to make up sentences in Swahili with Arkansas and M'uzuri in them, but now it seemed natural, no longer to be italicized, just as all the words came to seem the proper and natural words and there was nothing odd or unseemly in the stretching of the ears, in the tribal scars, or in a man carrying a spear. The tribal marks and the tattooed places seemed natural and handsome adornments and I regretted not having any of my own. My own scars were all informal, some irregular and sprawling, others simply puffy welts. I had one on my forehead that people still commented on, asking if I had bumped my head; but Droop had handsome ones beside his cheekbones and others, symmetrical and decorative, on his chest and belly. I was thinking that I had one good one, a sort of embossed Christmas tree, on the bottom of my right foot that only served to wear out socks, when we jumped two reedbuck. They went off through the trees and then stood at sixty yards, the thin, graceful buck looking back, and I shot him high and a touch behind the shoulder. He gave a jump and went off very fast.

"Piga." Droopy smiled. We had both heard the whunk of the bullet.

"Kufa," I told him. "Dead."

But when we came up to him, lying on his side, his heart was still beating strongly, although to all appearances he was dead. Droopy had no skinning knife and I had only a penknife to stick him with. I felt for the heart behind the foreleg with my fingers and feeling it beating under the hide slipped the knife in but it was short and pushed the heart away. I could feel it, hot and rubbery against my fingers, and feel the knife push it, but I felt around and cut the big artery and the blood came hot against my fingers. Once bled, I started to open him, with the little knife, still show-ing off to Droopy, and emptying him neatly took out the liver, cut away the gall, and laying the liver on a hummock of grass, put the kidneys beside it.

Droopy asked for the knife. Now he was going to show me something. Skilfully he slit open the stomach and turned it inside, tripe side, out, emptying the grass in it on the ground, shook it, then put the liver and kidneys inside it and with the knife cut a switch from the tree the buck lay under and sewed the stomach together with the withe so that the tripe made a bag to carry the other delicacies in. Then he cut a pole and put the bag on the end of it, running it through the flaps, and put it over his shoulder in the way tramps carried their property in a handkerchief on the end of a stick in Blue Jay corn plaster advertisements when we were children. It was a good trick and I thought how I would show it to John Staib in Wyoming some time and he would smile his deaf man's smile (you had to throw pebbles at him to make him stop when you heard a bull bugle), and I knew what John would say. He would say, "By Godd, Urnust, dot's smardt."

Droop handed me the stick, then took off his single garment, made a sling and got the buck up on his back. I tried to help him and suggested by signs that we cut a pole and sling him, carrying him between us, but he wanted to carry him alone. So we started for camp, me with the tripe bag on the end of a stick over my shoulder, my rifle slung, and Droopy staggering steadily ahead, sweating heavily, under the buck. I tried to get him to hang him in a tree and leave him until we could send out a couple of por-ters, and to that end we put him in the crotch of a tree. But when Droop saw that I meant to go off and leave him there rather than simply allow him to drain he got him down onto his shoulders again and we went on into camp, the boys, around the cooking fire, all laughing at the tripe bag over my shoulder as we came in.

This was the kind of hunting that I liked. No riding in cars, the country broken up instead of the plains, and I was completely happy. I had been quite ill and had that pleasant feeling of getting stronger each day. I was underweight, had a great appetite for meat, and could eat all I wanted without feeling stuffy. Each day I sweated out whatever we drank sitting at the fire at night, and in the heat of the day, now, I lay in the shade with a breeze in the trees and read with no obligation and no compulsion to write, happy in knowing that at four o'clock we would be starting out to hunt again. I would not even write a letter. The only person I really cared about, except the children, was with me and I had no wish to share this life with any one who was not there, only to live it, being completely happy and quite tired. I knew that I was shooting well and I had that feeling of well being and confidence that is so much more pleasant to have than to hear about.

As it turned out, we started soon after three to be on the hill by four. But it was nearly five before we saw the first rhino come bustling short-leggedly across the ridge of hill in almost the same place we had seen the rhino the night before. We saw where he went into the edge of the forest near where we had seen the two fighting and then took a course that would lead us down the hill, across the grown-over gully at the bottom, and up the steep slope to where there was a thorn tree with yellow blossoms that marked the place where we had seen the rhino go in.

Coming straight up the slope in sight of the thorn tree, the wind blowing across the hill, I tried to walk as slowly as I could and put a handkerchief inside the sweatband of my hat to keep the perspiration out of my glasses. I expected to shoot at any minute and I wanted to slow up enough so my heart would not be pounding. In shooting large animals there is no reason ever to miss if you have a clear shot and can shoot and know where to shoot, unless you are unsteady from a run or a climb or fog your glasses, break them or run out of cloth or paper to wipe them clean. The glasses were the biggest hazard and I used to carry four handkerchiefs and change them from the left to the right pocket when they were wet.

We came up to the yellow blossomed tree very carefully, like

people walking up to a covey of quail the dogs have pointed, and
the rhino was not in sight. We went all through the edge of the
forest and it was full of tracks and fresh rhino sign, but there
was no rhino. The sun was setting and it was getting too dark to
shoot, but we followed the forest around the side of the mountain, hoping to see a rhino in the open glades. When it was almost
too dark to shoot, I saw Droopy stop and crouch. With his head
down he motioned us forward. Crawling up, we saw a large rhino
and a small one standing chest deep in brush, facing us across a
little valley.

"Cow and calf," Pop said softly. "Can't shoot her. Let me
look at her horn." He took the glasses from M'Cola.

"Can she see us?" P. O. M. asked.

"No."

"How far are they?"

"Must be nearly five hundred yards."

"My God, she looks big," I whispered.

"She's a big cow," Pop said. "Wonder what became of the
bull?" He was pleased and excited by the sight of game. "Too
dark to shoot unless we're right on him."

The rhinos had turned and were feeding. They never seemed
to move slowly. They either bustled or stood still.

"What makes them so red?" P. O. M. asked.

"Rolling in the mud," Pop answered. "We better get along
while there's light."

The sun was down when we came out of the forest and looked
down the slope and across to the hill where we had watched from
with our glasses. We should have back-tracked and gone down,
crossed the gulch, and climbed back up the trail the way we had
come but we decided, like fools, to grade straight across the
mountain side below the edge of the forest. So in the dark, following this ideal line, we descended into steep ravines that showed
only as wooded patches until you were in them, slid down, clung
to vines, stumbled and climbed and slid again, down and down,
then steeply, impossibly, up, hearing the rustle of night things and
the cough of a leopard hunting baboons; me scared of snakes and
touching each root and branch with snake fear in the dark.

To go down and up two hands-and-knee-climbing ravines and
then out into the moonlight and the long, too-steep shoulder of

mountain that you climbed one foot up to the other, one foot after the other, one stride at a time, leaning forward against the grade and the altitude, dead tired and gun weary, single file in the moonlight across the slope, on up and to the top where it was easy, the country spread in the moonlight, then up and down and on, through the small hills, tired but now in sight of the fires and on into camp.

So then you sit, bundled against the evening chill, at the fire, with a whiskey and soda, waiting for the announcement that the canvas bath had been a quarter filled with hot water.

"*Bathi,* B'wana."

"God damn it, I could never hunt sheep again," you say.

"I never could," says P. O. M. "You all made me."

"You climbed a damn sight better than any of us."

"Do you suppose we could hunt sheep again, Pop?"

"I wonder," Pop said. "I suppose it's merely condition."

"It's riding in the damned cars that ruins us."

"If we did that walk every night we could come back in three nights from now and never feel it."

"Yes. But I'd be as scared of snakes if we did it every night for a year."

"You'd get over it."

"No," I said. "They scare me stiff. Do you remember that time we touched hands behind the tree?"

"Rather," said Pop. "You jumped two yards. Are you really afraid of them, or only talking?"

"They scare me sick," I said. "They always have."

"What's the matter with you men?" P. O. M. said. "Why haven't I heard anything about the war tonight?"

"We're too bloody tired. Were you in the war, Pop?"

"Not me," said Pop. "Where is that boy with the whiskey?" Then calling in that feeble, clowning falsetto, "Kayti—Katy-ay!"

"*Bathi,*" said Molo again softly, but insistently.

"Too tired."

"Memsahib *bathi,*" Molo said hopefully.

"I'll go," said P. O. M. "But you two hurry up with your drinking. I'm hungry."

"*Bathi,*" said Kayti severely to Pop.

"*Bathi* yourself," said Pop. "Don't bully me."

Kayti turned away in fire-lit slanting smile.

"All right. All right," said Pop. "Going to have one?" he asked.

"We'll have just one," I said, "and then we'll *bathi.*"

"Bathi, B'wana M'Kumba," Molo said. P. O. M. came toward the fire wearing her blue dressing gown and mosquito boots.

"Go on," she said. "You can have another when you come out. There's nice, warm, muddy water."

"They bully us," Pop said.

"Do you remember the time we were sheep hunting and your hat blew off and nearly fell onto the ram?" I asked her, the whiskey racing my mind back to Wyoming.

"Go take your bathi," P. O. M. said. "I'm going to have a gimlet."

In the morning we were dressed before daylight, ate breakfast, and were hunting the forest edge and the sunken valleys where Droop had seen the buffalo before the sun was up. But they were not there. It was a long hunt and we came back to camp and decided to send the trucks for porters and move with a foot safari to where there was supposed to be water in a stream that came down out of the mountain beyond where we had seen the rhinos the night before. Being camped there we could hunt a new country along the forest edge and we would be much closer to the mountain.

The trucks were to bring in Karl from his kudu camp where he seemed to be getting disgusted, or discouraged, or both, and he could go down to the Rift Valley the next day and kill some meat and try for an oryx. If we found good rhino we would send for him. We did not want to fire any shots where we were going except at rhino in order not to scare them, and we needed meat. The rhino seemed very shy and I knew from Wyoming how the shy game will all shift out of a small country, a country being an area, a valley or range of hills, a man can hunt in, after a shot or two. We planned this all out, Pop consulting with Droopy, and then sent the trucks off with Dan to recruit porters.

Late in the afternoon they were back with Karl, his outfit, and forty M'Bulus, good looking savages with a pompous headman who wore the only pair of shorts among them. Karl was thin now, his skin sallow, his eyes very tired looking and he seemed a little desperate. He had been eight days in the kudu camp in the hills, hunting hard, with no one with him who spoke any English, and they had only seen two cows and jumped a bull out of range. The guides claimed they had seen another bull but Karl had thought it was a kongoni, or that they said it was a kongoni, and had not shot. He was bitter about this and it was not a happy outfit.

"I never saw his horns. I don't believe it was a bull," he said. Kudu hunting was a touchy subject with him now and we let it alone.

"He'll get an oryx down there and he'll feel better," Pop said. "It's gotten on his nerves a little."

Karl agreed to the plan for us to move ahead into the new country and for him to go down for meat.

"Whatever you say," he said. "Absolutely whatever you say."

"It will give him some shooting," Pop said. "Then he'll feel better."

"We'll get one. Then you get one. Whoever gets his first can go on down after oryx. You'll probably get an oryx tomorrow anyway when you're hunting meat."

"Whatever you say," Karl said. His mind was bitterly revolving eight blank days of hill climbing in the heat, out before daylight, back at dark, hunting an animal whose Swahili name he could not then remember, with trackers in whom he had no confidence, coming back to eat alone, no one to whom he could talk, his wife nine thousand miles and three months away, and how was his dog and how was his job, and god-damn it where were they and what if he missed one when he got a shot, he wouldn't, you never missed when it was really important, he was sure of that, that was one of the tenets of his faith, but what if he got excited and missed, and why didn't he get any letters, what did the guide say kongoni for that time, they did, he knew they did, but he said nothing of all that, only, "Whatever you say," a little desperately.

"Come on, cheer up, you bastard," I said.

"I'm cheerful. What's the matter with you?"

"Have a drink."

"I don't want a drink. I want a god-damned kudu."

Later Pop said, "I thought he'd do well off by himself with no one to hurry him or rattle him. He'll be all right. He's a good lad."

"He wants some one to tell him exactly what to do and still leave him alone and not rattle him," I said. "It's hell for him to shoot in front of everybody. He's not a damned show-off like me."

"He made a damned fine shot at that leopard," Pop said.

"Two of them," I said. "The second was as good as the first. Hell, he can shoot. On the range he'll shoot the pants off of any of us. But he worries about it and I rattle him trying to get him to speed up."

"You're a little hard on him sometimes," Pop said.

"Hell, he knows me. He knows what I think of him. He doesn't mind."

"I still think he'll find himself off by himself," Pop said. "It's just a question of confidence. He's really a good shot."

"Hell, he's got the best buff, the best waterbuck, and the best lion, now," I said. "He's got nothing to worry about."

"The Memsahib has the best lion, brother. Don't make any mistake about that."

"I'm glad of that. But he's got a damned fine lion and a big leopard. Everything he has is good. We've got plenty of time. He's got nothing to worry about. What the hell is he so gloomy about?"

"We'll get an early start in the morning so we can finish it off before it gets too hot for the little Memsahib."

"She's in the best shape of any one."

"She's marvellous. She's like a little terrier."

We went out that afternoon and glassed the country from the hills and never saw a thing. That night after supper we were in the tent. P. O. M. disliked intensely being compared to a little terrier. If she must be like any dog, and she did not wish to be, she would prefer a wolfhound, something lean, racy, long-legged and ornamental. Her courage was so automatic and so much a simple state of being that she never thought of danger; then, too, danger was in the hands of Pop and for Pop she had a complete, clear-seeing, absolutely trusting adoration. Pop was her ideal of how a man should be, brave, gentle, comic, never losing his temper, never bragging, never complaining except in a joke, tolerant, understanding, intelligent, drinking a little too much as a good man should, and, to her eyes, very handsome.

"Don't you think Pop's handsome?"

"No," I said. "Droopy's handsome."

"Droopy's *beautiful*. But don't you *really* think Pop's handsome?"

"Hell, no. I like him as well as any man I've ever known, but I'm damned if he's handsome."

"I think he's lovely looking. But you understand about how I feel about him, don't you?"

"Sure. I'm as fond of the bastard myself."

"But *don't* you think he's handsome, really?"

"Nope."

Then, a little later:

"Well, who's handsome to you?"

"Belmonte and Pop. And you."

"Don't be patriotic," I said. "Who's a beautiful woman?"

"Garbo."

"Not any more. Josie is. Margot is."

"Yes, they are. I know I'm not."

"You're lovely."

"Let's talk about Mr. J. P. I don't like you to call him Pop. It's not dignified."

"He and I aren't dignified together."

"Yes, but I'm dignified with him. Don't you think he's wonderful?"

"Yes, and he doesn't have to read books written by some female he's tried to help get published saying how he's yellow."

"She's just jealous and malicious. You never should have helped her. Some people never forgive that."

"It's a damned shame, though, with all that talent gone to malice and nonsense and self-praise. It's a god-damned shame, really. It's a shame you never knew her before she went to pot. You know a funny thing; she never could write dialogue. It was terrible. She learned how to do it from my stuff and used it in that book. She had never written like that before. She never could forgive learning that and she was afraid people would notice it, where she'd learned it, so she had to attack me. It's a funny racket, really. But I swear she was damned nice before she got ambitious. You would have liked her then, really."

"Maybe, but I don't think so," said P. O. M. "We have fun though, don't we? Without all those people."

"God damn it if we don't. I've had a better time every year since I can remember."

"But isn't Mr. J. P. wonderful? Really?"

"Yes. He's wonderful."

"Oh, you're nice to say it. Poor Karl."

"Why?"

"Without his wife."

"Yes," I said. "Poor Karl."

CHAPTER

S O IN THE MORNING, again, we started ahead of the porters
and went down and across the hills and through a deeply
forested valley and then up and across a long rise of country with
high grass that made the walking difficult and on and up and
across, resting sometimes in the shade of a tree, and then on and
up and down and across, all in high grass, now, that you had
to break a trail in, and the sun was very hot. The five of us in
single file, Droop and M'Cola with a big gun apiece, hung with
musettes and water bottles and the cameras, we all sweating in
the sun, Pop and I with guns and the Memsahib trying to walk
like Droopy, her Stetson tilted on one side, happy to be on a trip,
pleased about how comfortable her boots were, we came finally
to a thicket of thorn trees over a ravine that ran down from the
side of a ridge to the water and we leaned the guns against the
trees and went in under the close shade and lay on the ground.
P. O. M. got the books out of one of the musettes and she and
Pop read while I followed the ravine down to the little stream that
came out of the mountain side, and found a fresh lion track and
many rhino tunnels in the tall grass that came higher than your

FOUR

head. It was very hot climbing back up the sandy ravine and I was glad to lean my back against the tree trunk and read in Tolstoi's *Sevastopol*. It was a very young book and had one fine description of fighting in it, where the French take the redoubt and I thought about Tolstoi and about what a great advantage an experience of war was to a writer. It was one of the major subjects and certainly one of the hardest to write truly of and those writers who had not seen it were always very jealous and tried to make it seem unimportant, or abnormal, or a disease as a subject, while, really, it was just something quite irreplaceable that they had missed. Then Sevastopol made me think of the Boulevard Sevastopol in Paris, about riding a bicycle down it in the rain on the way home from Strassburg and the slipperiness of the rails of the tram cars and the feeling of riding on greasy, slippery asphalt and cobble stones in traffic in the rain, and how we had nearly lived on the Boulevard du Temple that time, and I remembered the look of that apartment, how it was arranged, and the wall paper, and instead we had taken the upstairs of the pavilion in Notre Dame des Champs in the courtyard with the sawmill *(and the sudden whine of the saw, the smell of sawdust and the chestnut tree over the roof with a mad woman downstairs)* and the year worrying about money *(all of the stories back in the mail that came in through a slit in the saw-mill door, with notes of rejection that would never call them stories, but always anecdotes, sketches, contes, etc. They did not want them, and we lived on poireaux and drank cahors and water)* and how fine the fountains were at the Place de L'Observatoire *(water sheen rippling on the bronze of horses' manes, bronze breasts and shoulders, green under thin-flowing water)* and when they put up the bust of Flaubert in the Luxembourg on the short cut through the gardens on the way to the rue Soufflot *(one that we believed in, loved without criticism, heavy now in stone as an idol should be).* He had not seen war but he had seen a revolution and the Commune and a revolution is much the best if you do not become bigoted because every one speaks the same language. Just as civil war is the best war for a writer, the most complete. Stendhal had seen a war and Napoleon taught him to write. He was teaching everybody then; but no one else learned. Dostoevsky was made by being sent to Siberia. Writers are forged in injustice as a sword is forged. I wondered if it would make a writer of him, give him the necessary shock to cut the over-flow of words and give him a sense of proportion, if they sent Tom Wolfe to Siberia or to the Dry Tortugas. Maybe it would and maybe it wouldn't. He seemed sad, really, like Carnera. Tolstoi was a small man. Joyce was of medium height and he wore his eyes out. And that last night, drunk, with Joyce and the thing he kept quoting from Edgar Quinet, "Fraîche et rose comme au jour de la bataille." I didn't have it right I knew. And when you saw him he would take up a conversation interrupted three years before. It was nice to see a great writer in our time.

What I had to do was work. I did not care, particularly, how it all came out. I did not take my own life seriously any more, any one else's life, yes, but not mine. They all wanted something that I did not want and I would get it without wanting it, if I worked. To work was the only thing, it was the one thing that always made you feel good, and in the meantime it was my own damned life and I would lead it where and how I pleased. And where I had led it now pleased me very much. This was a better sky than Italy.

The hell it was. The best sky was in Italy and Spain and Northern Michigan in the fall and in the fall in the Gulf off Cuba. You could beat this sky; but not the country.

All I wanted to do now was get back to Africa. We had not left it, yet, but when I would wake in the night I would lie, listening, homesick for it already.

Now, looking out the tunnel of trees over the ravine at the sky with white clouds moving across in the wind, I loved the country so that I was happy as you are after you have been with a woman that you really love, when, empty, you feel it welling up again and there it is and you can never have it all and yet what there is, now, you can have, and you want more and more, to have, and be, and live in, to possess now again for always, for that long, sudden-ended always; making time stand still, sometimes so very still that afterwards you wait to hear it move, and it is slow in starting. But you are not alone, because if you have ever really loved her happy and untragic, she loves you always; no matter whom she loves nor where she goes she loves you more. So if you have loved some woman and some country you are very fortunate and, if you die afterwards it makes no difference. Now, being in Africa, I was hungry for more of it, the changes of the seasons, the rains with no need to travel, the discomforts that you paid to make it real, the names of the trees, of the small animals, and all the birds, to know the language and have time to be in it and to move slowly. I had loved country all my life; the country was always better than the people. I could only care about people a very few at a time.

P. O. M. was sleeping. She was always lovely to look at asleep, sleeping quietly, close curled like an animal, with nothing of the being dead look that Karl had asleep. Pop slept quietly too, you could see his soul was close in his body. His body no longer housed him fittingly. It had gone on and changed, thickening here, losing its lines, bloating a little there, but inside he was young and lean and tall and hard as when he galloped lion on the plain below Wami, and the pouches under his eyes were all outside, so that now I saw him asleep the way P. O. M. saw him always. M'Cola was an old man asleep, without history and without mystery. Droopy did not sleep. He sat on his heels and watched for the safari.

We saw them coming a long way off. At first the boxes just showed above the high grass, then a line of heads, then they were in a hollow, and there was only the point of a spear in the sun, then they came up a rise of ground and I could see the strung out line coming toward us. They had gone a little too far to the left and Droopy waved to signal them toward us. They made camp, Pop warning them to be quiet, and we sat under the dining tent and were comfortable in the chairs and talked. That night we hunted and saw nothing. The next morning we hunted and saw nothing and the next evening the same. It was very interesting but there were no results. The wind blew hard from the east and the ground was broken in short ridges of hills coming down close from the forest so you could not get above it without sending your scent on ahead of you on the wind to warn everything. You could not see into the sun in the evening, nor on the heavy shadowed hillsides to the west, beyond which the sun was setting at the time the rhino would be coming out of the forest; so all the country to the westward was a loss in the evening and in the country we could hunt we found nothing. Meat came in from Karl's camp by some porters we sent back. They came in carrying quarters of tommy, Grant, and wildebeeste, dusty, the meat seared dry by the sun, and the porters were happy, crouched around their fires roasting the meat on sticks. Pop was puzzled why the rhino were all gone. Each day we had seen less and we discussed whether it could be the full moon, that they fed out at night and were back in the forest in the morning before it was light, or that they winded us, or heard the men, and were simply shy and kept in the forest, or what was it? Me putting out the theories, Pop pricking them with his wit, sometimes considering them from politeness, sometimes with interest, like the one about the moon.

We went to bed early and in the night it rained a little, not a real rain but a shower from the mountains, and in the morning we were up before daylight and had climbed up to the top of the steep grassy ridge that looked down onto the camp, onto the ravine of the river bed, and across to the steep opposite bank of the stream, and from where we could see all the hilly slopes and the edge of the forest. It was not yet light when some geese flew overhead and the light was still too gray to be able to see the edge of the forest clearly in the glasses. We had scouts out on three different hill tops and we were waiting for it to be light enough for us to see them if they signalled.

Then Pop said, "Look at that son of a bitch," and shouted at M'Cola to bring the rifles. M'Cola went jumping down the hill, and across the stream, directly opposite us, a rhino was running with a quick trot along the top of the bank. As we watched he speeded up and came, fast trotting, angling down across the face of the bank. He was a muddy red, his horn showed clearly, and there was nothing ponderous in his quick, purposeful movement. I was very excited at seeing him.

"He'll cross the stream," Pop said. "He's shootable."

M'Cola put the Springfield in my hand and I opened it to make sure I had solids. The rhino was out of sight now but I could see the shaking of the high grass.

"How far would you call it?"

"All of three hundred."

"I'll bust the son of a bitch."

I was watching, freezing myself deliberately inside, stopping the excitement as you close a valve, going into that impersonal state you shoot from.

He showed, trotting into the shallow, boulder filled stream. Thinking of one thing, that the shot was perfectly possible, but that I must lead him enough, must get ahead, I got on him, then well ahead of him, and squeezed off. I heard the *whonk* of the bullet and, from his trot, he seemed to explode forward. With a whooshing snort he smashed ahead, splashing water and snorting. I shot again and raised a little column of water behind him, and shot again as he went into the grass; behind him again.

"Piga," M'Cola said. "Piga!"

Droopy agreed.

"Did you hit him?" Pop said.

"Absolutely," I said. "I think I've got him."

Droopy was running and I re-loaded and ran off after him. Half the camp was strung out across the hills waving and yelling. The rhino had come in right below where they were and gone on up the valley toward where the forest came close down into the head of the valley.

Pop and P. O. M. came up. Pop with his big gun and M'Cola carrying mine.

"Droopy will get the tracks," Pop said. "M'Cola swears you hit him."

"Piga!" M'Cola said.

"He snorted like a steam engine," P. O. M. said. "Didn't he look wonderful going along there?"

"He was late getting home with the milk," Pop said. "Are you *sure* you hit him? It was a godawful long shot."

"I *know* I hit him. I'm *pretty* sure I've killed him."

"Don't tell any one if you did," Pop said. "They'll never believe you. Look! Droopy's got blood."

Below, in the high grass Droop was holding up a grass blade toward us. Then, stooped, he went on trailing fast by the blood spoor.

"Piga," M'Cola said. "M'uzuri!"

"We'll keep up above where we can see if he makes a break," Pop said. "Look at Droopy."

Droop had removed his fez and held it in his hand.

"That's all the precautions he needs," Pop said. "We bring up a couple of heavy guns and Droopy goes in after him with one article less of clothing."

Below us Droopy and his partner who was trailing with him had stopped. Droopy held up his hand.

"They hear him," Pop said. "Come on."

We started toward them. Droopy came toward us and spoke to Pop.

"He's in there," Pop whispered. "They can hear the tick birds. One of the boys says he heard the faro, too. We'll go in against the wind. You go ahead with Droopy. Let the Memsahib stay behind me. Take the big gun. All right."

The rhino was in high grass, somewhere in there behind some bushes. As we went forward we heard a deep, moaning sort of groan. Droopy looked around at me and grinned. The noise came again, ending this time like a blood-choked sigh. Droopy was laughing. "Faro," he whispered and put his hand palm open on the side of his head in the gesture that means to go to sleep. Then in a jerky-flighted, sharp-beaked little flock we saw the tick birds rise and fly away. We knew where he was and, as we went slowly forward, parting the high grass, we saw him. He was on his side, dead.

"Better shoot him once to make sure," Pop said.

M'Cola handed me the Springfield he had been carrying. I noticed it was cocked, looked at M'Cola, furious with him, kneeled down and shot the rhino in the sticking place. He never moved. Droopy shook my hand and so did M'Cola.

"He had that damned Springfield cocked," I said to Pop. The cocked gun, behind my back, made me black angry.

That meant nothing to M'Cola. He was very happy, stroking the rhino's horn, measuring it with his fingers spread, looking for the bullet hole.

"It's on the side he's lying on," I said.

"You should have seen him when he was protecting Mama," Pop said. "That's why he had the gun cocked."

"Can he shoot?"

"No," Pop said. "But he would."

"Shoot me in the pants," I said. "Romantic bastard." When the whole outfit came up, we rolled the rhino into a sort of kneeling position and cut away the grass to take some pictures. The bullet hole was fairly high in the back, a little behind the lungs.

"That was a hell of a shot," Pop said. "A hell of a shot. Don't ever tell any one you made that one."

"You'll have to give me a certificate."

"That would just make us both liars. They're a strange beast, aren't they?"

There he was, long-hulked, heavy-sided, prehistoric looking, the hide like vulcanized rubber and faintly transparent looking, scarred with a badly healed horn wound that the birds had pecked at, his tail thick, round, and pointed, flat many-legged ticks crawling on him, his ears fringed with hair, tiny pig eyes, moss growing on the base of his horn that grew out forward from his nose. M'Cola looked at him and shook his head. I agreed with him. This was the hell of an animal.

"How is his horn?"

"It isn't bad," Pop said. "It's nothing extra. That was a hell of a shot you made on him though, brother."

"M'Cola's pleased with it," I said.

"You're pretty pleased with it yourself," P. O. M. said.

"I'm crazy about it," I said. "But don't let me start on it. Don't worry about how I feel about it. I can wake up and think about that any night."

"And you're a good tracker, and a hell of a fine bird shot, too," Pop said. "Tell us the rest of that."

"Lay off me. I only said that once when I was drunk."

"Once," said P. O. M. "Doesn't he tell us that every night?"

"By God, I *am* a good bird shot."

"Amazing," said Pop. "I never would have thought it. What else is it you do?"

"Oh, go to hell."

"Musn't ever let him realize what a shot that was or he'll get unbearable," Pop said to P. O. M.

"M'Cola and I know," I said.

M'Cola came up. "M'uzuri, B'wana," he said. "M'uzuri sana."

"He thinks you did it on purpose," Pop said.

"Don't you ever tell him different."

"Piga m'uzuri," M'Cola said. "M'uzuri."

"I believe he feels just the way you do about it," Pop said.

"He's my pal."

"I believe he is, you know," Pop said.

On our way back across country to our main camp I made a fancy shot on a reedbuck at about two hundred yards, offhand, breaking his neck at the base of the skull. M'Cola was very pleased and Droopy was delighted.

"We've got to put a stop to him," Pop said to P. O. M. "Where did you shoot for, really?"

"In the neck," I lied. I had held full on the center of the shoulder.

"It was awfully pretty," P. O. M. said. The bullet had made a crack when it hit like a baseball bat swung against a fast ball and the buck had collapsed without a move.

"I think he's a damned liar," Pop said.

"None of us great shots is appreciated. Wait till we're gone."

"His idea of being appreciated is for us to carry him on our shoulders," Pop said. "That rhino shot has ruined him."

"All right. You watch from now on. Hell, I've shot well the whole time."

"I seem to remember a Grant of some sort," Pop was teasing. So did I remember him. I'd followed a fine one out of the country missing shot after shot all morning after a series of stalks in the heat, then crawled up to an ant hill to shoot one that was not nearly as good, taken a rest on the ant hill, missed the buck at fifty yards, seen him stand facing me, absolutely still, his nose up, and shot him in the chest. He went over backwards and as I went up to him he jumped up and went off, staggering. I sat down and waited for him to stop and when he did, obviously anchored, I sat there, using the sling, and shot for his neck, slowly and carefully, missing him eight times straight in a mounting, stubborn rage, not making a correction but shooting exactly for the same place in the same way each time, the gun bearers all laughing, the truck that had come up with the outfit holding more amused niggers, P. O. M. and Pop saying nothing, me sitting there cold, crazy-stubborn-furious, determined to break his neck rather than walk up and perhaps start him off over that heat-hazy, baking, noontime plain. Nobody said anything. I reached up my hand to M'Cola for more cartridges, shot again, carefully, and missed, and on the tenth shot broke his damned neck. I turned away without looking toward him.

"Poor Papa," P. O. M. said.

"It's the light and the wind," Pop said. We had not known each other very well then. "They were all hitting the same place. I could see them throw the dust."

"I was a damned bloody stubborn fool," I said.

Anyway, I could shoot now. So far, and aided by flukes, my luck was running now.

We came on into sight of camp and shouted. No one came out. Finally Karl came out of his tent. He went back in as soon as he saw us, then came out again.

"Hey, Karl," I yelled. He waved and went back in the tent again. Then came toward us. He was shaky with excitement and I saw he had been washing blood off his hands.

"What is it?"

"Rhino," he said.

"Did you get in trouble with him?"

"No. We killed him."

"Fine. Where is he?"

"Over there behind that tree."

We went over. There was the newly severed head of a rhino that was a rhino. He was twice the size of the one I had killed. The little eyes were shut and a fresh drop of blood stood in the corner of one like a tear. The head bulked enormous and the horn swept up and back in a fine curve. The hide was an inch thick where it hung in a cape behind the head and was as white where it was cut as freshly sliced coconut.

"What is he? About thirty inches?"

"Hell, no," said Pop. "No thirty inches."

"But he iss a very fine one, Mr. Jackson," Dan said.

"Yes. He's a fine one," Pop said.

"Where did you get him?"

"Just outside of camp."

"He wass standing in some bush. We heard him grunt."

"We thought he was a buffalo," Karl said.

"He iss a very fine one," Dan repeated.

"I'm damned glad you got him," I said.

There we were, the three of us, wanting to congratulate, waiting to be good sports about this rhino whose smaller horn was longer than our big one, this huge, tear-eyed marvel of a rhino, this dead, head-severed dream rhino, and instead we all spoke like people who were about to become seasick on a boat, or people who had suffered some heavy financial loss. We were ashamed and could do nothing about it. I wanted to say something pleasant and hearty, instead, "How many times did you shoot him?" I asked.

"I don't know. We didn't count. Five or six, I guess."

"Five, I think," said Dan.

Poor Karl, faced by these three sad-faced congratulators, was beginning to feel his pleasure in the rhino drained away from him.

"We got one too," said P. O. M.

"That's fine," said Karl. "Is he bigger than this one?"

"Hell, no. He's a lousy runt."

"I'm sorry," Karl said. He meant it, simply and truly.

"What the hell have you got to be sorry about with a rhino like that? Goddamn it, he's a beauty. Let me get the camera and take some pictures of him."

I went after the camera. P. O. M. took me by the arm and walked close beside me.

"Papa, please try to act like a human being," she said. "Poor Karl. You're making him feel dreadfully."

"I know it," I said. "I'm trying not to act that way."

There was Pop. He shook his head. "I never felt more of a four-letter man," he said. "But it was like a kick in the stomach. I'm really delighted, of course."

"Me too," I said. "I'd rather have him beat me. You know that. Truly. But why couldn't he just get a good one, two or three inches longer? Why did he have to get one that makes mine ridiculous? It just makes ours silly."

"You can always remember that shot."

"The hell with that shot. That bloody fluke. God, what a beautiful rhino."

"Come on, let's pull ourselves together and try to act like white people with him."

"We were *awful*," P. O. M. said.

"I know it," I said. "And all the time I was trying to be jolly. You *know* I'm delighted he has it."

"You were certainly jolly. Both of you," P. O. M. said.

"But did you see M'Cola?" Pop asked. M'Cola had looked at the rhino dismally, shaken his head and walked away.

"He's a wonderful rhino," P. O. M. said. "We must act decently and make Karl feel good."

But it was too late. We could not make Karl feel good and for a long time we could not feel good ourselves. The porters came into camp with the loads and we could see them all, and all of our outfit, go over to where the rhino head lay in the shade. They were all very quiet. Only the skinner was delighted to see such a rhino head in camp.

"M'uzuri sana," he said to me. And measured the horn with shiftings of his widespread hand. "Kubwa sana!"

"N'Dio. M'uzuri sana," I agreed.

"B'wana Kabor shoot him?"

"Yes."

"M'uzuri sana."

"Yes," I agreed. "M'uzuri sana."

The skinner was the only gent in the outfit. We had tried, in all the shoot, never to be competitive. Karl and I had each tried to give the other the better chance on everything that came up. I was, truly, very fond of him and he was entirely unselfish and altogether self-sacrificing. I knew I could outshoot him and I could always outwalk him and, steadily, he got trophies that made mine dwarfs in comparison. He had done some of the worst shooting at game I had ever seen and I had shot badly twice on the trip, at that Grant, and at a bustard once on the plain, still he beat me on all the tangible things we had to show. For a while we had joked about it and I knew everything would even up. But it didn't even up. Now, on this rhino hunt, I had taken the first crack at the country. We had sent him after meat while we had gone into a new country. We had not treated him badly, but we had not treated him too well, and still he had beaten me. Not only beaten, beaten was all right. He had made my rhino look so small that I could never keep him in the same small town where we lived. He had wiped him out. I had the shot I had made on him to remember and nothing could take that away except that it was so bloody marvellous I knew I would wonder, sooner or later, if it was not really a fluke in spite of my unholy self-confidence. Old Karl had put it on us all right with that rhino. He was in his tent now, writing a letter.

Under the dining tent fly Pop and I talked over what we had better do.

"He's got his rhino anyway," Pop said. "That saves us time. Now you can't stand on that one."

"No."

"But this country is washed out. Something wrong with it. Droopy claims to know a good country about three hours from here in the trucks and another hour or so in with the porters. We can head for there this afternoon with a light outfit, send the trucks back, and Karl and Dan can move on down to M'uto Umbu and he can get his oryx."

"Fine."

"He has a chance to get a leopard on that rhino carcass this evening, too, or in the morning. Dan said they heard one. We'll try to get a rhino out of this country of Droopy's and then you join up with them and go on for kudu. We want to leave plenty of time for them."

"Fine."

"Even if you don't get an oryx. You'll pick one up some-where."

"Even if I don't get one at all, it's all right. We'll get one another time. I want a kudu, though."

"You'll get one. You're sure to."

"I'd rather get one, a good one, than all the rest. I don't give a damn about these rhino outside of the fun of hunting them. But I'd like to get one that wouldn't look silly beside that dream rhino of his."

"Absolutely."

So we told Karl and he said: "Whatever you say. Sure. I hope you get one twice as big." He really meant it. He was feeling bet-ter now and so were we all.

CHAPTER

DROOPY'S COUNTRY, when we reached it that evening, after a hot ride through red-soiled, bush-scrubby hills, looked awful. It was at the edge of a belt where all the trees had been girdled to kill the tse-tse flies. And across from camp was a dusty, dirty native village. The soil was red and eroded and seemed to be blowing away and camp was pitched in a high wind under the sketchy shade of some dead trees on a hillside overlooking a little stream and the mud village beyond. Before dark we followed Droopy and two local guides up past the village and in a long climb to the top of a rock-strewn ridge that overlooked a deep valley that was almost a canyon. Across, on the other side, were broken valleys that sloped steeply down into the canyon. There were heavy growths of trees in the valleys and grassy slopes on the ridges between, and above there was the thick bamboo forest of the mountain. The canyon ran down to the Rift Valley, seeming to narrow at the far end where it cut through the wall of the rift. Beyond, above the grassy ridges and slopes, were heavily forested hills. It looked a hell of a country to hunt.

"If you see one across there you have to go straight down to

FIVE

the bottom of the canyon. Then up one of those timber patches and across those damned gullies. You can't keep him in sight and you'll kill yourself climbing. It's too bloody steep. Those are the kind of innocent-looking gullies we got into that night coming home."

"It looks very bad," Pop agreed.

"I've hunted a country just like this for deer. The south slope of Timber Creek in Wyoming. The slopes are all too steep. It's hell. It's too broken. We'll take some punishment tomorrow."

P. O. M. said nothing. Pop had brought us here and Pop would bring us out. All she had to do was see her shoes did not hurt her feet. They hurt just a little now, and that was her only worry.

I went on to dilate on the difficulties the country showed and we went home to camp in the dark all very gloomy and full of prejudice against Droopy. The fire flamed brightly in the wind and we sat and watched the moon rise and listened to the hyenas. After we had a few drinks we did not feel so badly about the country.

"Droopy swears it's good," Pop said. "This isn't where he wanted to go though, he says. It was another place further on. But he swears this is good."

"I love Droopy," P. O. M. said. "I have perfect confidence in Droopy."

Droopy came up to the fire with two spear-carrying natives.

"What does he hear?" I asked.

There was some talk by the natives, then Pop said: "One of these sportsmen claims he was chased by a huge rhino today. Of course nearly any rhino would look huge when he was chasing him."

"Ask him how long the horn was."

The native showed that the horn was as long as his arm. Droopy grinned.

"Tell him to go," said Pop.

"Where did all this happen?"

"Oh, over there somewhere," Pop said. "You know. Over there. Way over there. Where these things always happen."

"That's marvellous. Just where we want to go."

"The good aspect is that Droopy's not at all depressed," Pop said. "He seems very confident. After all, it's his show."

"Yes, but we have to do the climbing."

"Cheer him up, will you?" Pop said to P. O. M. "He's getting me very depressed."

"Should we talk about how well he shoots?"

"Too bloody early in the evening. I'm not gloomy. I've just seen that kind of country before. It will be good for us all right. Take some of your belly off, Governor."

The next day I found that I was all wrong about that country.

We had breakfast before daylight and were started before sunrise, climbing the hill beyond the village in single file. Ahead there was the local guide with a spear, then Droopy with my heavy gun and a water bottle, then me with the Springfield, Pop with the Mannlicher, P. O. M. pleased, as always, to carry nothing, M'Cola with Pop's heavy gun and another water bottle, and finally two local citizens with spears, water bags, and a chop box with lunch. We planned to lay up in the heat of the middle of the day and not get back until dark. It was fine climbing in the cool fresh morning and very different from toiling up this same trail last evening in the sunset with all the rocks and dirt giving back the heat of the day. The trail was used regularly by cattle and the dust was powdered dry and, now, lightly moistened from the dew. There were many hyena tracks and, as the trail came onto a ridge of gray rock so that you could look down on both sides into a steep ravine, and then went on along the edge of the canyon, we saw a fresh rhino track in one of the dusty patches below the rocks.

"He's just gone on ahead," Pop said. "They must wander all over here at night."

Below, at the bottom of the canyon, we could see the tops of high trees and in an opening see the flash of water. Across were the steep hillside and the gullies we had studied last night. Droopy and the local guide, the one who had been chased by the rhino, were whispering together. Then they started down a steep path that went in long slants down the side of the canyon.

We stopped. I had not seen P. O. M. was limping, and in sudden whispered family bitterness there was a highly-righteous-on-both-sides clash, historically on unwearable shoes and boots in the past, and imperatively on these, which hurt. The hurt was lessened by cutting off the toes of the heavy short wool socks worn over ordinary socks, and then, by removing the socks entirely, the boots made possible. Going down-hill steeply made these Spanish shooting boots too short in the toe and there was an old argument, about this length of boot and whether the bootmaker, whose part I had taken, unwittingly first, only as interpreter, and finally embraced his theory patriotically as a whole and, I believed, by logic, had overcome it by adding onto the heel. But they hurt now, a stronger logic, and the situation was un-helped by the statement that men's new boots always hurt for weeks before they became comfortable. Now, heavy socks removed, stepping tentatively, trying the pressure of the leather against the toes, the argument past, she wanting not to suffer, but to keep up and please Mr. J. P., me ashamed at having been a four-letter man about boots, at being righteous against pain, at being righteous at all, at ever being righteous, stopping to whisper about it, both of us grinning at what was whispered, it all right now, the boots too, without the heavy socks, much better, me hating all righteous bastards now, one absent American friend especially, having just removed myself from that category, certainly never to be righteous again, watching Droopy ahead, we went down the long slant of the trail toward the bottom of the canyon where the trees were heavy and tall and the floor of the canyon, that from above had been a narrow gash, opened to a forest-banked stream.

We stood now in the shade of trees with great smooth trunks, circled at their base with the line of roots that showed in rounded ridges up the trunks like arteries; the trunks the yellow green of a French forest on a day in winter after rain. But these trees had a great spread of branches and were in leaf and below them, in the stream bed in the sun, reeds like papyrus grass grew thick as wheat and twelve feet tall. There was a game trail through the grass along the stream and Droopy was bent down looking at it. M'Cola went over and looked and they both followed it a little way, stooped close over it, then came back to us.

"Nyati," M'Cola whispered. "Buffalo." Droopy whispered to Pop and then Pop said, softly in his throaty, whiskey whisper, "They're buff gone down the river. Droop says there are some big bulls. They haven't come back."

"Let's follow them," I said. "I'd rather get another buff than rhino."

"It's as good a chance as any for rhino, too," Pop said.

"By God, isn't it a great looking country?" I said.

"Splendid," Pop said. "Who would have imagined it?"

"The trees are like André's pictures," P. O. M. said. "It's simply beautiful. Look at that green. It's Masson. Why can't a good painter see this country?"

"How are your boots?"

"Fine."

As we trailed the buffalo we went very slowly and quietly. There was no wind and we knew that when the breeze came up it would be from the east and blow up the canyon toward us. We followed the game trail down the river-bed and as we went the grass was much higher. Twice we had to get down to crawl and the reeds were so thick you could not see two feet into them.

Droop found a fresh rhino track, too, in the mud. I began to think about what would happen if a rhino came barging along this tunnel and who would do what. It was exciting but I did not like it. It was too much like being in a trap and there was P. O. M. to think about. Then as the stream made a bend and we came out of the high grass to the bank I smelled game very distinctly. I do not smoke, and hunting at home I have several times smelled elk in the rutting season before I have seen them and I can smell clearly where an old bull has lain in the forest. The bull elk has a strong musky smell. It is a strong but pleasant odor and I know it well, but this smell I did not know.

"I can smell them," I whispered to Pop. He believed me.

"What is it?"

"I don't know but it's plenty strong. Can't you?"

"No."

"Ask Droop."

Droopy nodded and grinned.

"They take snuff," Pop said. "I don't know whether they can scent or not."

We went on into another bed of reeds that were high over our heads, putting each foot down silently before lifting the other, walking as quietly as in a dream or a slow motion picture. I could smell whatever it was clearly now, all of the time, sometimes stronger than at others. I did not like it at all. We were close to the bank now, and, ahead the game trail went straight out into a long slough of higher reeds than any we had come through.

"I can smell them close as hell," I whispered to Pop. "No kidding. Really."

"I believe you," Pop said. "Should we get up here onto the bank and skirt this bit? We'll be above it."

"Good." Then, when we were up, I said, "That tall stuff had me spooked. I wouldn't like to hunt in that."

"How'd you like to hunt elephant in that?" Pop whispered.

"I wouldn't do it."

"Do you really hunt elephant in grass like that?" P. O. M. asked.

"Yes," Pop said. "Get up on somebody's shoulders to shoot."

Better men than I am do it, I thought. I wouldn't do it.

We went along the grassy right bank, on a sort of shelf, now in the open, skirting a slough of high dry reeds. Beyond on the opposite bank were the heavy trees and above them the steep bank of the canyon. You could not see the stream. Above us, on the right, were the hills, wooded in patches of orchard bush. Ahead, at the end of the slough of reeds the banks narrowed and the branches of the big trees almost covered the stream. Suddenly Droopy grabbed me and we both crouched down. He put the big gun in my hand and took the Springfield. He pointed and around a curve in the bank I saw the head of a rhino with a long, wonderful looking horn. The head was swaying and I could see the ears forward and twitching, and see the little pig eyes. I slipped the safety catch and motioned Droopy down. Then I heard M'Cola saying, "Toto! Toto!" and he grabbed my arm. Droopy was whispering, "Manamouki! Manamouki! Manamouki!" very fast and he and M'Cola were frantic that I should not shoot. It was a cow rhino with a calf and as I lowered the gun, she gave a snort, crashed in the reeds, and was gone. I never saw the calf. We could see the reeds swaying where the two of them were moving and then it was all quiet.

"Damn shame," Pop whispered. "She had a beautiful horn."

"I was all set to bust her," I said. "I couldn't tell she was a cow."

"M'Cola saw the calf."

M'Cola was whispering to Pop and nodding his head emphatically.

"He says there's another rhino in there," Pop said. "That he heard him snort."

"Let's get higher, where we can see them if they break, and throw something in," I said.

"Good idea," Pop agreed. "Maybe the bull's there."

We went a little higher up the bank where we could look out over the lake of high reeds and, with Pop holding his big gun ready and I with the safety off mine, M'Cola threw a club into the reeds where he had heard the snort. There was a wooshing snort and no movement, not a stir in the reeds. Then there was a crashing further away and we could see the reeds swaying with the rush of something through them toward the opposite bank, but could not see what was making the movement. Then I saw the black back, the wide-swept, point-lifted horns and then the quick-moving, climbing rush of a buffalo up the other bank. He went up, his neck up and out, his head horn-heavy, his withers rounded like a fighting bull, in fast strong-legged climb. I was holding on the point where his neck joined his shoulder when Pop stopped me.

"He's not a big one," he said softly. "I wouldn't take him unless you want him for meat."

He looked big to me and now he stood, his head up, broadside, his head swung toward us.

"I've got three more on the license and we're leaving their country," I said.

"It's awfully good meat," Pop whispered. "Go ahead then. Bust him. But be ready for the rhino after you shoot."

I sat down, the big gun feeling heavy and unfamiliar, held on the buff's shoulder, squeezed off and flinched without firing. Instead of the sweet clean pull of the Springfield with the smooth, unhesitant release at the end, this trigger came to what, in a squeeze, seemed metal stuck against metal. It was like when you shoot in a nightmare. I couldn't squeeze it and I corrected from my flinch, held my breath, and pulled the trigger. It pulled off with a jerk and the big gun made a rocking explosion out of which I came, seeing the buffalo still on his feet, and going out of sight to the left in a climbing run, to let off the second barrel and throw a burst of rock dust and dirt over his hind quarters. He was out of shot before I could reload the double-barrelled .470 and we had all heard the snorting and the crashing of another rhino that had gone out of the lower end of the reeds and on under the heavy trees on our side without showing more than a glimpse of his bulk in the reeds.

"It was the bull," Pop said. "He's gone down the stream."

"N'Dio. Doumi! Doumi!" Droopy insisted it was a bull.

"I hit the damned buff," I said. "God knows where. To hell with those heavy guns. The trigger pull put me off."

"You'd have killed him with the Springfield," Pop said.

"I'd know where I hit him anyway. I thought with the four-seventy I'd kill him or miss him," I said. "Instead, now we've got him wounded."

"He'll keep," Pop said. "We want to give him plenty of time."

"I'm afraid I gut-shot him."

"You can't tell. Going off fast like that he might be dead in a hundred yards."

"The hell with that four-seventy," I said. "I can't shoot it. The trigger's like the last turn of the key opening a sardine can."

"Come on," Pop said. "We've got God knows how many rhino scattered about here."

"What about the buff?"

"Plenty of time for him later. We must let him stiffen up. Let him get sick."

"Suppose we'd been down in there with all that stuff coming out."

"Yes," said Pop.

All this in whispers. I looked at P. O. M. She was like some one enjoying a good musical show.

"Did you see where it hit him?"

"I couldn't tell," she whispered. "Do you suppose there are any more in there?"

"Thousands," I said. "What do we do, Pop?"

"That bull may be just around the bend," Pop said. "Come on."

We went along the bank, our nerves cocked, and as we came to the narrow end of the reeds there was another rush of something heavy through the tall stalks. I had the gun up waiting for whatever it was to show. But there was only the waving of the reeds. M'Cola signalled with his hand not to shoot.

"The goddamned calf," Pop said. "Must have been two of them. Where's the bloody bull?"

"How the hell do you see them?"

"Tell by the size."

Then we were standing looking down into the stream bed, into the shadows under the branches of the big trees, and off ahead down the stream when M'Cola pointed up the hill on our right.

"Faro," he whispered and reached me the glasses.

There on the hillside, head-on, wide, black, looking straight toward us, ears twitching and head lifted, swaying as the nose searched for the wind, was another rhino. He looked huge in the glasses. Pop was studying him with his binoculars.

"He's no better than what you have," he said softly.

"I can bust him right in the sticking place," I whispered.

"You only have one more," Pop whispered. "You want a good one."

I offered the glasses to P. O. M.

"I can see him without," she said. "He's huge."

"He may charge," Pop said. "Then you'll have to take him."

Then, as we watched, another rhino came into sight from behind a wide feathery-topped tree. He was quite a bit smaller.

"By God, it's a calf," Pop said. "That one's a cow. Good thing you didn't shoot her. She bloody well may charge too."

"Is it the same cow?" I whispered.

"No. That other one had a hell of a horn."

We all had the nervous exhilaration, like a laughing drunk, that a sudden over-abundance, idiotic abundance of game makes. It is a feeling that can come from any sort of game or fish that is ordinarily rare and that, suddenly, you find in a ridiculously unbelievable abundance.

"Look at her. She knows there's something wrong. But she can't see us or smell us."

"She heard the shots."

"She knows we're here. But she can't make it out."

The rhino looked so huge, so ridiculous, and so fine to see, and I sighted on her chest.

"It's a nice shot."

"Perfect," Pop said.

"What are we going to do?" P. O. M. said. She was practical.

"We'll work around her," Pop said.

"If we keep low I don't believe our scent will carry up there once we're past."

"You can't tell," Pop said. "We don't want her to charge."

She did not charge, but dropped her head, finally, and worked up the hill followed by the nearly full-grown calf.

"Now," said Pop, "we'll let Droop go ahead and see if he can find the bull's tracks. We might as well sit down."

We sat in the shade and Droopy went up one side of the

stream and the local guide the other. They came back and said the bull had gone on down.

"Did any one ever see what sort of horn he had?" I asked.

"Droop said he was good."

M'Cola had gone up the hill a little way. Now he crouched and beckoned.

"Nyati," he said with his hand up to his face.

"Where?" Pop asked him. He pointed, crouched down, and as we crawled up to him he handed me the glasses. They were a long way away on the jutting ridge of one of the steep hillsides on the far side of the canyon, well down the stream. We could see six, then eight, buffalo, black, heavy necked, the horns shining, standing on the point of a ridge. Some were grazing and others stood, their heads up, watching.

"That one's a bull," Pop said, looking through the glasses.

"Which one?"

"Second from the right."

"They all look like bulls to me."

"They're a long way away. That one's a good bull. Now we've got to cross the stream and work down toward them and try to get above them."

"Will they stay there?"

"No. Probably they'll work down into this stream bed as soon as it's hot."

"Let's go."

We crossed the stream on a log and then another log and on the other side, half way up the hillside, there was a deeply worn game trail that graded along the bank under the heavily leafed branches of the trees. We went along quite fast, but walking carefully, and below us, now, the stream bed was covered solidly with foliage. It was still early in the morning but the breeze was rising and the leaves stirred over our heads. We crossed one ravine that came down to the stream, going into the thick bush to be out of sight and stooping as we crossed behind trees in the small open place, then, using the shoulder of the ravine as protection, we climbed so that we might get high up the hillside above the buffalo and work down to them. We stopped in the shelter of the ridge, me sweating heavily and fixing a handkerchief inside the sweatband of

my Stetson, and sent Droop ahead to look. He came back to say
they were gone. From above we could see nothing of them, so we
cut across the ravine and the hillside thinking we might intercept
them on their way down into the river bed. The next hillside had
been burned and at the bottom of the hill there was a burned area
of bush. In the ash dust were the tracks of the buffalo as they came
down and into the thick jungle of the stream bed. Here it was too
overgrown and there were too many vines to follow them. There
were no tracks going down the stream so we knew they were down
in that part of the stream bed we had looked down on from the
game trail. Pop said there was nothing to do about them in there.
It was so thick that if we jumped them we could not get a shot.
You could not tell one from another, he said. All you would see
would be a rush of black. An old bull would be gray but a good
herd bull might be as black as a cow. It wasn't any good to jump
them like that.

It was ten o'clock now and very hot in the open, the sun
pegged and the breeze lifted the ashes of the burned-over ground
as we walked. Everything would be in the thick cover now. We
decided to find a shady place and lie down and read in the cool; to
have lunch and kill the hot part of the day.

Beyond the burned place we came toward the stream and
stopped, sweating, in the shadow of some very large trees. We
unpacked our leather coats and our raincoats and spread them on
the grass at the foot of the trees so that we could lean back against
the trunks. P. O. M. got out the books and M'Cola made a small
fire and boiled water for tea.

The breeze was coming up and we could hear it in the high
branches. It was cool in the shade, but if you stirred into the sun,
or as the sun shifted the shadow while you read so that any part
of you was out of the shadow, the sun was heavy. Droopy had
gone on down the stream to have a look and as we lay there, reading, I could smell the heat of the day coming, the drying up of the
dew, the heat on the leaves, and the heaviness of the sun over the
stream.

P. O. M. was reading *Spanish Gold*, by George A. Birming-
ham, and she said it was no good. I still had the Sevastopol book
of Tolstoi and in the same volume I was reading a story called

"The Cossacks" that was very good. In it were the summer heat, the mosquitoes, the feel of the forest in the different seasons, and that river that the Tartars crossed, raiding, and I was living in that Russia again.

I was thinking how real that Russia of the time of our Civil War was, as real as any other place, as Michigan, or the prairie north of town and the woods around Evans's game farm, of how, through Turgenieff, I knew that I had lived there, as I had been in the family Buddenbrooks, and had climbed in and out of her window in *Le Rouge et le Noir,* or the morning we had come in the gates of Paris and seen Salcède torn apart by the horses at the Place de Grèves. I saw all that. And it was me they did not break on the rack that time because I had been polite to the executioner the time they killed Coconas and me, and I remember the Eve of St. Bartholomew's and how we hunted Huguenots that night, and when they trapped me at her house that time, and no feeling more true than finding the gate of the Louvre being closed, nor of looking down at his body in the water where he fell from the mast, and always, Italy, better than any book, lying in the chestnut woods, and in the fall mist behind the Duomo going across the town to the Ospedale Maggiore, the nails in my boots on the cobbles, and in the Spring sudden showers in the mountains and the smell of the regiment like a copper coin in your mouth. So in the heat the train stopped at Dezenzano and there was Lago de Garda and those troops are the Czech Legion, and the next time it was raining, and the next time it was in the dark, and the next time you passed it riding in a truck, and the next time you were coming from somewhere else, and the next time you walked to it in the dark from Sermione. For we have been there in the books and out of the books—and where we go, if we are any good, there you can go as we have been. A country, finally, erodes and the dust blows away, the people all die and none of them were of any importance permanently, except those who practised the arts, and these now wish to cease their work because it is too lonely, too hard to do, and is not fashionable. A thousand years makes economics silly and a work of art endures forever, but it is very difficult to do and now it is not fashionable. People do not want to do it any more because they will be out of fashion and the lice who crawl on literature will not praise them. Also it is very hard to do. So what? So I would go on reading about the river that the Tartars came across when raiding, and the drunken old hunter and the girl and how it was then in the different seasons.

Pop was reading *Richard Carvell*. We had bought what there was to buy in Nairobi and we were pretty well to the end of the books.

"I've read this before," Pop said. "But it's a good story."

"I can just remember it. But it was a good story then."

"It's a jolly good story but I wish I hadn't read it before."

"This is terrible," P. O. M. said. "You couldn't read it."

"Do you want this one?"

"Don't be ornamental," she said. "No. I'll finish this."

"Go on. Take it."

"I'll give it right back."

"Hey, M'Cola," I said. "Beer?"

"N'Dio," he said with great force, and from the chop box one of the natives had carried on his head produced, in its straw casing, a bottle of German beer, one of the sixty-four bottles Dan had bought from the German trading station. Its neck was wrapped in silver foil and on its black and yellow label there was a horseman in armor. It was still cool from the night and opened by the tin opener it creamed into three cups, thick-foamed, full-bodied.

"No," said Pop. "Very bad for the liver."

"Come on."

"All right."

We all drank and when M'Cola opened the second bottle Pop refused, firmly.

"Go on. It means more to you. I'm going to take a nap."

"Poor old Mama?"

"Just a little."

"All for me," I said. M'Cola smiled and shook his head at this drinking. I lay back against the tree and watched the wind bringing the clouds and drank the beer slowly out of the bottle. It was cooler that way and it was excellent beer. After a while Pop and P. O. M. were both asleep and I got back the Sevastopol book and read in the Cossacks again. It was a good story.

When they woke up we had lunch of cold sliced tenderloin,

bread, and mustard, and a can of plums, and drank the third, and last, bottle of beer. Then we read again and all went to sleep. I woke thirsty and was unscrewing the top from a water bottle when I heard a rhino snort and crash in the brush of the river bed. Pop was awake and heard it too and we took our guns, without speaking, and started toward where the noise had come from. M'Cola found the tracks. The rhino had come up the stream, evidently he had winded us when he was only about thirty yards away, and had gone on up. We could not follow the tracks the way the wind was blowing so we circled away from the stream and back to the edge of the burned place to get above him and then hunted very carefully against the wind along the stream through very thick bush, but we did not find him. Finally Droopy found where he had gone up the other side and on into the hills. From the tracks it did not seem a particularly large one.

We were a long way from camp, at least four hours as we had come, and much of it up-hill going back, certainly there would be that long climb out of the canyon; we had a wounded buffalo to deal with, and when we came out on the edge of the burned country again, we agreed that we should get P. O. M. and get started. It was still hot, but the sun was on its way down and for a good way we would be on the heavily shaded game trail on the high bank above the stream. When we found P. O. M. she pretended to be indignant at our going off and leaving her alone but she was only teasing us.

We started off, Droop and his spearsman in the lead, walking along the shadow of the trail that was broken by the sun through the leaves. Instead of the cool early morning smell of the forest there was a nasty stink like the mess cats make.

"What makes the stink?" I whispered to Pop.

"Baboons," he said.

A whole tribe of them had gone on just ahead of us and their droppings were everywhere. We came up to the place where the rhinos and the buff had come out of the reeds and I located where I thought the buff had been when I shot. M'Cola and Droopy were casting about like hounds and I thought they were at least fifty yards too high up the bank when Droop held up a leaf.

"He's got blood," Pop said. We went up to them. There was a

great quantity of blood, black now on the grass, and the trail was easy to follow. Droop and M'Cola trailed one on each side, leaving the trail between them, pointing to each blood spot formally with a long stem of grass. I always thought it would be better for one to trail slowly and the other cast ahead but this was the way they trailed, stooped heads, pointing each dried splash with their grass stems and occasionally, when they picked up the tracks after losing them, stooping to pluck a grass blade or a leaf that had the black stain on it. I followed them with the Springfield, then came Pop, with P. O. M. behind him. Droop carried my big gun and Pop had his. M'Cola had P. O. M.'s Mannlicher slung over his shoulder. None of us spoke and every one seemed to regard it as a pretty serious business. In some high grass we found blood, at a pretty good height on the grass leaves on both sides of the trail where the buff had gone through the grass. That meant he was shot clean through. You could not tell the original color of the blood now, but I had a moment of hoping he might be shot through the lungs. But further on we came on some droppings in the rocks with blood in them and then for a while he had dropped dung wherever he climbed and all of it was blood-spotted. It looked, now, like a gut shot or one through the paunch. I was more ashamed of it all the time.

"If he comes don't worry about Droopy or the others," Pop whispered. "They'll get out of his way. Stop him."

"Right up the nose," I said.

"Don't try anything fancy," Pop said. The trail climbed steadily, then twice looped back on itself and for a time seemed to wander, without plan, among some rocks. Once it led down to the stream, crossed a rivulet of it and then came back up on the same bank, grading up through the trees.

"I think we'll find him dead," I whispered to Pop. That aimless turn had made me see him, slow and hard hit, getting ready to go down.

"I hope so," Pop said.

But the trail went on, where there was little grass now, and trailing was much slower and more difficult. There were no tracks now that I could see, only the probable line he would take, verified by a shiny dark splatter of dried blood on a stone. Several times we lost it entirely and, the three of us making casts, one would find it, point and whisper "Damu," and we would go on again. Finally it led down from a rocky hillside with the last of the sun on it, down into the stream bed where there was a long, wide patch of the highest dead reeds that we had seen. These were higher and thicker even than the slough the buff had come out of in the morning and there were several game trails that went into them.

"Not good enough to take the little Memsahib in there," Pop said.

"Let her stay here with M'Cola," I said.

"It's not good enough for the little Memsahib," Pop repeated. "I don't know why we let her come."

"She can wait here. Droop wants to go on."

"Right you are. We'll have a look."

"You wait here with M'Cola," I whispered over my shoulder.

We followed Droopy into the thick, tall grass that was five feet above our heads, walking carefully on the game trail, stooping forward, trying to make no noise breathing. I was thinking of the buff the way I had seen them when we had gotten the three that time, how the old bull had come out of the bush, groggy as he was, and I could see the horns, the boss coming far down, the muzzle out, the little eyes, the roll of fat and muscle on his thin-haired, gray, scaly-hided neck, the heavy power and the rage in him, and I admired him and respected him, but he was slow, and all the while we shot I felt that it was fixed and that we had him. This was different, this was no rapid fire, no pouring it on him as he comes groggy into the open, if he comes now I must be quiet inside and put it down his nose as he comes with the head out. He will have to put the head down to hook, like any bull, and that will uncover the old place the boys wet their knuckles on and I will get one in there and then must go sideways into the grass and he would be Pop's from then on unless I could keep the rifle when I jumped. I was sure I could get that one in and jump if I could wait and watch his head come down. I knew I could do that and that the shot would kill him but how long would it take? That was the whole thing. How long would it take? Now, going forward, sure he was in here, I felt the elation, the best elation of all, of certain action to come, action in which you had something to do, in which you can kill and come out of it, doing something you are ignorant about and so not scared, no one to worry about and no responsibility except to perform something you feel sure you can perform, and I was walking softly ahead watching Droopy's back and remembering to keep the sweat out of my glasses when I heard a noise behind us and turned my head. It was P. O. M. with M'Cola coming on our tracks.

"For God's sake," Pop said. He was furious.

We got her back out of the grass and up onto the bank and made her realize that she must stay there. She had not understood that she was to stay behind. She had heard me whisper something but thought it was for her to come behind M'Cola.

"That spooked me," I said to Pop.

"She's like a little terrier," he said. "But it's not good enough."

We were looking out over that grass.

"Droop wants to go still," I said. "I'll go as far as he will. When he says no that lets us out. After all, I gut-shot the son of a bitch."

"Mustn't do anything silly, though."

"I can kill the son of a bitch if I get a shot at him. If he comes he's got to give me a shot."

The fright P. O. M. had given us about herself had made me noisy.

"Come on," said Pop. We followed Droopy back in and it got worse and worse and I do not know about Pop but about half way I changed to the big gun and kept the safety off and my hand over the trigger guard and I was plenty nervous by the time Droopy stopped and shook his head and whispered "Hapana." It had gotten so you could not see a foot ahead and it was all turns and twists. It was really bad and the sun was only on the hillside now. We both felt good because we had made Droopy do the calling off and I was relieved as well. What we had followed him into had made my fancy shooting plans seem very silly and I knew all we had in there was Pop to blast him over with the four-fifty number two after I'd maybe miss him with that lousy four-seventy. I had no confidence in anything but its noise any more.

We were back trailing when we heard the porters on the hillside shout and we ran crashing through the grass to try to get to a high enough place to see to shoot. They waved their arms and shouted that the buffalo had come out of the reeds and gone past them and then M'Cola and Droopy were pointing and Pop had me by the sleeve trying to pull me to where I could see them and then, in the sunlight, high up on the hillside against the rocks I saw two buffalo. They shone very black in the sun and one was much bigger than the other and I remember thinking this was our bull and that he had picked up a cow and she had made the pace and kept him going. Droop had handed me the Springfield and I slipped my arm through the sling and sighting, the buff now all seen through the aperture, I froze myself inside and held the bead on the top of his shoulder and as I started to squeeze he started running and I swung ahead of him and loosed off. I saw him lower his head and jump like a bucking horse as he comes out of the chutes and as I threw the shell, slammed the bolt forward and shot again, behind him as he went out of sight, I knew I had him. Droopy and I started to run and as we were running I heard a low bellow. I stopped and yelled at Pop, "Hear him? I've got him, I tell you!"

"You hit him," said Pop. "Yes."

"Goddamn it, I killed him. Didn't you hear him bellow?"

"No."

"Listen!" We stood listening and there it came, clear, a long, moaning, unmistakable bellow.

"By God," Pop said. It was a very sad noise.

M'Cola grabbed my hand and Droopy slapped my back and all laughing we started on a running scramble, sweating, rushing, up the ridge through the trees and over rocks. I had to stop for breath, my heart pounding, and wiped the sweat off my face and cleaned my glasses.

"Kufa!" M'Cola said, making the word for dead almost explosive in its force. "N'Dio! Kufa!"

"Kufa!" Droopy said grinning.

"Kufa!" M'Cola repeated and we shook hands again before we went on climbing. Then, ahead of us, we saw him, on his back, throat stretched out to the full, his weight on his horns, wedged against a tree. M'Cola put his finger in the bullet hole in the center of the shoulder and shook his head happily.

Pop and P. O. M. came up, followed by the porters.

"By God, he's a better bull than we thought," I said.

"He's not the same bull. This is a real bull. That must have been our bull with him."

"I thought he was with a cow. It was so far away I couldn't tell."

"It must have been four hundred yards. By God, you can shoot that little pipsqueak."

"When I saw him put his head down between his legs and buck I knew we had him. The light was wonderful on him."

"I knew you had hit him, and I knew he wasn't the same bull. So I thought we had two wounded buffalo to deal with. I didn't hear the first bellow."

"It was wonderful when we heard him bellow," P. O. M. said. "It's such a sad sound. It's like hearing a horn in the woods."

"It sounded awfully jolly to me," Pop said. "By God, we deserve a drink on this. That was a shot. Why didn't you ever tell us you could shoot?"

"Go to hell."

"You know he's a damned good tracker, too, and what kind of a bird shot?" he asked P. O. M.

"Isn't he a beautiful bull?" P. O. M. asked.

"He's a fine one. He's not old but it's a fine head."

We tried to take pictures but there was only the little box camera and the shutter stuck and there was a bitter argument about the shutter while the light failed, and I was nervous now, irritable, righteous, pompous about the shutter and inclined to be abused because we could get no picture. You cannot live on a plane of the sort of elation I had felt in the reeds and having killed, even when it is only a buffalo, you feel a little quiet inside. Killing is not a feeling that you share and I took a drink of water and told P. O. M. I was sorry I was such a bastard about the camera. She said it was all right and we were all right again looking at the buff with M'Cola making the cuts for the headskin and we standing close together and feeling fond of each other and understanding everything, camera and all. I took a drink of the whiskey and it had no taste and I felt no kick from it.

"Let me have another," I said. The second one was all right.

We were going on ahead to camp with the chased-by-a-rhino spearsman as guide and Droop was going to skin out the head and they were going to butcher and cache the meat in trees so the hyenas would not get it. They were afraid to travel in the dark and I told Droopy he could keep my big gun. He said he knew how to shoot so I took out the shells and put on the safety and handing it to him told him to shoot. He put it to his shoulder, shut the wrong eye, and pulled hard on the trigger, and again, and again. Then I showed him about the safety and had him put it on and off and snap the gun a couple of times. M'Cola became very superior during Droopy's struggle to fire with the safety on and Droopy seemed to get much smaller. I left him the gun and two cartridges and they were all busy butchering in the dusk when we followed the spearsman and the tracks of the smaller buff, which had no blood on them, up to the top of the hill and on our way toward home. We climbed around the tops of valleys, went across gulches, up and down ravines and finally came onto the main ridge, it dark and cold in the evening, the moon not yet up, we plodded along, all tired. Once M'Cola, in the dark, loaded with Pop's heavy gun and an assortment of water bottles, binoculars, and a musette bag of books, sung out a stream of what sounded like curses at the guide who was striding ahead.

"What's he say?" I asked Pop.

"He's telling him not to show off his speed. That there is an old man in the party."

"Who does he mean, you or himself?"

"Both of us."

We saw the moon come up, smoky red over the brown hills, and we came down through the chinky lights of the village, the mud houses all closed tight, and the smells of goats and sheep, and then across the stream and up the bare slope to where the fire was burning in front of our tents. It was a cold night with much wind.

In the morning we hunted, picked up a track at a spring and trailed a rhino all over the high orchard country before he went down into a valley that led, steeply, into the canyon. It was very hot and the tight boots of the day before had chafed P. O. M.'s feet. She did not complain about them but I could see they hurt her. We were all luxuriantly, restfully tired.

"The hell with them," I said to Pop. "I don't want to kill another one unless he's big. We might hunt a week for a good one. Let's stand on the one we have and pull out and join Karl. We can hunt oryx down there and get those zebra hides and get on after the kudu."

We were sitting under a tree on the summit of a hill and could see off over all the country and the canyon running down to the Rift Valley and Lake Manyara.

"It would be good fun to take porters and a light outfit and hunt on ahead of them down through that valley and out to the lake," Pop said.

"That would be swell. We could send the trucks around to meet us at what's the name of the place?"

"Maji-Moto."

"Why don't we do that?" P. O. M. asked.

"We'll ask Droopy how the valley is."

Droopy didn't know but the spearsman said it was very rough and bad going where the stream came down through the rift wall. He did not think we could get the loads through. We gave it up.

"That's the sort of trip to make, though," Pop said. "Porters don't cost as much as petrol."

"Can't we make trips like that when we come back?" P. O. M. asked.

"Yes," Pop said. "But for a big rhino you want to go up on Mount Kenya. You'll get a real one there. Kudu's the prize here. You'd have to go up to Kalal to get one in Kenya. Then if we get them we'll have time to go on down in that Handeni country for sable."

"Let's get going," I said without moving.

Since a long time we had all felt good about Karl's rhino. We were glad he had it and all of that had taken on a correct perspective. Maybe he had his oryx by now. I hoped so. He was a fine fellow, Karl, and it was good he got these extra fine heads.

"How do you feel, poor old Mama?"

"I'm fine. If we *are* going I'll be just as glad to rest my feet. But I love this kind of hunting."

"Let's get back, eat, break camp, and get down there tonight."

That night we got into our old camp at M'utu-Umbo, under the big trees, not far from the road. It had been our first camp in Africa and the trees were as big, as spreading, and as green, the stream as clear and fast flowing, and the camp as fine as when we had first been there. The only difference was that now it was hotter at night, the road in was hub-deep in dust, and we had seen a lot of country.

CHAPTER

WE HAD COME down to the Rift Valley by a sandy red road across a high plateau, then up and down through orchard-bushed hills, around a slope of forest to the top of the rift wall where we could look down and see the plain, the heavy forest below the wall, and the long, dried-up edged shine of Lake Manyara rose-colored at one end with a half million tiny dots that were flamingoes. From there the road dropped steeply along the face of the wall, down into the forest, onto the flatness of the valley, through cultivated patches of green corn, bananas, and trees I did not know the names of, walled thick with forest, past a Hindu's trading store and many huts, over two bridges where clear, fast-flowing streams ran, through more forest, thinning now to open glades, and into a dusty turn-off that led into a deeply rutted, dust-filled track through bushes to the shade of M'utu-Umbu camp.

That night after dinner we heard the flamingoes flighting in the dark. It was like the sound the wings of ducks make as they go over before it is light, but slower, with a steady beat, and multiplied a thousand times. Pop and I were a little drunk and P. O. M. was

SIX

very tired. Karl was gloomy again. We had taken the edge from his victory over rhino and now that was past anyway and he was facing possible defeat by oryx. Then, too, they had found not a leopard but a marvellous lion, a huge, black-maned lion that did not want to leave, on the rhino carcass when they had gone there the next morning and could not shoot him because he was in some sort of forest reserve.

"That's rotten," I said and I tried to feel bad about it but I was still feeling much too good to appreciate any one else's gloom and Pop and I sat, tired through to our bones, drinking whiskey and soda and talking.

The next day we hunted oryx in the dried-up dustiness of the Rift Valley and finally found a herd way off at the edge of the wooded hills on the far side above a Masai village. They were like a bunch of Masai donkeys except for the beautiful straight-slanting black horns and all the heads looked good. When you looked closely two or three were obviously better than the others and sitting on the ground I picked what I thought was the very best of the lot and as they strung out I made sure of this one. I heard the bullet smack and watched the oryx circle out away from the others, the circle quickening, and knew I had it. So I did not shoot again.

This was the one Karl had picked, too. I did not know that, but had shot, deliberately selfish, to make sure of the best this time at least, but he got another good one and they went off in a wind-lifted cloud of gray dust as they galloped. Except for the miracle of their horns there was no more excitement in shooting them than if they had been donkeys and after the truck came up and M'Cola and Charo had skinned the heads out and cut up the meat we rode home in the blowing dust, our faces gray with it, and the valley one long heat mirage.

We stayed at that camp two days. We had to get some zebra hides that we had promised friends at home and it needed time for the skinner to handle them properly. Getting the zebra was no fun; the plain was dull, now that the grass had dried, hot and dusty after the hills, and the picture that remains is of sitting against an ant hill with, in the distance, a herd of zebra galloping in the gray heat haze, raising a dust, and on the yellow plain, the birds circling over a white patch there, another beyond, there a third, and looking back, the plume of dust of the truck coming with the skinners and the men to cut up the meat for the village. I did some bad shooting in the heat on a Grant's gazelle that the volunteer skinners asked me to kill them for meat, wounding him in a running shot after missing him three or four times, and then following him across the plain until almost noon in that heat until I got within range and killed him.

But that afternoon we went out along the road that ran through the settlement and past the corner of the Hindu's general store, where he smiled at us in well-oiled, unsuccessful-storekeeping, brotherly humanity, and hopeful salesmanship, turned the car off to the left onto a track that went into the deep forest, a narrow brush-bordered track through the heavy timber, that crossed a stream on an unsound log and pole bridge and went on until the timber thinned and we came out into a grassy savannah that stretched ahead to the reed-edged, dried-up bed of the lake with, far beyond, the shine of the water and the rose-pink of the flamingoes. There were some grass huts of fishermen in the shade of the last trees and ahead the wind blew across the grass of the savannah and the dried bed of the lake showed a white-gray with many small animals humping across its baked surface as our car alarmed them. They were reed buck and they looked strange and awkward as they moved in the distance but trim and graceful as you saw them standing close. We turned the car out through the thick, short grass and onto the dried lake floor and everywhere, to the left and to the right, where the streams flowed out into the lake and made a reedy marsh that ran down toward the receded lake, cut by canals of water, ducks were flying and we could see big flocks of geese spread over the grassy hummocks that rose above the marsh. The dried bed was hard and firm and we drove the car until it commenced to look moist and soft ahead, then left the motor car standing there, and, Karl taking Charo and I, M'Cola to carry shells and birds, we agreed to work one on one side and one the other of the marsh and try to shoot and keep the birds moving while Pop and P. O. M. went into the edge of the high reeds on the left shore of the lake where another stream made a thick marsh to which we thought the ducks might fly.

We saw them walk across the open, a big bulky figure in a faded corduroy coat and a very small one in trousers, gray khaki jacket, boots, and a big hat, and then disappear as they crouched in a point of dried reeds before we started. But as we went out to reach the edge of the stream we soon saw the plan was no good. Even watching carefully for the firmest footing you sunk down in the cool mud to the knees and, as it became less mucky and there were more hummocks broken by water, sometimes I went in to the waist. The ducks and geese flew up out of range and after the first flock had swung across toward where the others were hidden in the reeds and we heard the sharp, small, double report of P. O. M.'s 28-gauge and saw the ducks wheel off and go out toward the lake, the other scattered flocks and the geese all went out toward the open water. A flock of dark ibises, looking, with their dipped bills, like great curlews, flew over from the marsh on the side of the stream where Karl was and circled high above us before they went back into the reeds. All through the bog were snipe and black and white godwits and finally, not being able to get within range of the ducks, I began to shoot snipe to M'Cola's great disgust. We followed the marsh out and then I crossed another stream, shoulder high, holding my gun and shooting coat with shells in the pocket above my head and finally trying to work toward where P. O. M. and Pop were, found a deep flowing stream where teal were flying, and killed three. It was nearly dark now and I found Pop and P. O. M. on the far bank of this stream at the edge of the dried lake bed. It all looked too deep to wade and the bottom was soft but finally I found a heavily worn hippo trail that went into the stream and treading on this, the bottom fairly firm under foot, I made it, the water coming just under my armpits. As I came out on the grass and stood dripping a flock of teal came over very fast and, crouching to shoot in the dusk at the same time Pop did, we cut down three that fell hard in a long slant ahead in the tall grass. We hunted carefully and found them all. Their speed had carried them much farther than we expected and then, almost dark now, we started for the car across the gray dried mud of the lake bed, me soaked and my boots squashing water, P. O. M. pleased with the ducks, the first we'd had since the Serengetti, we all remembering how marvellous they were to eat, and ahead we could see the car looking very small and beyond it a stretch of flat, baked mud and then the grassy savannah and the forest.

Next day we came in from the zebra business gray and sweat-caked with dust that the car raised and the wind blew over us on the way home across the plain.

P. O. M. and Pop had not gone out, there was nothing for them to do and no need for them to eat that dust, and Karl and I out on the plain in the too much sun and dust had gone through one of those rows that starts like this, "What was the matter?"

"They were too far."

"Not at the start."

"They were too far, I tell you."

"They get hard if you don't take them."

"You shoot them."

"I've got enough. We only want twelve hides altogether. You go ahead."

Then some one, angry, shooting too fast to show he was being asked to shoot too fast, getting up from behind the ant hill and turning away in disgust, walking toward his partner, who says, smugly, "What's the matter with them?"

"They're too damned far, I tell you," desperately.

The smug one, complacently, "Look at them."

The zebra that had galloped off had seen the approaching truck of the skinners and had circled and were standing now, broadside, in easy range.

The one looks, says nothing, too angry now to shoot. Then says, "Go ahead. Shoot."

The smug one, more righteous now than ever, refuses. "Go ahead," he says.

"I'm through," says the other. He knows he is too angry to shoot and he feels he has been tricked. Something is always tricking him, the need to do things other than in a regular order, or by an inexact command in which details are not specified, or to have to do it in front of people, or to be hurried.

"We've got eleven," says smug face, sorry now. He knows he should not hurry him, that he should leave him alone, that he only upsets him by trying to speed him up, and that he has been a smugly righteous bastard again. "We can pick up the other one any time. Come on, Bo, we'll go in."

"No, let's get him. You get him."

"No, let's go in."

And as the car comes up and you ride in through the dust the bitterness goes and there is only the feeling of shortness of time again.

"What you thinking about now?" you ask. "What a son of a bitch I am, still?"

"About this afternoon," he says and grins, making wrinkles in the caked dust on his face.

"Me too," you say.

Finally the afternoon comes and you start.

This time you wear canvas ankle-high boots, light to pull out when you sink, you work out from hummock to hummock, picking a way across the marsh and wade and flounder through the canals and the ducks fly as before out to the lake, but you make a long circle to the right and come out into the lake itself and find the bottom hard and firm and walking knee deep in the water get outside the big flocks, then there is a shot and you and M'Cola crouch, heads bent, and then the air is full of them, and you cut down two, then two again, and then a high one straight overhead, then miss a fast one straight and low to the right, then they come whistling back, passing faster than you can load and shoot, you brown a bunch to get cripples for decoys and then take only fancy shots because you know now you can get all that we can use or carry. You try the high one, straight overhead and almost leaning backward, the *coup de roi,* and splash a big black duck down beside M'Cola, him laughing, then, the four cripples swimming away, you decide you better kill them and pick up. You have to run in water to your knees to get in range of the last cripple and you slip and go face down and are sitting, enjoying being completely wet finally, water cool on your behind, soaked with muddy water, wiping off glasses and then getting the water out of the gun, wondering if you can shoot up the shells before they will swell, M'Cola delighted with the spill. He, with the shooting coat now full of ducks, crouches and a flock of geese pass over in easy range while you try to pump a wet shell in. You get a shell in, shoot, but it is too far, or you were behind, and at the shot you see the cloud of flamingoes rise in the sun, making the whole horizon of the lake pink. Then they settle. But after that each time after you shoot you turn and look out into the sun on the water and see that quick rise of the unbelievable cloud and then the slow settling.

" 'Cola," you say and point.

"N'Dio," he says, watching them. "M'uzuri!" and hands you more shells.

We all had good shooting but it was best out on the lake and for three days afterward, travelling, we had cold teal, the best of ducks to eat, fine, plump, and tender, cold with Pan-Yan pickles, and the red wine we bought at Babati sitting by the road waiting for the trucks to come up, sitting on the shady porch of the little hotel at Babati, then late at night when the trucks finally came in and we were at the house of an absent friend of a friend, high up in the hills, cold at night, wearing coats at the table, having waited so long for the broken-down truck to come that we all drank much too much and were unspeakably hungry, P. O. M. dancing with the manager of the coffee shamba, and with Karl, to the gramophone, me shot full of emetine and with a ringing headache drowning it successfully in whiskey-soda with Pop on the porch, it dark and the wind blowing a gale, and then those teal coming on the table, smoking hot and with fresh vegetables. Guinea hen were all right, and I had one now in the lunch box in the back of the car that I would eat tonight; but those teal were the finest of all.

From Babati we had driven through the hills to the edge of a plain, wooded in a long stretch of glade beyond a small village where there was a mission station at the foot of a mountain. Here we had made a camp to hunt kudu which were supposed to be in the wooded hills and in the forest on the flats that stretched out to the edge of the open plain.

CHAPTER

I T WAS A hot place to camp, under trees that had been girdled to kill them so that the tse-tse fly would leave, and there was hard hunting in the hills, which were steep, brushy, and very broken, with a hard climb before you got up into them, and easy hunting on the wooded flats where you wandered as though through a deer park. But everywhere were tse-tse flies, swarming around you, biting hard on your neck, through your shirt, on arms, and behind the ears. I carried a leafy branch and swished away at the back of my neck as we walked and we hunted five days, from daylight until dark, coming home after dark, dead tired but glad of the coolness and of the darkness that stopped the tse-tse from biting. We took turns hunting the hills and the flats and Karl became steadily gloomier although he killed a very fine roan antelope. He had gotten a very complicated personal feeling about kudu and, as always when he was confused, it was some one's fault, the guides, the choice of beat, the hills; these all betrayed him. The hills punished him and he did not believe in the flats. Each day I hoped he would get one and that the atmosphere would clear but each day his feelings about the kudu complicated the hunting. He

SEVEN

was never a climber and took real punishment in the hills. I tried
to take the bulk of the hill beats to relieve him but I could see,
now that he was tired he felt they probably *were* in the hills and
he was missing his chance.

In the five days I saw a dozen or more kudu cows and one
young bull with a string of cows. The cows were big, gray,
striped-flanked antelope with ridiculously small heads, big ears,
and a soft, fast-rushing gait that moved them in big-bellied panic
through the trees. The young bull had the start of a spiral on his
horns but they were short and dumpy and as he ran past us at the
end of a glade in the dusk, third in a string of six cows, he was
no more like a real bull than a spike elk is like a big, old, thick-
necked, dark-maned, wonder-horned, tawny-hided, beer-horse-
built bugler of a bull-elk.

Another time, headed home as the sun went down along a
steep valley in the hills, the guides pointed to two gray, white-
striped, moving animals, against the sun at the top of the hill,
showing only their flanks through the trunks of the trees and said
they were kudu bulls. We could not see the horns and when we

got up to the top of the hill the sun was gone and on the rocky ground we could not find their tracks. But from the glimpse we had they looked higher in the legs than the cows we saw and they might have been bulls. We hunted the ridges until dark but never saw them again nor did Karl find them the next day when we sent him there.

We jumped many water buck and once, still hunting along a ridge with a steep gully below, we came on a water buck that had heard us, but not scented us, and as we stood, perfectly quiet, M'Cola holding his hand on mine, we watched him, only a dozen feet away, standing, beautiful, dark, full-necked, a dark ruff on his neck, his horns up, trembling all over as his nostrils widened searching for the scent. M'Cola was grinning, pressing his fingers tight on my wrist and we watched the big buck shiver from the danger that he could not locate. Then there was the distant, heavy boom of a native black powder gun and the buck jumped and almost ran over us as he crashed up the ridge.

Another day, with P. O. M. along, we had hunted all through the timbered flat and come out to the edge of the plain where there were only clumps of bush and sanseviera when we heard a deep, throaty, cough. I looked at M'Cola.

"Simba," he said and did not look pleased.

"Wapi?" I whispered. "Where?"

He pointed.

I whispered to P. O. M., "It's a lion. Probably the one we heard early this morning. You go back to those trees."

We had heard a lion roaring just before daylight when we were getting up.

"I'd rather stay with you."

"It wouldn't be fair to Pop," I said. "You wait back there."

"All right. But you *will* be careful."

"I won't take anything but a standing shot and I won't shoot unless I'm sure of him."

"All right."

"Come on," I said to M'Cola.

He looked very grave and did not like it at all.

"Wapi Simba?" I whispered.

"Here," he said dismally and pointed at the broken islands

of thick, green spiky cover. I motioned to one of the guides to go back with P. O. M. and we watched them go back a couple of hundred yards to the edge of the forest.

"Come on," I said. M'Cola shook his head without smiling but followed. We went forward very slowly, looking into and trying to see through the senseviera. We could see nothing. Then we heard the cough again, a little ahead and to the right.

"*No!*" M'Cola whispered. "*Hapana, B'wana!*"

"Come on," I said. I pointed my forefinger into my neck and wriggled the thumb down. "Kufa," I whispered, meaning that I would shoot the bastard in the neck and kill him dead. M'Cola shook his head, his face dead grave and sweating. "Hapana!" he whispered.

There was an ant hill ahead and we climbed the furrowed clay and from the top looked all around. We could not make out anything in the green cactus-like cover. I had believed we might see him from the ant hill and after we came down we went on for about two hundred yards into the broken cactus. Once again we heard him cough ahead of us and once, a little farther on, we heard a growl. It was very deep and very impressive. Since the ant heap my heart had not been in it. Until that had failed I had believed I might have a close and good shot and I knew that if I could kill one alone, without Pop along, I would feel good about it for a long time. I had made up my mind absolutely not to shoot unless I knew I could kill him, I had killed three and knew what it consisted in, but I was getting more excitement from this one than the whole trip. I felt it was perfectly fair to Pop to take it on as long as I had a chance to call the shot but what we were getting into now was bad. He kept moving away as we came on, but slowly. Evidently he did not want to move, having fed, probably, when we had heard him roaring in the early morning, and he wanted to settle down now. M'Cola hated it. How much of it was the responsibility he felt for me to Pop and how much was his own acute feeling of misery about the dangerous game I did not know. But he felt very miserable. Finally he put his hand on my shoulder, put his face almost into mine and shook his head violently three times.

"Hapana! Hapana! Hapana! B'wana!" he protested, sorrowed, and pled.

After all, I had no business taking him where I could not call the shot and it was a profound personal relief to turn back.

"All right," I said. We turned around and came back out the same way we had gone in, then crossed the open prairie to the trees where P. O. M. was waiting.

"Did you see him?"

"No," I told her. "We heard him three or four times."

"Weren't you frightened?"

"Pee-less," I said, "at the last. But I'd rather have shot him in there than any damned thing in the world."

"My, I'm glad you're back," she said. I got the dictionary out of my pocket and made a sentence in pigeon Swahili. "Like" was the word I wanted.

"M'Cola like Simba?"

M'Cola could grin again now and the smile moved the Chinese hairs at the corner of his mouth.

"Hapana," he said, and waved his hand in front of his face. "Hapana!"

"Hapana" is a negative.

"Shoot a kudu?" I suggested.

"Good," said M'Cola feelingly in Swahili. "Better. Best. Tendalla, yes. Tendalla."

But we never saw a kudu bull out of that camp and we left two days later to go into Babati and then down to Kondoa and strike across country toward Handeni and the coast.

I never liked that camp, nor the guides, nor the country. It had that picked-over, shot-out feeling. We knew there were kudu there and the Prince of Wales had killed his kudu from that camp, but there had been three other parties in that season, and the natives were hunting, supposedly defending their crops from baboons, but on meeting a native with a brass-bound musket it seemed odd that he should follow the baboons ten miles away from his shamba up into the kudu hills to have a shot at them, and I was all for pulling out and trying the new country toward Handeni where none of us had ever been.

"Let's go then," Pop said.

It seemed this new country was a gift. Kudu came out into the open and you sat and waited for the more enormous ones and selecting a suitable head, blasted him over. Then there were sable and we agreed that whoever killed the first kudu should move on in the sable country. I was beginning to feel awfully good and Karl was very cheerful at the prospect of this new miraculous country where they were so unsophisticated that it was really a shame to topple them over.

We left, soon after daylight, ahead of the outfit, who were to strike camp and follow in the two lorries. We stopped in Babati at the little hotel overlooking the lake and bought some more Pan-Yan pickles and had some cold beer. Then we started south on the Cape to Cairo road, here well graded, smooth, and carefully cut through wooded hills overlooking the long yellow stretch of plains of the Masai Steppes, down and through farming country, where the dried-breasted old women and the shrunken-flanked, hollow-ribbed old men hoed in the cornfields, through miles and dusty miles of this, and then into a valley of sun-baked, eroded land where the soil was blowing away in clouds as you looked, into the tree-shaded, pretty, whitewashed, German model-garrison town of Kandoa-Irangi.

We left M'Cola at the crossroads to hold up our lorries when they came, put the car into some shade and visited the military cemetery. We intended to call on the D. O. but they were at lunch, and we did not want to bother them, so after the military cemetery which was a pleasant, clean, well-kept place and as good as another to be dead in, we had some beer under a tree in shade that seemed liquid cool after the white glare of a sun that you could feel the weight of on your neck and shoulders, started the car and went out to the crossroads to pick up the lorries and head to the east into the new country.

CHAPTER

I T WAS A new country to us but it had the marks of the oldest
countries. The road was a track over shelves of solid rock, worn
by the feet of the caravans and the cattle, and it rose in the boulder-
strewn un-roadliness through a double line of trees and into the
hills. The country was so much like Aragon that I could not believe
that we were not in Spain until, instead of mules with saddle bags,
we met a dozen natives bare-legged and bare-headed dressed in
white cotton cloth they wore gathered over the shoulder like a
toga; but when they were past, the high trees beside the track over
those rocks was Spain and I had followed this same route forced
on ahead and following close behind a horse one time watching
the horror of the flies scuttling around his crupper. They were the
same camel flies we found here on the lions. In Spain if one got
inside your shirt you had to get the shirt off to kill him. He'd go
inside the neckband, down the back, around and under one arm,
make for the navel and the belly band, and if you did not get him he
would move with such intelligence and speed that, scuttling flat and
uncrushable he would make you undress completely to kill him.

That day of watching the camel flies working under the horse's
tail, having had them myself, gave me more horror than anything

EIGHT

I could remember except one time in a hospital with my right arm broken off short between the elbow and the shoulder, the back of the hand having hung down against my back, the points of the bone having cut up the flesh of the biceps until it finally rotted, swelled, burst, and sloughed off in pus. Alone with the pain in the night in the fifth week of not sleeping I thought suddenly how a bull elk must feel if you break a shoulder and he gets away and in that night I lay and felt it all, the whole thing as it would happen from the shock of the bullet to the end of the business and, being a little out of my head, thought perhaps what I was going through was a punishment for all hunters. Then, getting well, decided if it was a punishment I had paid it and at least I knew what I was doing. I did nothing that had not been done to me. I had been shot and I had been crippled and gotten away. I expected, always, to be killed by one thing or another and I, truly, did not mind that any more. Since I still loved to hunt I resolved that I would only shoot as long as I could kill cleanly and as soon as I lost that ability I would stop.

If you serve time for society, democracy, and the other things quite young, and declining any further enlistment make yourself responsible only to yourself, you exchange the pleasant, comforting stench of comrades for something you can never feel in any other way than by yourself. That something I cannot yet define completely but the feeling comes when you write well and truly of something and know impersonally you have written in that way and those who are paid to read it and report on it do not like the subject so they say it is all a fake, yet you know its value absolutely; or when you do something which people do not consider a serious occupation and yet you know, truly, that it is as important and has always been as important as all the things that are in fashion, and when, on the sea, you are alone with it and know that this Gulf Stream you are living with, knowing, learning about, and loving, has moved, as it moves, since before man, and that it has gone by the shoreline of that long, beautiful, unhappy island since before Columbus sighted it and that the things you find out about it, and those that have always lived in it are permanent and of value because that stream will flow, as it has flowed, after the Indians, after the Spaniards, after the British, after the Americans and after all the Cubans and all the systems of governments, the richness, the poverty, the martyrdom, the sacrifice and the venality and the cruelty are all gone as the high-piled scow of garbage, bright-colored, white-flecked, ill-smelling, now tilted on its side, spills off its load into the blue water, turning it a pale green to a depth of four or five fathoms as the load spreads across the surface, the sinkable part going down and the flotsam of palm fronds, corks, bottles, and used electric light globes, seasoned with an occasional condom or a deep floating corset, the torn leaves of a student's exercise book, a well-inflated dog, the occasional rat, the no-longer-distinguished cat; all this well shepherded by the boats of the garbage pickers who pluck their prizes with long poles, as interested, as intelligent, and as accurate as historians; they have the viewpoint; the stream, with no visible flow, takes five loads of this a day when things are going well in La Habana and in ten miles along the coast it is as clear and blue and unimpressed as it was ever before the tug hauled out the scow; and the palm fronds of our victories, the worn light bulbs of our discoveries and the empty condoms of our great loves float with no significance against one single, lasting thing—the stream.

So, in the front seat, thinking of the sea and of the country, in a little while we ran out of Aragon and down to the bank of a sand river, half a mile wide, of golden-colored sand, shored by green trees and broken by islands of timber and in this river the water is underneath the sand and the game comes down at night and digs in the sand with sharp-pointed hoofs and water flows in and they drink. We crossed this river and by now it was getting to be afternoon and we passed many people on the road who were leaving the country ahead where there was a famine and there were small trees and close brush now beside the road and then it commenced to climb and we came into some blue hills, old, worn, wooded hills with trees like beeches and clusters of huts with fire smoking and cattle home driven, flocks of sheep and goats and patches of corn and I said to P. O. M., "It's like Galicia."

"Exactly," she said. "We've been through three provinces of Spain today."

"Is it really?" Pop asked.

"There's no bloody difference," I said. "Only the buildings. It was like Navarre in Droopy's country too. The limestone out-cropping in the same way, the way the land lies, the trees along the watercourses and the springs."

"It's damned strange how you can love a country," Pop said.

"You two are very profound fellows," P. O. M. said. "But where are we going to camp?"

"Here," said Pop. "As well as any place. We'll just find some water."

We camped under some trees near three big wells where native women came for water and, after drawing lots for location, Karl and I hunted in the dusk around two of the hills across the road above the native village.

"It's all kudu country," Pop said. "You're liable to jump one anywhere."

But we saw nothing but some Masai cattle in the timber and came home, in the dark, glad of the walk after a day in the car, to find camp up, Pop and P. O. M. in pyjamas by the fire, and Karl not yet in.

He came in, furious for some reason, no kudu possibly, pale, and gaunt looking and speaking to nobody.

Later, at the fire, he asked me where we had gone and I said we had hunted around our hill until our guide had heard them; then cut up to the top of the hill, down, and across country to camp.

"What do you mean, heard us?"

"He said he heard you. So did M'Cola."

"I thought we drew lots for where we would hunt."

"We did," I said. "But we didn't know we had gotten around to your side until we heard you."

"Did *you* hear us?"

"I heard something," I said. "And when I put my hand up to my ear to listen the guide said something to M'Cola and M'Cola said, 'B'wana.' I said, 'What B'wana?' and he said, 'B'wana Kabor.' That's you. So we figured we'd come to our limit and went up to the top and came back."

He said nothing and looked very angry.

"Don't get sore about it," I said.

"I'm not sore. I'm tired," he said. I could believe it because of all people no one can be gentler, more understanding, more self-sacrificing, than Karl, but the kudu had become an obsession to him and he was not himself, nor anything like himself.

"He better get one pretty quick," P. O. M. said when he had gone in to his tent to bathe.

"Did you cut in on his country?" Pop asked me.

"Hell, no," I said.

"He'll get one where we're going," Pop said. "He'll probably get a fifty-incher."

"All the better," I said. "But by God, I want to get one too."

"You will, Old Timer," Pop said. "I haven't a thought but what you will."

"What the hell. We've got ten days."

"We'll get sable too, you'll see. Once our luck starts to run."

"How long have you ever had them hunt them in a good country?"

"Three weeks and leave without seeing one. And I've had them get them the first half day. It's still hunting, the way you hunt a big buck at home."

"I love it," I said. "But I don't want that guy to beat me. Pop, he's got the best buff, the best rhino, the best water-buck—"

"You beat him on oryx," Pop said.

"What's an oryx?"

"He'll look damned handsome when you get him home."

"I'm just kidding."

"You beat him on impala, on eland. You've got a first-rate bushbuck. Your leopard's as good as his. But he'll beat you on anything where there's luck. He's got damned wonderful luck and he's a good lad. I think he's off his feed a little."

"You know how fond I am of him. I like him as well as I like any one. But I want to see him have a good time. It's no fun to hunt if we get that way about it."

"You'll see. He'll get a kudu at this next camp and he'll be on top of the wave."

"I'm just a crabby bastard," I said.

"Of course you are," said Pop. "But why not have a drink?"

"Right," I said.

Karl came out, quiet, friendly, gentle, and understandingly delicate.

"It will be fine when we get to that new country," he said.

"It will be swell," I said.

"Tell me what it's like, Mr. Phillips," he said to Pop.

"I don't know," said Pop. "But they say it's very pleasant hunting. They're supposed to feed right out in the open. That old Dutchman claims there are some remarkable heads."

"I hope you get a sixty-incher, kid," Karl said to me.

"You'll get a sixty-incher."

"No," said Karl. "Don't kid me. I'll be happy with any kudu."

"You'll probably get a hell of a one," Pop said.

"Don't kid me," Karl said. "I know how lucky I've been. I would be happy with any kudu. Any bull at all."

He was very gentle and he could tell what was in your mind, forgive you for it, and understand it.

"Good old Karl," I said, warmed with whiskey, understanding, and sentiment.

"We're having a swell time, aren't we?" Karl said. "Where's poor old Mama?"

"I'm here," said P. O. M. from the shadow. "I'm one of those quiet people."

"By God if you're not," Pop said. "But you can puncture the old man quick enough when he gets started."

"That's what makes a woman a universal favorite," P. O. M. told him. "Give me another compliment, Mr. J."

"By God, you're brave as a little terrier." Pop and I had both been drinking, it seemed.

"That's lovely," P. O. M. sat far back in her chair, holding her hands clasped around her mosquito boots. I looked at her, seeing her quilted blue robe in the firelight now, and the light on her black hair. "I love it when you all reach the little terrier stage. Then I know the war can't be far away. Were either of you gentlemen in the war by any chance?"

"Were we not," said Pop. "A couple of the bravest bastards that ever lived and your husband's an extraordinary wing shot and an excellent tracker."

"Now he's drunk, we get the truth," I said.

"Let's eat," said P. O. M. "I'm really frightfully hungry."

We were out in the car at daylight, out onto the road and beyond the village and, passing through a stretch of heavy bush, we came to the edge of a plain, still misty before the sunrise, where we could see, a long way off, eland feeding, looking huge and gray in the early morning light. We stopped the car at the edge of the bush and getting out and sitting down with the glasses saw there was a herd of kongoni scattered between us and the eland and with the kongoni a single bull oryx, like a fat, plum-colored, Masai donkey with marvellous long, black, straight, back-slanting horns that showed each time he lifted his head from feeding.

"You want to go after him?" I asked Karl.

"No. You go on."

I knew he hated to make a stalk and to shoot in front of people and so I said, "All right." Also I wanted to shoot, selfishly, and Karl was unselfish. We wanted meat badly.

I walked along the road, not looking toward the game, trying to look casual, holding the rifle slung straight up and down from the left shoulder away from the game. They seemed to pay no attention but fed away steadily. I knew that if I moved toward them they would at once move off out of range so, when from the tail of my eye I saw the oryx drop his head to feed again, and, the shot looking possible, I sat down, slipped my arm through the sling and as he looked up and started to move off, quartering away, I held for the top of his back and squeezed off. You do not hear the noise of the shot on game but the slap of the bullet sounded as he started running across and to the right, the whole plain backgrounding into moving animals against the rise of the sun, the rocking-horse canter of the long-legged, grotesque kongoni, the heavy swinging trot into gallop of the eland, and another oryx I had not seen before running with the kongoni. This sudden life and panic all made background for the one I wanted, now trotting, three-quartering away, his horns held high now and I stood to shoot running, got on him, the whole animal miniatured in the aperture and I held above his shoulders, swung ahead and squeezed and he was down, kicking, before the crack of the bullet striking bone came back. It was a very long and even more lucky shot that broke a hind leg.

I ran toward him, then slowed to walk up carefully, in order not to be blown if he jumped and ran; but he was down for good. He had gone down so suddenly and the bullet had made such a crack as it landed that I was afraid I had hit him on the horns but when I reached him he was dead from the first shot behind the shoulders high up in the back and I saw it was cutting the leg from under him that brought him down. They all came up and Charo stuck him to make him legal meat.

"Where did you hold on him the second time?" Karl asked.

"Nowhere. A touch above and quite a way ahead and swung with him."

"It was very pretty," Dan said.

"By evening," Pop said, "he'll tell us that he broke that off leg on purpose. That's one of his favorite shots, you know. Did you ever hear him explain it?"

While M'Cola was skinning the head out and Charo was butchering out the meat, a long, thin Masai with a spear came up, said good morning, and stood, on one leg, watching the skinning. He spoke to me at some length and I called to Pop. The Masai repeated it to Pop.

"He wants to know if you are going to shoot something else,"

Pop said. "He would like some hides but he doesn't care about oryx hide. It is almost worthless, he says. He wonders if you would like to shoot a couple of kongoni or an eland. He likes those hides."

"Tell him on our way back."

Pop told him solemnly. The Masai shook my hand.

"Tell him he can always find me around Harry's New York Bar," I said.

The Masai said something else and scratched one leg with the other.

"He says why did you shoot him twice?" Pop asked.

"Tell him in the morning in our tribe we always shoot them twice. Later in the day we shoot them once. In the evening we are often half shot ourselves. Tell him he can always find me at the New Stanley or at Torr's."

"He says what do you do with the horns?"

"Tell him in our tribe we give the horns to our wealthiest friends. Tell him it is very exciting and sometimes members of the tribe are chased across vast spaces with empty pistols. Tell him he can find me in the book."

Pop told the Masai something and we shook hands again, parting on a most excellent basis. Looking across the plain through the mist we could see some other Masai coming along the road; earth-brown skins, and knee-ing forward stride and spears thin in the morning light.

Back in the car, the oryx head wrapped in a burlap sack, the meat tied inside the mudguards, the blood drying, the meat dusting over, the road of red sand now, the plain gone, the bush again close to the edge of the road, we came up into some hills and through the little village of Kibaya where there was a white rest house and a general store and much farming land. It was here Dan had sat on a haystack one time waiting for a kudu to feed out into the edge of a patch of mealy-corn and a lion had stalked Dan while he sat and nearly gotten him. This gave us a strong historical feeling for the village of Kibaya and as it was still cool and the sun had not yet burned off the dew from the grass I suggested we drink a bottle of that silver-paper-necked, yellow-and-black-labelled German beer with the horseman in armor on it in order that we might remember the place better and even appreciate it more. This done, full of historical admiration for Kibaya, we learned the road was possible ahead, left word for the lorries to follow on to the eastward and headed on toward the coast and the kudu country.

For a long time, while the sun rose and the day became hot we drove through what Pop had described, when I asked him what the country was like to the south, as a million miles of bloody Africa, bush close to the road that was impenetrable, solid, scrubby-looking undergrowth.

"There are very big elephant in there," Pop said, "But it's impossible to hunt them. That's why they're very big. Simple, isn't it?"

After a long stretch of the million-mile country, the country began to open out into dry, sandy, bush-bordered prairies that dried into a typical desert country with occasional patches of bush where there was water, that Pop said was like the northern frontier province of Kenya. We watched for gerenuk, that long-necked antelope that resembles a praying mantis in its way of carrying itself, and for the lesser kudu that we knew lived in this desert bush, but the sun was high now and we saw nothing. Finally the road began to lift gradually into the hills again, low, blue, wooded hills now, with miles of sparse bush, a little thicker than orchard bush, between, and ahead a pair of high, heavy, timbered hills that were big enough to be mountains. These were on each side of the road and as we climbed in the car where the red road narrowed there was a herd of hundreds of cattle ahead being driven down to the coast by Somali cattle buyers, the principal buyer walked ahead, tall, good-looking in white turban and coast clothing, carrying an umbrella as a symbol of authority. We worked the car through the herd, finally, and coming out wound our way through pleasant looking bush, up and out into the open between the two mountains and on, a half a mile, to a mud and thatched village in the open clearing on a little low plateau beyond the two mountains. Looking back, the mountains looked very fine with timber up their slopes, out-croppings of limestone and open glades and meadows above the timber.

"Is this the place?"

"Yes," said Dan. "We will find where the camping place is."

A very old, worn, and faded black man, with a stubble of white beard, a farmer, dressed in a dirty once-white cloth gathered at the shoulder in the manner of a Roman toga, came out from behind one of the mud and wattle huts, and guided us back down the road and off it to the left to a very good camp site. He was a very discouraged-looking old man and after Pop and Dan had talked with him he went off, seeming more discouraged than before, to bring some guides whose names Dan had written on a piece of paper as being recommended by a Dutch hunter who had been here a year ago and who was Dan's great friend.

We took the seats out of the car to use as a table and benches and spreading our coats to sit on had a lunch in the deep shade of a big tree, drank some beer, and slept or read while we waited for the lorries to come up. Before the lorries arrived the old man came back with the skinniest, hungriest, most unsuccessful looking of Wanderobos who stood on one leg, scratched the back of his neck and carried a bow and quiver of arrows and a spear. Queried as to whether this was the guide whose name we had the old man admitted he was not and went off, more discouraged than ever, to get the official guides.

When we woke next the old man was standing with the two official and highly clothed in khaki guides and two others, quite naked, from the village. There was a long palaver and the head one of the two khaki-panted guides showed his credentials a To Whom It May Concern stating the bearer knew the country well and was a reliable boy and capable tracker. This was signed by so and so, professional hunter. The khaki-clothed guide referred to this professional hunter as B'wana Simba and the name infuriated us all.

"Some bloke that killed a lion once," Pop said.

"Tell him I am B'wana Fisi, the hyena slaughterer," I told Dan. "B'wana Fisi chokes them with his naked hands."

Dan was telling them something else.

"Ask them if they would like to meet B'wana Hop-Toad, the inventor of the hoptoads and Mama Tziggi, who owns all these locusts."

Dan ignored this. It seemed they were discussing money. After ascertaining their customary daily wage, Pop told them if either of us killed a kudu the guide would receive fifteen shillings.

"You mean a pound," said the leading guide.

"They seem to know what they're up to," Pop said. "I must say I don't care for this sportsman in spite of what B'wana Simba says."

B'wana Simba, by the way, we later found out to be an excellent hunter with a wonderful reputation on the coast.

"We'll put them into two lots and you draw from them," Pop suggested, "one naked one and one with breeches in each lot. I'm all for the naked savage, myself, as a guide."

On suggesting to the two testimonial-equipped, breeched guides that they select an unclothed partner, we found this would not work out. Loud Mouth, the financial and, now, theatrical, genius who was giving a gesture-by-gesture reproduction of How B'wana Simba Killed His Last Kudu interrupted it long enough to state he would only hunt with Abdullah. Abdullah, the short, thick-nosed, educated one, was His Tracker. They always hunted together. He himself did not track. He resumed the pantomime of B'wana Simba and another character known as B'wana Doktor and the horned beasts.

"We'll take the two savages as one lot and these two Oxonians as the other," Pop said.

"I *hate* that theatrical bastard," I said.

"He may be marvellous," Pop said doubtfully. "Anyway, you're a tracker, you know. The old man says the other two are good."

"Thank you. Go to hell. Will you hold the straws?"

Pop arranged two grass stems in his fist. "The long one is for David Garrick and his pal," he explained. "The short one is the two nudist sportsmen."

"Do you want to draw first?"

"Go ahead," Karl said.

I drew David Garrick and Abdullah.

"I got the bloody tragedian."

"He may be very good," Karl said.

"Do you want to trade?"

"No. He may be a marvel."

"Now we'll draw for choice of beats. The long straw gets first choice," Pop explained.

"Go ahead and draw."

Karl drew the short one.

"What are the beats?" I asked Pop.

There was a long conversation in which our David simulated the killing of half a dozen kudu from different types of ambush, surprise, stalks in the open, and jumping them in the bush.

Finally Pop said, "It seems there's some sort of a salt-lick where they come to lick salt and thousands are slain. Then sometimes you just stroll around the hill there and pot the poor buggers in the open. If you're feeling frightfully fit, you climb for them and up in the crags you knock them over as they stroll out to feed."

"I'll take the salt-lick."

"Mind you only shoot the very biggest sort," Pop said.

"When do we start?" Karl asked.

"The salt-lick is supposed to be an early morning show," Pop told us. "But Old Hem might as well have a look at it tonight. It's about five miles down the road before you start to walk. He'll start first and take the car. You can start back in the hills any time after the sun gets a little farther down."

"What about the Memsahib?" I asked. "Should she go with me?"

"I don't think it's advisable," Pop said seriously. "The fewer people when you're after kudu the better."

M'Cola, Theatre Business, Abdullah, and I came back that evening late in the cool of the night and full of excitement as we came up to the fire. The dust of the salt-lick had been cut up and printed deep with fresh kudu tracks and there were several big bull tracks. The blind made a marvellous ambush and I was as confident and as sure of a shot at kudu the next morning as I would be sure of a shot at ducks from a good blind, with a fine stock of decoys out, cold weather, and the certainty of a flight on.

"It's airtight. It's foolproof. It's even a shame. What's his name, Booth, Barrett, McCullough—you know who I mean—"

"Charles Laughton," said Pop, pulling on his pipe.

"That's the one. Fred Astaire. Society's hoofer and the world's. He's an ace. Found the blind and everything. Knew where the salt-lick was. Could tell which way the wind blew by simply scattering dust. He's a marvel. B'wana Simba trains 'em, pal. Pop, we have them in the container. It's only a question of not spoiling the meat and selecting the more rugged specimens. I'll kill you two tomorrow on that lick. Citizens, I feel very well."

"What *have* you been drinking?"

"Not a damned thing, really. Call Garrick. Tell him I'll put him in the cinema. Got a part for him. Little thing I thought up on the way home. It may not work out but I like the plot. Othello or The Moor of Venice. D'you like it? It's got a wonderful idea. You see this jig we call Othello falls in love with this girl who's never been around at all so we call her Desdemona. Like it? They've been after me to write it for years but I drew the color line. Let him go out and get a reputation, I told them. Harry Wills, hell. Paulino beat him. Sharkey beat him. Dempsey beat Sharkey. Carnera knocked him out. What if nobody saw the punch? Where the hell were we, Pop? Harry Greb is dead you know."

"We were just coming into Town," Pop said. "Chaps were throwing things at you and we couldn't find out why."

"I remember," P. O. M. said. "Why didn't you make him draw the color line, Mr. J. P.?"

"I was frightfully tired," Pop said.

"You're very distinguished looking, though," P. O. M. said. "What are we going to do with this goofy?"

"Throw a drink into the brute and see if he'll quiet down."

"I'm quiet now," I said. "But by God I feel awfully good about tomorrow."

Just then who should come into camp but old Karl with his two naked savages and his half-size, very devout Mohammedan gun bearer, Charo. In the firelight old Karl looked a grayish, yellowish white in the face and he took off his Stetson.

"Well, did you get one?" he asked.

"No. But they're there. What did you do?"

"Walked along a god-damned road. How do they expect to find kudu along a road with nothing but cattle and huts and people?"

He did not look like himself and I thought he must be ill. But coming in like a death's head when we had been clowning made me behave badly again and I said, "We drew lots, you know."

"Of course," he said bitterly. "We hunted along a road. What would you expect to see? Does that seem the way to hunt kudu to you?"

"But you'll get one on the salt-lick in the morning," P. O. M. told him very cheerfully.

I drank off the glass of whiskey and soda and heard my voice say very cheerfully, "You'll be sure to get one on the salt-lick in the morning."

"You're hunting it in the morning," Karl said.

"No. You're hunting it. I had it tonight. We're changing off. That's been understood. Isn't it, Pop?"

"Quite," Pop said. No one was looking at any one else.

"Have a whiskey and soda, Karl," P. O. M. said.

"All right," Karl said.

We had one of those quiet meals. In bed in the tent, I said, "What in God's name prompted you to say that about him having the lick in the morning?"

"I don't know. I don't think that's what I meant to say. I got mixed up. Let's not talk about it."

"I won the damned thing drawing lots. You can't go against lots. That's the only way the luck has a chance to even up, ever."

"Don't let's talk about it."

"I don't think he's well now and he doesn't feel himself. The damned things have gotten his goat and he's liable to blow that salt-lick higher than a kite in the state he's in."

"Please stop talking about it."

"I will."

"Good."

"Well, we made him feel good anyway."

"I don't know that we did. Please stop talking about it."

"I will."

"Good."

"Good night," she said.

"The hell with it," I said. "Good night."

"Good night."

CHAPTER

IN THE MORNING Karl and his outfit started for the salt-lick and Garrick, Abdullah, M'Cola and I crossed the road, angled behind the village up a dry watercourse and started climbing the mountains in a mist. We headed up a pebbly, boulder-filled, dry stream bed overgrown with vines and brush so that, climbing, you walked, stooping, in a steep tunnel of vines and foliage. I sweated so that I was soaked through my shirt and undergarments and when we came out on the shoulder of the mountain and stood, looking down at the bank of clouds quilting over the entire valley below us, the morning breeze chilled me and I had to put on my raincoat while we glassed the country. I was too wet with sweat to sit down and I signed Garrick to keep on going. We went around one side of the mountain, doubled back on a higher grade and crossed over, out of the sun that was drying my wet shirt and along the top of a series of grassy valleys, stopping to search each one thoroughly with the field glasses. Finally we came to a sort of amphitheatre, a bowl-like valley of very green grass with a small stream down the middle and timber along the far side and all the lower edge. We sat in the shadow against some rocks, out of any

NINE

breeze, watching with the glasses as the sun rose and lighted the opposite slopes, seeing two kudu cows and a calf feed out from the timber, moving with the quickly browsing, then head lifted, long staring vigilance of all browsing animals in a forest. Animals on a plain can see so far that they have confidence and feed very differently from animals in the woods. We could see the vertical white stripes on their gray flanks and it was very satisfying to watch them and to be high in the mountain that early in the morning. Then, while we watched, there was a boom, like a rockslide. I thought at first it was a boulder falling, but M'Cola whispered.

"B'wana Kibor! Piga!" We listened for another shot but we did not hear one and I was sure Karl had his kudu. The cows we were watching had heard the shot and stood, listening, then went on feeding. But they fed into the timber. I remembered the old saying of the Indian in camp, "One shot, meat. Two shots, maybe. Three shots, heap shit," and I got out the dictionary to translate it for M'Cola. However it came out seemed to amuse him and he laughed and shook his head. We glassed that valley until the sun came onto us, then hunted around the other side of the mountain and in another fine valley saw the place where the other B'wana, B'wana Doktor he still sounded like, had shot a fine bull kudu, but a Masai walked down the center of the valley while we were glassing it and when I pretended I was going to shoot him Garrick became very dramatic insisting it was a man, a man, a man!

"Don't shoot men?" I asked him.

"No! No! No!" he said putting his hand to his head. I took the gun down with great reluctance, clowning for M'Cola who was grinning and, it very hot now, we walked across a meadow where the grass was knee high and truly swarming with long, rose-colored, gauze-winged locusts that rose in clouds about us, making a whirring like a mowing machine and, climbing small hills and going down a long steep slope, we made our way back to camp to find the air of the valley drifting with flying locusts and Karl already in camp with his kudu.

Passing the skinner's tent he showed me the head which looked, body-less and neck-less, the cape of hide hanging loose, wet and heavy from where the base of the skull had been severed from the vertebral column, a very strange and unfortunate kudu. Only the skin running from the eyes down to the nostrils, smooth gray and delicately marked with white, and the big, graceful ears were beautiful. The eyes were already dusty and there were flies around them and the horns were heavy, coarse, and instead of spiralling high they made a heavy turn and slanted straight out. It was a freak head, heavy and ugly.

Pop was sitting under the dining tent smoking and reading.

"Where's Karl?" I asked him.

"In his tent, I think. What did you do?"

"Worked around the hill. Saw a couple of cows."

"I'm awfully glad you got him," I told Karl at the mouth of his tent. "How was it?"

"We were in the blind and they motioned me to keep my head down and then when I looked up there he was right beside us. He looked huge."

"We heard you shoot. Where did you hit him?"

"In the leg first, I think. Then we trailed him and finally I hit him a couple of more times and we got him."

"I heard only one shot."

"There were three or four," Karl said.

"I guess the mountain shut off some if you were gone the other way trailing him. He's got a heavy beam and a big spread."

"Thanks," Karl said. "I hope you get a lot better one. They said there was another one but I didn't see him."

I went back to the dining tent where Pop and P. O. M. were. They did not seem very elated about the kudu.

"What's the matter with you?" I asked.

"Did you see the head?" P. O. M. asked.

"Sure."

"It's *awful* looking," she said.

"It's a kudu. He's got another one still to go."

"Charo and the trackers said there was another bull with this one. A big bull with a wonderful head."

"That's all right. I'll shoot him."

"If he ever comes back."

"It's fine he has one," P. O. M. said.

"I'll bet he'll get the biggest one ever known, now," I said.

"I'm sending him down with Dan to the sable country," Pop said. "That was the agreement. The first to kill a kudu to get first crack at the sable."

"That's fine."

"Then as soon as you get your kudu we'll move down there too."

"*Good.*"

GREEN HILLS OF AFRICA

PART III

Pursuit and Failure

CHAPTER

THAT ALL SEEMED a year ago. Now, this afternoon in the car, on the way out to the twenty-eight-mile salt-lick, the sun on our faces, just having shot the guinea fowl, having, in the last five days, failed on the lick where Karl shot his bull, having failed in the hills, the big hills and the small hills, having failed on the flats, losing a shot the night before on this lick because of the Austrian's truck, I knew there were only two days more to hunt before we must leave. M'Cola knew it too, and we were hunting together now, with no feeling of superiority on either side any more, only a shortness of time and our disgust that we did not know the country and were saddled with these farcical bastards as guides.

Kamau, the driver, was a Kikuyu, a quiet man of about thirty-five who, with an old brown tweed coat some shooter had discarded, trousers heavily patched on the knees and ripped open again, and a very ragged shirt, managed always to give an impression of great elegance. Kamau was very modest, quiet, and an excellent driver and now, as we came out of the bush country, and into an open, scrubby, desert-looking stretch, I looked at him,

TEN

whose elegance, achieved with an old coat and a safety pin, whose
modesty, pleasantness and skill I admired so much now, and
thought how, when we first were out, he had very nearly died of
fever, and that if he had died it would have meant nothing to me
except that we would be short a driver; while now whenever or
wherever he should die I would feel badly. Then abandoning the
sweet sentiment of the distant and improbable death of Kamau,
I thought what a pleasure it would be to shoot David Garrick in
the behind, just to see the look on his face, sometime when he
was dramatizing a stalk and, just then, we put up another flock of
guineas. M'Cola handed me the shotgun and I shook my head. He
nodded violently and said, "Good. Very good," and I told Kamau
to go on. This confused Garrick who began an oration. Didn't we
want guineas? Those were guineas. The finest kind. I had seen by
the speedometer that we were only about three miles from the salt
and had no desire to spook a bull off of it, by a shot, to frighten
him in the way we had seen the lesser kudu leave the salt when he
heard the truck noise while we were in the blind.

We left the truck under some scrubby trees about two miles

from the lick and walked along the sandy road toward the first salt place which was in the open to the left of the trail. We had gone about a mile keeping absolutely quiet and walking in single file, Abdullah the educated tracker leading, then me, M'Cola, and Garrick, when we saw the road was wet ahead of us. Where the sand was thin over the clay there was a pool of water and you could see that a heavy rain had drenched it all on ahead. I did not realize what this meant but Garrick threw his arms wide, looked up to the sky and bared his teeth in anger.

"It's no good," M'Cola whispered.

Garrick started to talk in a loud voice.

"Shut up, you bastard," I said, and put my hand to my mouth. He kept on talking in above normal tones and I looked up "shut up" in the dictionary while he pointed to the sky and the rained-out road. I couldn't find "shut up" so I put the back of my hand against his mouth with some firmness and he closed it in surprise.

" 'Cola," I said.

"Yes," said M'Cola.

"What's the matter?"

"Salt no good."

"Ah."

So that was it. I had thought of the rain only as something that made tracking easy.

"When the rain?" I asked.

"Last night," M'Cola said.

Garrick started to talk and I placed the back of my hand against his mouth.

" 'Cola."

"Yes."

"Other salt," pointing in the direction of the big lick in the woods, which I knew was a good bit higher because we went very slightly up-hill through the brush to reach it. "Other salt good?"

"Maybe."

M'Cola said something in a very low voice to Garrick who seemed deeply hurt but kept his mouth shut and we went on down the road, walking around the wet places, to where, sure enough, the deep depression of the salt-lick was half filled with water. Garrick started to whisper a speech here but M'Cola shut him up again.

"Come on," I said, and, M'Cola ahead, we started trailing up the damp, sandy, ordinarily dry watercourse that led through the trees to the upper lick.

M'Cola stopped dead, leaned over to look at the damp sand, then whispered, "Man," to me. There was the track.

"Shenzi," he said, which meant a wild man.

We trailed the man, moving slowly through the trees and stalking the lick carefully, up and into the blind. M'Cola shook his head.

"No good," he said. "Come on."

We went over to the lick. There it was all written plainly. There were the tracks of three big bull kudu in the moist bank beyond the lick where they had come to the salt. Then there were the sudden, deep, knifely-cut tracks where they made a spring when the bow twanged and the slashing heavily cut prints of their hoofs as they had gone off up the bank and then, far-spaced, the tracks running into the bush. We trailed them, all three, but no man's track joined theirs. The bow-man missed them.

M'Cola said, "Shenzi!" putting great hate into the word. We picked up the shenzi's tracks and saw where he had gone on back to the road. We settled down in the blind and waited there until it was dark and a light rain began to fall. Nothing came to the salt. In the rain we made our way back to the truck. Some wild-man had shot at our kudu and spooked them away from the salt and now the lick was being ruined.

Kamau had rigged a tent out of a big canvas ground cloth, hung my mosquito net inside, and set up the canvas cot. M'Cola brought the food inside the shelter tent.

Garrick and Abdullah built a fire and they, Kamau and M'Cola, cooked over it. They were going to sleep in the truck. It rained drizzlingly and I undressed, got into mosquito boots and heavy pyjamas and sat on the cot, ate a breast of roast guinea hen and drank a couple of tin cups of half whiskey and water.

M'Cola came in, grave, solicitous, and very awkward inside of a tent and took my clothes out from where I had folded them to make a pillow and folded them again, very un-neatly, and put them under the blankets. He brought three tins to see if I did not want them opened.

"No."

"Chai?" he asked.

"The hell with it."

"No chai?"

"Whiskey better."

"Yes," he said feelingly. "Yes."

"Chai in the morning. Before the sun."

"Yes, B'wana M'Kumba."

"You sleep here. Out of the rain," I pointed to the canvas where the rain was making the finest sound that we, who live much outside of houses, ever hear. It was a lovely sound, even though it was bitching us.

"Yes."

"Go on. Eat."

"Yes. No chai?"

"The hell with tea."

"Whiskey?" he asked hopefully.

"Whiskey finish."

"Whiskey," he said confidently.

"All right," I said. "Go eat," and pouring the cup half and half with water got in under the mosquito bar, found my clothes and again made them into a pillow, and lying on my side drank the whiskey very slowly, resting on one elbow, then dropped the cup down under the bar onto the ground, felt under the cot for the Springfield, put the searchlight beside me in the bed under the blanket, and went to sleep listening to the rain. I woke when I heard M'Cola come in, make his bed and go to sleep, and I woke once in the night and heard him sleeping by me; but in the morning he was up and had made the tea before I was awake.

"Chai," he said, pulling on my blanket.

"Bloody chai," I said, sitting up still asleep.

It was a gray, wet morning. The rain had stopped but the mist hung over the ground and we found the salt-lick rained out and not a track near it. Then we hunted through the wet scrub on the flat hoping to find a track in the soaked earth and trail a bull until we could see him. There were no tracks. We crossed the road and followed the edge of the scrub around a moor-like open stretch. I hoped we might find the rhino but while we came on much fresh rhino dung there were no tracks since the rain. Once we heard tick birds and looking up saw them in jerky flight above us headed to the northward over the heavy scrub. We made a long circle through there but found nothing but a fresh hyena track and a cow kudu track. In a tree M'Cola pointed out a lesser kudu skull with one beautiful, long, curling horn. We found the other horn below in the grass and I screwed it back onto its bone base.

"Shenzi," M'Cola said and imitated a man pulling a bow. The skull was quite clean but the hollow horns had some damp residue in them, smelled unbearably foul and, giving no sign of having noticed the stench, I handed them to Garrick who promptly, without sign, gave them to Abdullah. Abdullah wrinkled the edge of his flat nose and shook his head. They really smelled abominably. M'Cola and I grinned and Garrick looked virtuous.

I decided a good idea might be to drive along the road in the car, watching for kudu, and hunt any likely looking clearings. We went back to the car and did this, working several clearings with no luck. By then the sun was up and the road was becoming populous with travellers, both white-clothed and naked, and we decided to head for camp. On our way in, we stopped and stalked the other salt-lick. There was an impala on it looking very red where the sun struck his hide in the patches between the gray trees and there were many kudu tracks. We smoothed them over and drove on in to camp to find a sky full of locusts passing over, going to the westward, making the sky, as you looked up, seem a pink dither of flickering passage, flickering like an old cinema film, but pink instead of gray. P. O. M. and Pop came out and were very disappointed. No rain had fallen in camp and they had been sure we would have something when we came in.

"Did my literary pal get off?"

"Yes," Pop said. "He's gone into Handeni."

"He told me all about American women," P. O. M. said. "Poor old Poppa, I was sure you'd get one. Damn the rain."

"How are American women?"

"He thinks they're terrible."

"Very sound fellow," said Pop. "Tell me just what happened today."

We sat in the shade of the dining tent and I told them.

"A Wanderobo," Pop said. "They're frightful shots. Bad luck."

"I thought it might be one of those travelling sportsmen you see with their bows slung going along the road. He saw the lick by the road and trailed up to the other one."

"Not very likely. They carry those bows and arrows as protection. They're not hunters."

"Well, whoever it was put it on us."

"Bad luck. That and the rain. I've had scouts out here on both the hills but they've seen nothing."

"Well, we're not bitched until tomorrow night. When do we have to leave?"

"After tomorrow."

"That bloody savage."

"I suppose Karl is blasting up the sable down there."

"We won't be able to get into camp for the horns. Have you heard anything?"

"No."

"I'm going to give up smoking for six months for you to get one," P. O. M. said. "I've started already."

We had lunch and afterwards I went into the tent and lay down and read. I knew we still had a chance on the lick in the morning and I was not going to worry about it. But I was worried and I did not want to go to sleep and wake up feeling dopey so I came out and sat in one of the canvas chairs under the open dining tent and read somebody's life of Charles the Second and looked up every once in a while to watch the locusts. The locusts were exciting to see and it was difficult for me to take them as a matter of course.

Finally I went to sleep in the chair with my feet on a chop-box and when I woke there was Garrick, the bastard, wearing a large, very floppy, black and white ostrich-plume head-dress.

"Go away," I said in English.

He stood smirking proudly, then turned so I could see the head-dress from the side.

I saw Pop coming out of his tent with a pipe in his mouth. "Look what we have," I called to him.

He looked, said, "Christ," and went back into the tent.

"Come on," I said. "We'll just ignore it."

Pop came out, finally, with a book and we took no notice of Garrick's head-dress at all, sitting and talking, while he posed with it.

"Bastard's been drinking, too," I said.

"Probably."

"I can smell it."

Pop, without looking at him, spoke a few words to Garrick in a very soft voice.

"What did you tell him?"

"To go and get dressed properly and be ready to start."

Garrick walked off, his plumes waving.

"Not the moment for his bloody ostrich plumes," Pop said.

"Some people probably like them."

"That's it. Start photographing them."

"Awful," I said.

"Frightful," Pop agreed.

"On the last day if we don't get anything, I'm going to shoot Garrick in the ass. What would that cost me?"

"Might make lots of trouble. If you shoot one, you have to shoot the other, too."

"Only Garrick."

"Better not shoot then. Remember it's me you get into trouble."

"Joking, Pop."

Garrick, un-head-dressed and with Abdullah, appeared and Pop spoke with them.

"They want to hunt around the hill a new way."

"Splendid. When?"

"Any time now. It looks like rain. You might get going."

I sent Molo for my boots and a raincoat, M'Cola came out with the Springfield; and we walked down to the car. It had been heavily cloudy all day although the sun had come through the clouds in the forenoon for a time and again at noon. The rains were moving up on us. Now it was starting to rain and the locusts were no longer flying.

"I'm dopey with sleep," I told Pop. "I'm going to have a drink."

We were standing under the big tree by the cooking fire with the light rain pattering in the leaves. M'Cola brought the whiskey flask and handed it to me very solemnly.

"Have one?"

"I don't see what harm it can do."

We both drank and Pop said, "The hell with them."

"The hell with them."

"You may find some bloody tracks."

"We'll run them out of the country."

In the car we turned to the right on the road, drove on up past the mud village and turned off the road to the left onto a red, hard, clay track that circled the edge of the hills and was close bordered on either side with trees. It was raining fairly hard now and we drove slowly. There seemed to be enough sand in the clay to keep the car from slipping. Suddenly, from the back seat, Abdullah, very excited, told Kamau to stop. We stopped with a skid, all got out, and walked back. There was a freshly cut kudu track in the wet clay. It could not have been made more than five minutes before as it was sharp-edged and the dirt, that had been picked up by the inside of the hoof, was not yet softened by the rain.

"Doumi," Garrick said and threw back his head and spread his arms wide to show horns that hung back over his withers. "Kubwa Sana!" Abdullah agreed it was a bull; a huge bull.

"Come on," I said.

It was easy tracking and we knew we were close. In rain or snow it is much easier to come up close to animals and I was sure we were going to get a shot. We followed the tracks through thick brush and then out into an open patch. I stopped to wipe the rain off my glasses and blew through the aperture in the rear sight of the Springfield. It was raining hard now, and I pulled my hat low down over my eyes to keep my glasses dry. We skirted the edge of the open patch and then, ahead, there was a crash and I saw a gray, white-striped animal making off through the brush. I threw the gun up and M'Cola grabbed my arm, "Manamouki!" he whispered. It was a cow kudu. But when we came up to where it had jumped there were no other tracks. The same tracks we had followed led, logically and with no possibility of doubt, from the road to that cow.

"Doumi Kubwa Sana!" I said, full of sarcasm and disgust to

Garrick and made a gesture of giant horns flowing back from behind his ears.

"Manamouki Kubwa Sana," he said very sorrowfully and patiently. "What an enormous cow."

"You lousy ostrich-plumed punk," I told him in English. "Manamouki! Manamouki! Manamouki!"

"Manamouki," said M'Cola and nodded his head.

I got out the dictionary, couldn't find the words, and made it clear to M'Cola with signs that we would circle back in a long swing to the road and see if we could find another track. We circled back in the rain getting thoroughly soaked, saw nothing, found the car, and as the rain lessened and the road still seemed firm decided to go on until it was dark. Puffs of cloud hung on the hillside after the rain and the trees dripped but we saw nothing. Not in the open glades, not in the fields where the bush thinned, not on the green hillsides. Finally it was dark and we went back to camp. The Springfield was very wet when we got out of the car and I told M'Cola to clean it carefully and oil it well. He said he would and I went on and into the tent where a lantern was burning, took off my clothes, had a bath in the canvas tub and came out to the fire comfortable and relaxed in pyjamas, dressing gown and mosquito boots.

P. O. M. and Pop were sitting in their chairs by the fire and P. O. M. got up to make me a whiskey and soda.

"M'Cola told me," Pop said from his chair by the fire.

"A damned big cow," I told him. "I nearly busted her. What do you think about the morning?"

"The lick I suppose. We've scouts out to watch both of these hills. You remember that old man from the village? He's on a wild-goose chase after them in some country over beyond the hills. He and the Wanderobo. They've been gone three days."

"There's no reason why we shouldn't get one on the lick where Karl shot his. One day is as good as another."

"Quite."

"It's the last damned day though and the lick may be rained out. As soon as it's wet there's no salt. Just mud."

"That's it."

"I'd like to see one."

"When you do, take your time and make sure of him. Take your time and kill him."

"I don't worry about that."

"Let's talk about something else," P. O. M. said. "This makes me too nervous."

"I wish we had old Leather Pants," Pop said. "God, he was a talker. He made the old man here talk too. Give us that spiel on modern writers again."

"Go to hell."

"Why don't we have some intellectual life?" P. O. M. asked. "Why don't you men ever discuss world topics? Why am I kept in ignorance of everything that goes on?"

"World's in a hell of a shape," Pop stated.

"Awful."

"What's going on in America?"

"Damned if I know! Some sort of Y. M. C. A. show. Starry eyed bastards spending money that somebody will have to pay. Everybody in our town quit work to go on relief. Fishermen all turned carpenters. Reverse of the Bible."

"How are things in Turkey?"

"Frightful. Took the fezzes away. Hanged any amount of old pals. Ismet's still around though."

"Been in France lately?"

"Didn't like it. Gloomy as hell. Been a bad show there just now."

"By God," said Pop, "it must have been if you can believe the papers."

"When they riot they really riot. Hell, they've got a tradition."

"Were you in Spain for the revolution?"

"I got there late. Then we waited for two that didn't come. Then we missed another."

"Did you see the one in Cuba?"

"From the start."

"How was it?"

"Beautiful. Then lousy. You couldn't believe how lousy."

"Stop it," P. O. M. said. "I know about those things. I was crouched down behind a marble-topped table while they were shooting in Havana. They came by in cars shooting at everybody they saw. I took my drink with me and I was very proud not to have spilled it or forgotten it. The children said, 'Mother, can we go out in the afternoon to see the shooting?' They got so worked up about revolution we had to stop mentioning it. Bumby got so bloodthirsty about Mr. M. he had terrible dreams."

"Extraordinary," Pop said.

"Don't make fun of me. I don't want to just hear about revolutions. All we see or hear is revolutions. I'm sick of them."

"The old man must like them."

"I'm sick of them."

"You know, I've never seen one," Pop said.

"They're beautiful. Really. For quite a while. Then they go bad."

"They're very exciting," P. O. M. said. "I'll admit that. But I'm sick of them. Really, I don't care anything about them."

"I've been studying them a little."

"What did you find out?" Pop asked.

"They were all very different but there were some things you could co-ordinate. I'm going to try to write a study of them."

"It could be damned interesting."

"If you have enough material. You need an awful lot of past performances. It's very hard to get anything true on anything you haven't seen yourself because the ones that fail have such a bad press and the winners always lie so. Then you can only really follow anything in places where you speak the language. That limits you of course. That's why I would never go to Russia. When you can't overhear it's no good. All you get are handouts and sight-seeing. Any one who knows a foreign language in any country is damned liable to lie to you. You get your good dope always from the people and when you can't talk with people and can't overhear you don't get anything that's of anything but journalistic value."

"You want to knuckle down on your Swahili then."

"I'm trying to."

"Even then you can't overhear because they're always talking their own language."

"But if I ever write anything about this it will just be landscape painting until I know something about it. Your first seeing of a country is a very valuable one. Probably more valuable to yourself than to any one else, is the hell of it. But you ought to always write it to try to get it stated. No matter what you do with it."

"Most of the damned Safari books are most awful bloody bores."

"They're terrible."

"The only one I ever liked was Streeter's. What did he call it? Denatured Africa. He made you feel what it was like. That's the best."

"I liked Charlie Curtis's. It was very honest and it made a fine picture."

"That man Streeter was damned funny though. Do you remember when he shot the kongoni?"

"It was very funny."

"I've never read anything, though, that could make you feel about the country the way we feel about it. They all have this damned Nairobi fast life or else bloody rot about shooting beasts with horns half an inch longer than some one else shot. Or muck about danger."

"I'd like to try to write something about the country and the animals and what it's like to some one who knows nothing about it."

"Have a try at it. Can't do any harm. You know I wrote a diary of that Alaskan trip."

"I'd love to read it," P. O. M. said. "I didn't know you were a writer, Mr. J. P."

"No bloody fear," said Pop. "If you'd read it, though, I'll send for it. You know it's just what we did each day and how Alaska looked to an Englishman from Africa. It'd bore you."

"Not if you wrote it," P. O. M. said.

"Little woman's giving us compliments," Pop said.

"Not me. You."

"I've read things by him," she said. "I want to read what Mr. J. P. writes."

"Is the old man really a writer?" Pop asked her. "I haven't seen anything to prove it. You're sure he doesn't support you by tracking and wing shooting?"

"Oh, yes. He writes. When he's going well he's awfully easy

to get along with. But just before he gets going he's frightful. His temper has to go bad before he can write. When he talks about never writing again I know he's about to get started."

"We ought to get more literary conversation from him," Pop said. "Leather Breeches was the lad. Give us some literary anecdotes."

"Well, the last night we were in Paris I'd been out shooting at Ben Gallagher's in the Sologne the day before and he had a *fermée*, you know, they put up a low fence while they're out feeding, and shot rabbits in the morning and in the afternoon we had several drives and shot pheasants and I shot a chevreuil."

"That isn't literary."

"Wait. The last night Joyce and his wife came to dinner and we had a pheasant and a quarter of the chevreuil with the saddle and Joyce and I got drunk because we were off for Africa the next day. God, we had a night."

"That's a hell of a literary anecdote," Pop said. "Who's Joyce?"

"Wonderful guy," I said. "Wrote *Ulysses*."

"Homer wrote Ulysses," Pop said.

"Who wrote *Æschylus*?"

"Homer," said Pop. "Don't try to trap me. D'you know many more literary anecdotes?"

"Ever heard of Pound?"

"No," said Pop. "Absolutely no."

"I know some good ones about Pound."

"Suppose you and he ate some funny-sounding beast and then got drunk."

"Several times," I said.

"Literary life must be awfully jolly. Think I'd make a writer?"

"Rather."

"We're going to chuck all this," Pop told P. O. M., "and both be writers. Give us another anecdote."

"Ever heard of George Moore?"

"Chap that wrote 'But before I go, George Moore, here's a last long health to you?'"

"That's him."

"What about him."

"He's dead."

"That's a damned dismal anecdote. You can do better than that."

"I saw him in a book-shop once."

"That's better. See how lively he can make them?"

"I went to call on him once in Dublin," P. O. M. said, "with Clara Dunn."

"What happened?"

"He wasn't in."

"By God. I tell you the literary life's the thing," Pop said. "You can't beat it."

"I hate Clara Dunn," I said.

"So do I," said Pop. "What did she write?"

"Letters," I said. "You know Dos Passos?"

"Never heard of him."

"He and I used to drink hot kirsch in the winter time."

"What happened then?"

"People objected, finally."

"Only writer I ever met was Stewart Edward White," Pop said. "Used to admire his writing no end. Damned good, you know. Then I met him. Didn't like him."

"You're coming on," I said. "See. There's no trick to a literary anecdote."

"Why didn't you like him?" P. O. M. asked.

"Do I have to tell? Isn't the anecdote complete? It's just like the old man tells them."

"Go ahead and tell."

"Too much the old timer about him. Eyes used to vast distances and that sort of thing. Killed too many bloody lions. No credit kill so many lions. Gallop 'em, yes. Couldn't kill that many. Bloody lion kill you instead. Writes damned fine things in *The Saturday Evening Post* about what's the bloke's name, Andy Burnett. Oh, damned fine. Took an awful dislike to him, though. See him in Nairobi with his eyes used to vast distances. Wore his oldest clothes in town. Hell of a fine shot, everybody says."

"Why you're a literary bastard," I said. "Look at that for an anecdote."

"He's marvellous," P. O. M. said. "Aren't we ever going to eat?"

"Thought by God we'd eaten," Pop said. "Start these anecdotes. No end to 'em."

After dinner we sat by the fire a little while and then went to bed. One thing seemed to be on Pop's mind and before I went in the tent he said, "After you've waited so long, when you get a shot take it easy. You're fast enough so you can take your time, remember. Take it easy."

"All right."

"I'll have them get you up early."

"All right. I'm plenty sleepy."

"Good night, Mr. J. P.," P. O. M. called from the tent.

"Good night," Pop said. He moved toward his tent carrying himself with comic stiffness, walking in the dark as carefully as though he were an opened bottle.

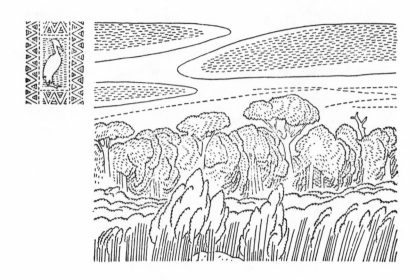

CHAPTER

MOLO WAKED ME by pulling on the blanket in the morning and I was dressing, dressed, and out washing the sleep out of my eyes before I was really awake. It was still very dark and I could see Pop's back shadowed against the fire. I walked over holding the early morning cup of hot tea and milk in my hand waiting for it to be cool enough to drink.

"Morning," I said.

"Morning," he answered in that husky whisper.

"Sleep?"

"Very well. Feeling fit?"

"Sleepy is all."

I drank the tea and spat the leaves into the fire.

"Tell your bloody fortune with those," Pop said.

"No fear."

Breakfast in the dark with a lantern, cool juice-slippery apricots, hash, hot-centered, brown, and catsup spread, two fried eggs and the warm promise-keeping coffee. On the third cup Pop, watching, smoking his pipe, said, "Too early for me to face it yet."

"Get you?"

ELEVEN

"A little."

"I'm getting exercise," I said. "It doesn't bother me."

"Bloody anecdotes," Pop said. "Memsahib must think we're silly buggars."

"I'll think up some more."

"Nothing better than drinking. Don't know why it should make you feel bad."

"Are you bad?"

"Not too."

"Take a spot of Enos?"

"It's this damned riding in cars."

"Well, today's the day."

"Remember to take it very easy."

"You're not worried about that, are you?"

"Just a touch."

"Don't. It never worries me a minute. Truly."

"Good. Better get going."

"Have to make a trip first."

Standing in front of the canvas circle of the latrine I looked, as each morning, at that fuzzy blur of stars that the romanticists of astronomers called the Southern Cross. Each morning at this moment I observed the Southern Cross in solemn ceremony.

Pop was at the car. M'Cola handed me the Springfield and I got in the front. The tragedian and his tracker were in the back. M'Cola climbed in with them.

"Good luck," Pop said. Someone was coming from toward the tents. It was P. O. M. in her blue robe and mosquito boots. "*Oh,* good luck," she said. "*Please,* good luck."

I waved and we started, the headlights showing the way to the road.

There was nothing on the salt when we came up to it after leaving the car about three miles away and making a very careful stalk. Nothing came all morning. We sat with our heads down in the blind, each covering a different direction through openings in the thatched withes, and always I expected the miracle of a bull kudu coming majestic and beautiful through the open scrub to the gray, dusty opening in the trees where the salt-lick was worn, grooved, and trampled. There were many trails to it through the trees and on any one a bull might come silently. But nothing came. When the sun was up and we were warmed after the misty cold of the morning I settled my rump deeper in the dust and lay back against the wall of the hole, resting against the small of my back and my shoulders and still able to see out through the slit in the blind. Putting the Springfield across my knees I noticed that there was rust on the barrel. Slowly I pulled it along and looked at the muzzle. It was freshly brown with rust.

"The bastard never cleaned it last night after that rain," I thought and, very angry, I lifted the lug and slipped the bolt out. M'Cola was watching me with his head down. The other two were looking out through the blind. I held the rifle in one hand for him to look through the breech and then put the bolt back in and shoved it forward softly, lowering it with my finger on the trigger so that it was ready to cock rather than keeping it on the safety.

M'Cola had seen the rusty bore. His face had not changed and I had said nothing but I was full of contempt and there had been indictment, evidence, and condemnation without a word being spoken. So we sat there, he with his head bent so only the bald top showed, me leaning back and looking out through the slit, and we were no longer partners, no longer good friends; and nothing came to the salt.

At ten o'clock the breeze, which had come up in the east, began to shift around and we knew it was no use. Our scent was being scattered in all directions around the blind as sure to frighten any animals as though we were revolving a searchlight in the dark. We got up out of the blind and went over to look in the dust of the lick for tracks. The rain had moistened it but it was not soaked and we saw several kudu tracks, probably made early in the night and one big bull track, long, narrow, heart-shaped; clearly, deeply cut.

We took the track and followed it on the damp reddish earth for two hours in thick bush that was like second-growth timber at home. Finally we had to leave it in stuff we could not move through. All this time I was angry about the uncleaned rifle and yet happy and eager with anticipation that we might jump the bull and get a snap at him in the brush. But we did not see him and now, in the big heat of noon, we made three long circles around some hills and finally came out into a meadow full of little, humpy Masai cattle and, leaving all shade behind, trailed back across the open country under the noon sun to the car.

Kamau, sitting in the car, had seen a kudu bull pass a hundred yards away. He was headed toward the salt-lick at about nine o'clock when the wind began to be tricky, had evidently caught our scent and gone back into the hills. Tired, sweating, and feeling more sunk than angry now, I got in beside Kamau and we headed the car toward camp. There was only one evening left now, and no reason to expect we would have any better luck than we were having. As we came to camp, and the shade of the heavy trees cool as a pool, I took the bolt out of the Springfield and handed the rifle, boltless, to M'Cola without speaking or looking at him. The bolt I tossed inside the opening of our tent onto my cot.

Pop and P. O. M. were sitting under the dining tent.

"No luck?" Pop asked gently.

"Not a damn bit. Bull went by the car headed toward the salt. Must have spooked off. We hunted all over hell."

"Didn't you see anything?" P. O. M. asked. "Once we thought we heard you shoot."

"That was Garrick shooting his mouth off. Did the scouts get anything?"

"Not a thing. We've been watching both hills."

"Hear from Karl?"

"Not a word."

"I'd like to have seen one," I said. I was tired out and slipping into bitterness fast. "God damn them. What the hell did he have to blow that lick to hell for the first morning and gut-shoot a lousy bull and chase him all over the son-of-a-bitching country spooking it to holy bloody hell?"

"Bastards," said P. O. M., staying with me in my unreasonableness. "Sonsabitches."

"You're a good girl," I said. "I'm all right. Or I will be."

"It's been awful," she said. "Poor old Poppa."

"You have a drink," Pop said. "That's what you need."

"I've hunted them hard, Pop. I swear to God I have. I've enjoyed it and I haven't worried up until today. I was so damned sure. Those damned tracks all the time—what if I never see one? How the hell do I know we can ever get back here again?"

"You'll be back," Pop said. "You don't have to worry about that. Go ahead. Drink it."

"I'm just a lousy belly-aching bastard but I swear they haven't gotten on my nerves until today."

"Belly-ache," said Pop. "Better to get it out."

"What about lunch?" asked P. O. M. "Aren't you frightfully hungry?"

"The hell with lunch. The thing is, Pop, we've never seen them on the salt in the evening and we've never seen a bull in the hills. I've only got tonight. It looks washed up. Three times I've had them cold and Karl and the Austrian and the Wanderobo beat us."

"We're not beaten," said Pop. "Drink another one of those."

We had lunch, a very good lunch, and it was just over when Kati came and said there was some one to see Pop. We could see their shadows on the tent fly, then they came around to the front of the tent. It was the old man of the first day, the old farmer, but now he was gotten up as a hunter and carried a long bow and a sealed quiver of arrows.

He looked older, more disreputable and tired-er than ever and his get-up was obviously a disguise. With him was the skinny, dirty, Wanderobo with the slit and curled-up ears who stood on one leg and scratched the back of his knee with his toes. His head was on one side and he had a narrow, foolish, and depraved-looking face.

The old man was talking earnestly to Pop, looking him in the eye and speaking slowly, without gestures.

"What's he done? Gotten himself up like that to get some of the scout money?" I asked.

"Wait," Pop said.

"Look at the pair of them," I said. "That goofy Wanderobo and that lousy old fake. What's he say, Pop?"

"He hasn't finished," Pop said.

Finally the old man was finished and he stood there leaning on his property bow. They both looked very tired but I remember thinking they looked a couple of disgusting fakes.

"He says," Pop began, "They have found a country where there are kudu and sable. He has been there three days. They know where there is a big kudu bull and he has a man watching him now."

"Do you believe it?" I could feel the liquor and the fatigue drain out of me and the excitement come in.

"God knows," said Pop.

"How far away is the country?"

"One day's march. I suppose that's three or four hours in the car if the car can go."

"Does he think the car can get in?"

"None ever has been in but he thinks you can make it."

"When did they leave the man watching the kudu?"

"This morning."

"Where are the sable?"

"There in the hills."

"How do we get in?"

"I can't make out except that you cross the plain, go around that mountain and then south. He says no one has ever hunted there. He hunted there when he was young."

"Do you believe it?"

"Of course natives lie like hell, but he tells it very straight."

"Let's go."

"You'd better start right away. Go as far as you can in the car and then use it for a base and hunt on from there. The Memsahib and I will break camp in the morning, move the outfit and go on to where Dan and Mr. T. are. Once the outfit is over that black cotton stretch we're all right if the rain catches us. You come on and join us. If you're caught we can always send the car back by Kandoa, if worst comes, and the trucks down to Tanga and around."

"Don't you want to come?"

"No. You're better off alone on a show like this. The more people the less game you'll see. You should hunt kudu alone. I'll move the outfit and look after the little Memsahib."

"All right," I said. "And I don't have to take Garrick or Abdullah?"

"Hell, no. Take M'Cola, Kamau and these two. I'll tell Molo to pack your things. Go light as hell."

"God damn it, Pop. Do you think it could be true?"

"Maybe," said Pop. "We have to play it."

"How do you say sable?"

"Tarahalla."

"Valhalla, I can remember. Do the females have horns?"

"Sure, but you can't make a mistake. The bull is black and they're brown. You can't go wrong."

"Has M'Cola ever seen one?"

"I don't think so. You've got four on your license. Any time you can better one, go ahead."

"Are they hard to kill?"

"They're tough. They're not like a kudu. If you've got one down be careful how you walk up to him."

"What about time?"

"We've got to get out. Make it back tomorrow night if you can. Use your own judgment. I think this is the turning point. You'll get a kudu."

"Do you know what it's like?" I said. "It's just like when we were kids and we heard about a river no one had ever fished out on the huckleberry plains beyond the Sturgeon and the Pigeon."

"How did the river turn out?"

"Listen. We had a hell of a time to get in and the night we got there, just before dark, and saw it, there was a deep pool and a long straight stretch and the water so cold you couldn't keep your hand in it and I threw a cigarette butt in and a big trout hit it and they kept snapping it up and spitting it out as it floated until it went to pieces."

"Big trout?"

"The biggest kind."

"God save us," said Pop. "What did you do then?"

"Rigged up my rod and made a cast and it was dark and there was a nighthawk swooping around and it was cold as a bastard and then I was fast to three fish the second the flies hit the water."

"Did you land them?"

"The three of them."

"You damned liar."

"I swear to God."

"I believe you. Tell me the rest when you come back. Were they big trout?"

"The biggest bloody kind."

"God save us," said Pop. "You're going to get a kudu. Get started."

In the tent I found P. O. M. and told her.

"Not really?"

"Yes."

"Hurry up," she said. "Don't talk. Get started."

I found raincoat, extra boots, socks, bathrobe, bottle of quinine tablets, citronella, notebook, a pencil, my solids, the cameras, the emergency kit, knife, matches, extra shirt and undershirt, a book, two candles, money, the flask—

"What else?"

"Have you got soap? Take a comb and a towel. Got handkerchiefs?"

"All right."

Molo had everything packed in a ruck-sack and I found my field glasses, M'Cola taking Pop's big field glasses, a canteen with water and Kati sending a chop-box with food. "Take plenty of beer," Pop said. "You can leave it in the car. We're short on whiskey but there's a bottle."

"How will that leave you?"

"All right. There's more at the other camp. We sent two bottles on with Mr. K."

"I'll only need the flask," I said. "We'll split the bottle."

"Take plenty of beer then. There's any amount of it."

"What's the bastard doing?" I said, pointing at Garrick who was getting into the car.

"He says you and M'Cola won't be able to talk with the natives there. You'll have to have some one to interpret."

"He's poison."

"You *will* need some one to interpret whatever they speak into Swahili."

"All right. But tell him he's not running the show and to keep his bloody mouth shut."

"We'll go to the top of the hill with you," Pop said and we started off, the Wanderobo hanging to the side of the car. "Going to pick the old man up in the village."

Every one in camp was out to watch us go.

"Have we got plenty of salt?"

"Yes."

Now we were standing by the car on the road in the village waiting for the old man and Garrick to come back from their huts. It was early afternoon and the sky was clouding over and I was looking at P. O. M., very desirable, cool, and neat-looking in her khaki and her boots, her Stetson on one side of her head, and at Pop, big, thick, in the faded corduroy sleeveless jacket that was almost white now from washing and the sun.

"You be a good girl."

"Don't ever worry. I wish I could go."

"It's a one-man show," Pop said. "You want to get in fast and do the dirty and get out fast. You've a big load as it is."

The old man appeared and got into the back of the car with M'Cola who was wearing my old khaki sleeveless, quail-shooting coat.

"M'Cola's got the old man's coat," Pop said.

"He likes to carry things in the game pockets," I said.

M'Cola saw we were talking about him. I had forgotten about the uncleaned rifle. Now I remembered it and said to Pop, "Ask him where he got the new coat."

M'Cola grinned and said something.

"He says it is his property."

I grinned at him and he shook his old bald head and it was understood that I had said nothing about the rifle.

"Where's that bastard Garrick?" I asked.

Finally he came with his blanket and got in with M'Cola and the old man behind. The Wanderobo sat with me in front beside Kamau.

"That's a lovely-looking friend you have," P. O. M. said. "You be good too."

I kissed her good-bye and we whispered something.

"Billing and coo-ing," Pop said. "Disgusting."

"Good-bye, you old bastard."

"Good-bye, you damned bullfighter."

"Good-bye, sweet."

"Good-bye and good luck."

"You've plenty of petrol and we'll leave some here," Pop called.

I waved and we were starting down hill through the village on a narrow track that led down and onto the scrubby dry plain that spread out below the two great blue hills.

I looked back as we went down the hill and saw the two figures, the tall thick one and the small neat one, each wearing big Stetson hats, silhouetted on the road as they walked back toward camp, then I looked ahead at the dried-up, scrubby plain.

GREEN HILLS OF AFRICA

PART IV

Pursuit as Happiness

CHAPTER

THE ROAD WAS only a track and the plain was very discouraging to see. As we went on we saw a few thin Grant's gazelles showing white against the burnt yellow of the grass and the gray trees. My exhilaration died with the stretching out of this plain, the typical poor game country, and it all began to seem very impossible and romantic and quite untrue. The Wanderobo had a very strong odor and I looked at the way the lobes of his ears were stretched and then neatly wrapped on themselves and at his strange un-negroid, thin-lipped face. When he saw me studying his face he smiled pleasantly and scratched his chest. I looked around at the back of the car. M'Cola was asleep. Garrick was sitting straight up, dramatizing his awakeness, and the old man was trying to see the road.

By now there was no more road, only a cattle track, but we were coming to the edge of the plain. Then the plain was behind us and ahead there were big trees and we were entering a country the loveliest that I had seen in Africa. The grass was green and smooth, short as a meadow that has been mown and is newly grown, and the trees were big, high-trunked, and old with no

TWELVE

undergrowth but only the smooth green of the turf like a deer park and we drove on through shade and patches of sunlight following a faint trail the Wanderobo pointed out. I could not believe we had suddenly come to any such wonderful country. It was a country to wake from, happy to have had the dream and, seeing if it would clown away, I reached up and touched the Wanderobo's ear. He jumped and Kamau snickered. M'Cola nudged me from the back seat and pointed and there, standing in an open space between the trees, his head up, staring at us, the bristles on his back erect, long, thick, white tusks up-curving, his eyes showing bright, was a very large wart-hog boar watching us from less than twenty yards. I motioned to Kamau to stop and we sat looking at him and he at us. I put the rifle up and sighted on his chest. He watched and did not move. Then I motioned to Kamau to throw in the clutch and we went on and made a curve to the right and left the wart-hog, who had never moved, nor showed any fright at seeing us.

I could see that Kamau was excited and, looking back, M'Cola nodded his head up and down in agreement. None of us had ever seen a wart-hog that would not bolt off, fast-trotting, tail in air. This was a virgin country, an un-hunted pocket in the million miles of bloody Africa. I was ready to stop and make camp anywhere.

This was the finest country I had seen but we went on, winding along through the big trees over the softly rolling grass. Then ahead and to the right we saw the high stockade of a Masai village. It was a very large village and out of it came running long-legged, brown, smooth-moving men who all seemed to be of the same age and who wore their hair in a heavy club-like queue that swung against their shoulders as they ran. They came up to the car and surrounded it, all laughing and smiling and talking. They all were tall, their teeth were white and good, and their hair was stained a red brown and arranged in a looped fringe on their foreheads. They carried spears and they were very handsome and extremely jolly, not sullen, nor contemptuous like the northern Masai, and they wanted to know what we were going to do. The Wanderobo evidently said we were hunting kudu and were in a hurry. They had the car surrounded so we could not move. One said something and three or four others joined in and Kamau explained to me that they had seen two kudu bulls go along the trail in the afternoon.

"It can't be true," I said to myself. "It can't be."

I told Kamau to start and slowly we pushed through them, they all laughing and trying to stop the car, making it all but run over them. They were the tallest, best-built, handsomest people I had ever seen and the first truly light-hearted happy people I had seen in Africa. Finally, when we were moving, they started to run beside the car smiling and laughing and showing how easily they could run and then, as the going was better, up the smooth valley of a stream, it became a contest and one after another dropped out of the running, waving and smiling as they left until there were only two still running with us, the finest runners of the lot, who kept pace easily with the car as they moved long-legged, smoothly, loosely, and with pride. They were running too, at the pace of a fast miler, and carrying their spears as well. Then we had to turn to the right and climb out of the putting-green smoothness of the valley into a rolling meadow and, as we slowed, climbing

in first gear, the whole pack came up again, laughing and trying
not to seem winded. We went through a little knot of brush and
a small rabbit started out, zig-zagging wildly and all the Masai
behind now in a mad sprint. They caught the rabbit and the tallest runner came up with him to the car and handed him to me.
I held him and could feel the thumping of his heart through the
soft, warm, furry body, and as I stroked him the Masai patted
my arm. Holding him by the ears I handed him back. No, no,
he was mine. He was a present. I handed him to M'Cola. 'Cola
did not take him seriously and handed him to one of the Masai.
We were moving and they were running again now. The Masai
stooped and put the rabbit on the ground and as he ran free they
all laughed. M'Cola shook his head. We were all very impressed
by these Masai.

"Good Masai," M'Cola said, very moved. "Masai many cattle. Masai no kill to eat. Masai kill man."

The Wanderobo patted himself on the chest.

"Wanderobo—Masai," he said, very proudly, claiming kin.
His ears were curled in the same way theirs were. Seeing them
running and so damned handsome and so happy made us all
happy. I had never seen such quick disinterested friendliness, nor
such fine looking people.

"*Good* Masai," M'Cola repeated, nodding his head emphatically. "*Good, good* Masai." Only Garrick seemed impressed
in a different way. For all his khaki clothes and his letter from
B'wana Simba, I believe these Masai frightened him in a very old
place. They were our friends, not his. They certainly were our
friends though. They had that attitude that makes brothers, that
unexpressed but instant and complete acceptance that you must
be Masai wherever it is you come from. That attitude you only
get from the best of the English, the best of the Hungarians and
the very best Spaniards; the thing that used to be the most clear
distinction of nobility when there was nobility. It is an ignorant
attitude and the people who have it do not survive, but very few
pleasanter things ever happen to you than the encountering of it.

So now there were only the two of them left again, running,
and it was hard going and the machine was beating them. They
were still running well and still loose and long but the machine was

a cruel pacemaker. So I told Kamau to speed it up and get it over with because a sudden burst of speed was not the humiliation of a steady using. They sprinted, were beaten, laughed, and then we were leaning out, waving, and they stood leaning on their spears and waved. We were still great friends but now we were alone again and there was no track, only the general direction to follow around clumps of trees and along the run of this green valley.

After a little the trees grew closer and we left the idyllic country behind and now were picking our way along a faint trail through thick second-growth. Sometimes we came to a dead halt and had to get out and pull a log out of the way or cut a tree that blocked the body of the car. Sometimes we had to back out of bush and look for a way to circle around and come upon the trail again, chopping our way through with the long brush knives that are called pangas. The Wanderobo was a pitiful chopper and Garrick was little better. M'Cola did everything well in which a knife was used and he swung a panga with a fast yet heavy and vindictive stroke. I used it badly. There was too much wrist in it to learn it quickly; your wrist tired and the blade seemed to have a weight it did not have. I wished that I had a Michigan double-bitted ax, honed razor-sharp, to chop with instead of this sabering of trees.

Chopping through when we were stopped, avoiding all we could, Kamau driving with intelligence and a sound feeling for the country, we came through the difficult going and out into another open-meadow stretch and could see a range of hills off to our right. But here there had been a recent heavy rain and we had to be very careful about the low parts of the meadow where the tires cut in through the turf to mud and spun in the slick greasiness. We cut brush and shovelled out twice and then, having learned not to trust any low part, we skirted the high edge of the meadow and then were in timber again. As we came out, after several long circles in the woods to find places where we could get the car through, we were on the bank of a stream, where there was a sort of brushy bridging across the bed built like a beaver dam and evidently designed to hold back the water. On the other side was a thorn-brush-fenced cornfield, a steep, stump-scattered bank with corn planted all over it, and some abandoned looking corrals or thorn-bush-fenced enclosures with mud and stick buildings and to the right there were cone-shaped grass huts projecting above a heavy thorn fence. We all got out, for this stream was a problem and, on the other side, the only place we could get up the bank led through the stump-filled maize field.

The old man said the rain had come that day. There had been no water going over the brushy dam when they had passed that morning. I was feeling fairly depressed. Here we had come through a beautiful country of virgin timber where kudu had been seen walking along the trail to end up stuck on the bank of a little creek in some one's cornfield. I had not expected any cornfield and I resented it. I thought we would have to get permission to drive through the maize, provided we could make it across the stream and up the bank and I took off my shoes and waded across the stream to test it underfoot. The brush and saplings on the bottom were packed hard and firm and I was sure we could cross if we took it fairly fast. M'Cola and Kamau agreed and we walked up the bank to see how it would be. The mud of the bank was soft but there was dry earth underneath and I figured we could shovel our way up if we could get through the stumps. But we would need to unload before we tried it.

Coming toward us, from the direction of the huts, were two men and a boy. I said "Jambo," as they came up. They answered, "Jambo," and then the old man and the Wanderobo talked with them. M'Cola shook his head at me. He did not understand a word. I thought we were asking permission to go through the corn. When the old man finished talking the two men came closer and we shook hands.

They looked like no negroes I had ever seen. Their faces were a gray brown, the oldest looked to be about fifty, had thin lips, an almost Grecian nose, rather high cheekbones, and large, intelligent eyes. He had great poise and dignity and seemed to be very intelligent. The younger man had the same cast of features and I took him for a younger brother. He looked about thirty-five. The boy was as pretty as a girl and looked rather shy and stupid. I had thought he was a girl from his face for an instant when he first came up, as they all wore a sort of Roman toga of unbleached muslin gathered at the shoulder that revealed no line of their bodies.

They were talking with the old man, who, now that I looked

at him standing with them, seemed to bear a sort of wrinkled and degenerate resemblance to the classic-featured owner of the shamba; just as the Wanderobo-Masai was a shrivelled caricature of the handsome Masai we had met in the forest.

Then we all went down to the stream and Kamau and I rigged ropes around the tires to act as chains while the Roman elder and the rest unloaded the car and carried the heaviest things up the steep bank. Then we crossed in a wild, water-throwing smash and, all pushing heavily, made it halfway up the bank before we stuck. We chopped and dug out and finally made it to the top of the bank but ahead was that maize field and I could not figure where we were to go from there.

"Where do we go?" I asked the Roman elder.

They did not understand Garrick's interpreting and the old man made the question clear.

The Roman pointed toward the heavy thorn-bush fence to the left at the edge of the woods.

"We can't get through there in the car."

"Campi," said M'Cola, meaning we were going to camp there.

"Hell of a place," I said.

"Campi," M'Cola said firmly and they all nodded.

"Campi! Campi!" said the old man.

"There we camp," Garrick announced pompously.

"You go to hell," I told him cheerfully.

I walked toward the camp site with the Roman who was talking steadily in a language I could not understand a word of. M'Cola was with me and the others were loading and following with the car. I was remembering that I had read you must never camp in abandoned native quarters because of ticks and other hazards and I was preparing to hold out against this camp. We entered a break in the thorn-bush fence and inside was a building of logs and saplings stuck in the ground and crossed with branches. It looked like a big chicken coop. The Roman made us free of this and of the enclosure with a wave of his hand and kept on talking.

"Bugs," I said to M'Cola in Swahili, speaking with strong disapproval.

"No," he said, dismissing the idea. "No bugs."

"Bad bugs. Many bugs. Sickness."

"No bugs," he said firmly.

The no-bugs had it and with the Roman talking steadily, I hoped on some congenial topic, the car came up, stopped under a huge tree about fifty yards from the thorn-bush fence and they all commenced carrying the necessities in for the making of camp. My ground-sheet tent was slung between a tree and one side of the chicken coop and I sat down on a petrol case to discuss the shooting situation with the Roman, the old man, and Garrick while Kamau and M'Cola fixed up a camp and the Wanderobo-Masai stood on one leg and let his mouth hang open.

"Where were kudu?"

"Back there," waving his arm.

"Big ones?"

Arms spread to show hugeness of horns and a torrent from the Roman.

Me, dictionary-ing heavily, "Where was the one they were watching?"

No results on this but a long speech from the Roman which I took to mean they were watching them all.

It was late afternoon now and the sky was heavy with clouds. I was wet to the waist and my socks were mud soaked. Also I was sweating from pushing on the car and from chopping.

"When do we start?" I asked.

"Tomorrow," Garrick answered without bothering to question the Roman.

"No," I said. "Tonight."

"Tomorrow," Garrick said. "Late now. One hour light." He showed me one hour on my watch.

I dictionaried. "Hunt tonight. Last hour best hour."

Garrick implied that the kudu were too far away. That it was impossible to hunt and return, all this with gestures, "Hunt tomorrow."

"You bastard," I said in English. All this time the Roman and the old man had been standing saying nothing. I shivered. It was cold with the sun under the clouds in spite of the heaviness of the air after rain.

"Old man," I said.

"Yes, Master," said the old man. Dictionary-ing carefully, I said, "Hunt kudu tonight. Last hour best hour. Kudu close?"

"Maybe."

"Hunt now?"

They talked together.

"Hunt tomorrow," Garrick put in.

"Shut up, you actor," I said. "Old man. Little hunt now?"

"Yes," said old man and Roman nodded. "Little while."

"Good," I said and went to find a shirt and undershirt and a pair of socks.

"Hunt now," I told M'Cola.

"Good," he said. "M'uzuri."

With the clean feeling of dry shirt, fresh socks and a change of boots I sat on the petrol case and drank a whiskey and water while I waited for the Roman to come back. I felt certain I was going to have a shot at kudu and I wanted to take the edge off so I would not be nervous. Also I wanted not to catch a cold. Also I wanted the whiskey for itself, because I loved the taste of it and because, being as happy as I could be, it made me feel even better.

I saw the Roman coming and I pulled the zippers up on my boots, checked the cartridges in the magazine of the Springfield, took off the foresight protector and blew through the rear aperture. Then I drank what was left in the tin cup that was on the ground by the box and stood up, checking that I had a pair of handkerchiefs in my shirt pockets.

M'Cola came carrying his knife and Pop's big glasses.

"You stay here," I said to Garrick. He did not mind. He thought we were silly to go out so late and he was glad to prove us wrong. The Wanderobo wanted to go.

"That's plenty," I said and waved the old man back and we started out of the corral with the Roman ahead, carrying a spear, then me, then M'Cola with glasses and the Mannlicher, full of solids, and last the Wanderobo-Masai with another spear.

It was after five when we struck off across the maize field and down to the stream, crossing where it narrowed in high grass a hundred yards above the dam and then, walking slowly and carefully, went up the grassy bank on the far side getting soaked to the waist as we stooped going through the wet grass and bracken. We had not been gone ten minutes and were moving carefully up the stream bank, when, without warning, the Roman grabbed my arm and pulled me bodily down to the ground as he crouched; me pulling back the bolt to cock the rifle as I dropped. Holding his breath he pointed and across the stream on the far bank at the edge of the trees was a large, gray animal, white stripes showing on his flanks and huge horns curling back from his head as he stood, broadside to us, head up, seeming to be listening. I raised the rifle but there was a bush in the way of the shot. I could not shoot over the bush without standing.

"Piga," whispered M'Cola. I shook my finger and commenced to crawl forward to be clear of the bush, sick afraid the bull would jump while I was trying to make the shot certain, but remembering Pop's "Take your time." When I saw I was clear I got on one knee, saw the bull through the aperture, marvelling at how big he looked and then, remembering not to have it matter, that it was the same as any other shot, I saw the bead centered exactly where it should be just below the top of the shoulder and squeezed off. At the roar he jumped and was going into the brush, but I knew I had hit him. I shot at a show of gray between the trees as he went in and M'Cola was shouting, "Piga! Piga!" meaning, "He's hit! He's hit!" and the Roman was slapping me on the shoulder, then he had his toga up around his neck and was running naked, and the four of us were running now, full speed, like hounds, splashing across the stream, tearing up the bank, the Roman ahead, crashing naked through the brush, then stooping and holding up a leaf with bright blood, slamming me on the back, M'Cola saying, "Damu! Damu!" blood, blood, then the deep cut tracks off to the right, me reloading, we all trailing in a dead run, it almost dark in the timber, the Roman, confused a moment by the trail, making a cast off to the right, then picking up blood once more, then pulling me down again with a jerk on my arm and none of us breathing as we saw him standing in a clearing a hundred yards ahead, looking to me hard-hit and looking back, wide ears spread, big, gray, white-striped, his horns a marvel, as he looked straight toward us over his shoulder. I thought I must make absolutely sure this time, now, with the

dark coming and I held my breath and shot him a touch behind
the fore-shoulder. We heard the bullet smack and saw him buck
heavily with the shot. M'Cola shouted, "Piga! Piga! Piga!" as he
went out of sight and as we ran again, like hounds, we almost
fell over something. It was a huge, beautiful kudu bull, stone-
dead, on his side, his horns in great dark spirals, wide-spread and
unbelievable as he lay dead five yards from where we stood when
I had just that instant shot. I looked at him, big, long-legged, a
smooth gray with the white stripes and the great, curling, sweeping horns, brown as walnut meats, and ivory pointed, at the big
ears and the great, lovely heavy-maned neck the white chevron
between his eyes and the white of his muzzle and I stooped over
and touched him to try to believe it. He was lying on the side
where the bullet had gone in and there was not a mark on him
and he smelled sweet and lovely like the breath of cattle and the
odor of thyme after rain.

Then the Roman had his arms around my neck and M'Cola
was shouting in a strange high sing-song voice and Wanderobo-
Masai kept slapping me on the shoulder and jumping up and down
and then one after the other they all shook hands in a strange way
that I had never known in which they took your thumb in their
fist and held it and shook it and pulled it and held it again, while
they looked you in the eyes, fiercely.

We all looked at him and M'Cola knelt and traced the curve
of his horns with his finger and measured the spread with his arms
and kept crooning, "Oo-oo-eee-eee," making small high noises of
ecstasy and stroking the kudu's muzzle and his mane.

I slapped the Roman on the back and we went through the
thumb pulling again; me pulling his thumb too. I embraced the
Wanderobo-Masai and he, after a thumb-pulling of great intensity
and feeling, slapped his chest and said very proudly, "Wanderobo-
Masai wonderful guide."

"Wanderobo-Masai wonderful Masai," I said.

M'Cola kept shaking his head, looking at the kudu and making the strange small noises. Then he said, "Doumi, Doumi,
Doumi! B'wana Kabor Kidogo, Kidogo." Meaning this was a bull
of bulls. That Karl's had been a little one, a nothing.

We all knew we had killed the other kudu that I had mistaken for this one, while this first one was lying dead from the first shot, and it seemed of no importance beside the miracle of this kudu. But I wanted to see the other.

"Come on, kudu," I said.

"He's dead," said M'Cola, "Kufa!"

"Come on."

"This one best."

"Come on."

"Measure," M'Cola pleaded. I ran the steel tape around the curve of one horn, M'Cola holding it down. It was well over fifty inches. M'Cola looked at me anxiously.

"Big! Big!" I said. "Twice as big as B'wana Kabor."

"Eee-eee," he crooned.

"Come on," I said. The Roman was off already.

We cut for where we saw the bull when I shot and there were the tracks with blood breast high on the leaves in the brush from the start. In a hundred yards we came on him absolutely dead. He was not quite as big as the first bull. The horns were as long, but narrower, but he was as beautiful, and he lay on his side, bending down the brush where he fell.

We all shook hands again, using the thumb which evidently denoted extreme emotion.

"This askari," M'Cola explained. This bull was the policeman or bodyguard for the bigger one. He had evidently been in the timber when we had seen the first bull, had run with him, and had looked back to see why the big bull did not follow.

I wanted pictures and told M'Cola to go back to camp with the Roman and bring the two cameras, the Graflex and the cinema camera and my flashlight. I knew we were on the same side of the stream and above the camp and I hoped the Roman could make a short cut and get back before the sun set.

They went off and now, at the end of the day, the sun came out brightly below the clouds and the Wanderobo-Masai and I looked at this kudu, measured his horns smelled the fine smell of him, sweeter than an eland, even, stroked his nose, his neck, and his shoulder, marvelling at the great ears, and the smoothness and cleanness of his hide, looked at his hooves, that were built long, narrow, and springy so he seemed to walk on tip-toe, felt under his shoulder for the bullet-hole and then shook hands again while the Wanderobo-Masai told what a man he was and I told him he was my pal and gave him my best four-bladed pocket knife.

"Let's go look at the first one, Wanderobo-Masai," I said in English.

The Wanderobo-Masai nodded, understanding perfectly, and we trailed back to where the big one lay in the edge of the little clearing. We circled him, looking at him and then the Wanderobo-Masai, reaching underneath while I held the shoulder up, found the bullet hole and put his finger in. Then he touched his forehead with the bloody finger and made the speech about "Wanderobo-Masai wonderful guide!"

"Wanderobo-Masai king of guides," I said. "Wanderobo-Masai my pal."

I was wet through with sweat and I put on my raincoat that M'Cola had been carrying and left behind and turned the collar up around my neck. I was watching the sun now and worrying about it being gone before they got up with the cameras. In a little while we could hear them coming in the brush and I shouted to let them know where we were. M'Cola answered and we shouted back and forth and I could hear them talking and crashing in the brush while I would shout and watch the sun which was almost down. Finally I saw them and I shouted to M'Cola, "Run, run," and pointed to the sun, but there was no run left in them. They had made a fast trip uphill, through heavy brush, and when I got the camera, opened the lens wide and focused on the bull the sun was only lighting the tops of the trees. I took a half a dozen exposures and used the cinema while they all dragged the kudu to where there seemed to be a little more light, then the sun was down and, obligation to try to get a picture over, I put the camera into its case and settled, happily, with the darkness into the unresponsibility of victory; only emerging to direct M'Cola in where to cut to make a full enough cape when skinning out the head-skin. M'Cola used a knife beautifully and I liked to watch him skin-out, but tonight, after I had shown him where to make the first cut, well down on the legs, around the lower chest where it joined the belly and well back over the withers I did not watch him because I wanted to remember the bull as I had first seen him, so I went, in the dusk, to the second kudu and waited there until they came, with the flashlight and then, remembering that I had skinned-out or seen skinned-out every animal that I had ever shot, yet remembered every one exactly as he was at every moment, that one memory does not destroy another, and that the not-watching idea was only laziness and a form of putting the dishes in the sink until morning, I held the flashlight for M'Cola while he worked on the second bull and, although tired, enjoyed as always his fast, clean, delicate scalpeling with the knife, until, the cape all clear and spread back he nocked through the connection of the skull and the spine and then, twisting with the horns, swung the head loose and lifted it, cape and all, free from the neck, the cape hanging heavy and wet in the light of the electric torch that shone on his red hands and on the dirty khaki of his tunic. We left the Wanderobo-Masai, Garrick, the Roman, and his brother with a lantern to skin out and pack in the meat and M'Cola with a head, the old man with a head, and me with the flashlight and the two guns, we started in the dark back for camp.

In the dark the old man fell flat and M'Cola laughed; then the cape unrolled and came down over his face and he almost choked and we both laughed. The old man laughed too. Then M'Cola fell in the dark and the old man and I laughed. A little farther on I went through the covering on some sort of game pit and went flat on my face and got up to hear M'Cola chuckling and choking and the old man giggling.

"What the hell is this? A Chaplin comedy?" I asked them in English. They were both laughing under the heads. We got to the thorn-bush fence, finally, after a nightmare march through the brush and saw the fire at the camp and M'Cola seemed to be delighted when the old man fell going through the thorns and got up cursing and seeming barely able to lift the head as I shone the flash ahead of him to show him the opening.

We came up to the fire and I could see the old man's face bleeding as he put the head down against the stick and mud cabin. M'Cola put his head down, pointed at the old man's face and laughed and shook his head. I looked at the old man. He was completely done-in, his face was badly scratched, covered with mud and bleeding, and he was chuckling happily.

"B'wana fell down," M'Cola said and imitated me pitching forward. They both chuckled.

I made as though to take a swing at him and said, "Shenzi!"

He imitated me falling down again and then there was Kamau shaking hands very gently and respectfully and saying, "Good, B'wana! Very good, B'wana!" and then going over to the heads, his eyes shining and kneeling, stroking the horns and feeling the ears and crooning the same, sighing, "Ooo-ooo! Eee-eee!" noises M'Cola had made.

I went into the dark of the tent, we had left the lantern with the meat bringers, and washed, took off my wet clothes and feeling in the dark in my ruck-sack found a pair of pyjamas and a bath-robe. I came out to the fire wearing these and mosquito boots. I brought my wet things and my boots to the fire and Kamau spread them on sticks and put the boots, each one, leg-down, on a stick and back far enough from the blaze where the fire would not scorch them.

In the firelight I sat on a petrol box with my back against a tree and Kamau brought the whiskey flask and poured some in a cup and I added water from the canteen and sat drinking and looking in the fire, not thinking, in complete happiness, feeling the whiskey warm me and smooth me inside as you straighten the wrinkled sheet in a bed, while Kamau brought tins from the provisions to see what I would eat for supper. There were three tins of Christmas special mince meat, three tins of salmon, and three of mixed fruit, there were also a number of cakes of chocolate and a tin of Special Christmas Plum Pudding. I sent these back wondering what Kati had imagined the mince-meat to be. We had been looking for that plum pudding for two months.

"Meat?" I asked.

Kamau brought a thick, long chunk of roast Grant gazelle tenderloin from one of the Grant Pop had shot on the plain while we had been hunting the twenty-five-mile salt-lick, and some bread.

"Beer?"

He brought one of the big German liter bottles and opened it.

It seemed too complicated sitting on the petrol case and I spread my raincoat on the ground in front of the fire where the ground had been dried by the heat and stretched my legs out, leaning my back against the wooden case. The old man was roasting meat on a stick. It was a choice piece he had brought with him wrapped in his toga. In a little while they all began to come in carrying meat and the hides and then I was stretched out drinking beer and watching the fire and all around they were talking and roasting meat on sticks. It was getting cold and the night was clear and there was the smell of the roasting meat, the smell of the smoke of the fire, the smell of my boots steaming, and, where he squatted close, the smell of the good old Wanderobo-Masai. But I could remember the odor of the kudu as he lay in the woods.

Each man had his own meat or collection of pieces of meat on sticks stuck around the fire, they turned them and tended them, and there was much talking. Two others that I had not seen had come over from the huts and the boy we had seen in the afternoon was with them. I was eating a piece of hot broiled liver I had lifted from one of the sticks of the Wanderobo-Masai and wondering where the kidneys were. The liver was delicious. I was wondering whether it was worth while getting up to get the dictionary to ask about the kidneys when

M'Cola said, "Beer?"

"All right."

He brought the bottle, opened it, and I lifted it and drank half of it off to chase down that liver.

"It's a hell of a life," I told him in English.

He grinned and said, "More beer?" in Swahili.

My talking English to him was an acceptable joke.

"Watch," I said, and tipped the bottle up and let it all go down. It was an old trick we learned in Spain drinking out of wine skins without swallowing. This impressed the Roman greatly. He came over, squatted down by the raincoat and started to talk. He talked for a long time.

"Absolutely," I told him in English. "And furthermore he can take the sleigh."

"More beer?" M'Cola asked.

"You want to see the old man tight I suppose?"

"N'Dio," he said, "Yes," pretending to understand the English.

"Watch it, Roman," I started to let the beer go down, saw the Roman following the motion with his own throat, started to choke, barely recovered and lowered the bottle.

"That's all. Can't do it more than twice in an evening. Makes you liverish."

The Roman went on talking in his language. I heard him say Simba twice.

"Simba here?"

"No," he said. "Over there," waving at the dark, and I could not make out the story. But it sounded very good.

"Me plenty Simba," I said. "Hell of a man with Simba. Ask M'Cola." I could feel that I was getting the evening braggies but Pop and P. O. M. weren't here to listen. It was not nearly so satisfactory to brag when you could not be understood, still it was better than nothing. I definitely had the braggies, on beer, too.

"Amazing," I told the Roman. He went on with his own story. There was a little beer in the bottom of the bottle.

"Old Man," I said. "Mzee."

"Yes, B'wana," said the old man.

"Here's some beer for you. You're old enough so it can't hurt you."

I had seen the old man's eyes while he watched me drink and I knew he was another of the same. He took the bottle, drained it to the last bit of froth and crouched by his meat sticks holding the bottle lovingly.

"More beer?" asked M'Cola.

"Yes," I said. "And my cartridges."

The Roman had gone on steadily talking. He could tell a longer story even than Carlos in Cuba.

"That's mighty interesting," I told him. "You're a hell of a fellow, too. We're both good. Listen." M'Cola had brought the beer and my khaki coat with the cartridges in the pocket. I drank a little beer, noted the old man watching and spread out six cartridges. "I've got the braggies," I said. "You have to stand for this, look!" I touched each of the cartridges in turn, "Simba, Simba, Faro, Nyati, Tendalla, Tendalla. What do you think of that? You don't have to believe it. Look, M'Cola!" and I named the six cartridges again. "Lion, lion, rhino, buffalo, kudu, kudu."

"Ayee!" said the Roman excitedly.

"N'Dio," said M'Cola solemnly. "Yes, it is true."

"Ayee!" said the Roman and grabbed me by the thumb.

"God's truth," I said. "Highly improbable, isn't it?"

"N'Dio," said M'Cola, counting them over himself. "Simba, Simba, Faro, Nyati, Tendalla, Tendalla!"

"You can tell the others," I said in English. "That's a hell of a big piece of bragging. That'll hold me for tonight."

The Roman went on talking to me again and I listened carefully and ate another piece of the broiled liver.

M'Cola was working on the heads now, skinning out one skull and showing Kamau how to skin out the easy part of the other. It was a big job to do for the two of them, working carefully around the eyes and the muzzle and the cartilage of the ears, and afterwards flesh all of the head skins so they would not spoil, and they were working at it very delicately and carefully in the firelight. I do not remember going to bed, nor if we went to bed.

I remember getting the dictionary and asking M'Cola to ask the boy if he had a sister and M'Cola saying, "No. No," to me very firmly and solemnly.

"Nothing tendacious, you understand. Curiosity."

M'Cola was firm. "No," he said and shook his head. "Hapana," in the same tone he used when we followed the lion into the sanseviera that time.

That disposed of the opportunities for social life and I looked up kidneys and the Roman's brother produced some from his lot and I put a piece between two pieces of liver on a stick and started it broiling.

"Make an admirable breakfast," I said out loud. "Much better than mince-meat."

Then we had a long talk about sable. The Roman did not call them Tarahalla and that name meant nothing to him. There was some confusion about buffalo because the Roman kept saying, "nyati," but he meant they were black like the buff. Then we drew pictures in the dust of ashes from the fire and what he meant were sable all right. The horns curved back like scimitars, way back over their withers.

"Bulls?" I said.

"Bulls and cows."

With the old man and Garrick interpreting, I believed I made out that there were two herds.

"Tomorrow."

"Yes," the Roman said. "Tomorrow."

" 'Cola," I said. "Today, kudu. Tomorrow, sable, buffalo, Simba."

"Hapana, buffalo!" he said and shook his head. "Hapana, Simba!"

"Me and the Wanderobo-Masai buffalo," I said.

"Yes," said the Wanderobo-Masai excitedly. "Yes."

"There are very big elephants near here," Garrick said.

"Tomorrow elephants," I said, teasing M'Cola.

"Hapana elephants!" he knew it was teasing but he did not even want to hear it said.

"Elephants," I said. "Buffalo, Simba, leopard."

The Wanderobo-Masai was nodding excitedly. "Rhino," he put in.

"Hapana!" M'Cola said shaking his head. He was beginning to suffer.

"In those hills many buffalo," the old man interpreted for the now very excited Roman who was standing and pointing beyond where the huts were.

"Hapana! Hapana! Hapana!" M'Cola said definitely and finally. "More beer?" putting down his knife.

"All right," I said. "I'm just kidding you."

M'Cola was crouched close talking, making an explanation. I heard Pop's title and I thought it was that Pop would not like it. That Pop would not want it.

"I was just kidding you," I said in English. Then in Swahili, "Tomorrow sable?"

"Yes," he said feelingly. "Yes."

After that the Roman and I had a long talk in which I spoke Spanish and he spoke whatever it was he spoke and I believe we planned the entire campaign for the next day.

CHAPTER

I DO NOT REMEMBER going to bed nor getting up, only being by the fire in the gray before daylight with a tin cup of hot tea in my hand and my breakfast, on the stick, not looking nearly so admirable and very over-blown with ashes. The Roman was standing making an oration with gestures in the direction where the light was beginning to show and I remember wondering if the bastard had talked all night.

The head skins were all spread and neatly salted and the skulls with the horns were leaning against the log and stick house. M'Cola was folding the head skins. Kamau brought me the tins and I told him to open one of fruit. It was cold from the night and the mixed fruit and the cold syrupy juice sucked down smoothly. I drank another cup of tea, went in the tent, dressed, put on my dry boots and we were ready to start. The Roman had said we would be back before lunch.

We had the Roman's brother as guide. The Roman was going, as near as I could make out, to spy on one of the herds of sable and we were going to locate the other. We started out with the brother ahead, wearing a toga and carrying a spear, then me with the Springfield slung and my small Zeiss glasses in my pocket,

THIRTEEN

then M'Cola with Pop's glasses, slung on one side, water canteen on the other, skinning knife, whetstone, extra box of cartridges, and cakes of chocolates in his pockets, and the big gun over his shoulder, then the old man with the Graflex, Garrick with the movie camera, and the Wanderobo-Masai with a spear and bow and arrows.

We said good-bye to the Roman and started out of the thorn-bush fence just as the sun came through the gap in the hills and shone on the cornfield, the huts and the blue hills beyond. It promised to be a fine clear day.

The brother led the way through some heavy brush that soaked us all; then through the open forest, then steeply uphill until we were well up on the slope that rose behind the edge of the field where we were camped. Then we were on a good, smooth trail that graded back into these hills above which the sun had not yet risen. I was enjoying the early morning, still a little sleepy, going along a little mechanically and starting to think that we were a very big outfit to hunt quietly, although every one seemed to move quietly enough, when we saw two people coming toward us.

They were a tall, good-looking man with features like the Roman's, but slightly less noble, wearing a toga and carrying a bow and quiver of arrows, and behind him, his wife, very pretty, very modest, very wifely, wearing a garment of brown tanned skins and neck ornament of concentric copper wire circles and many wire circles on her arms and ankles. We halted, said "Jambo," and the brother talked to this seeming tribesman who had the air of a business man on the way downtown to his office and, as they spoke in rapid question and answer, I watched the most freshly brideful wife who stood a little in profile so that I saw her pretty pear-shaped breasts and the long, clean niggery legs and was studying her pleasant profile most profitably until her husband spoke to her suddenly and sharply, then in explanation and quiet command, and she moved around us, her eyes down, and went on along the trail that we had come, alone, we all watching her. The husband was going on with us, it seemed. He had seen the sable that morning and, slightly suspicious, obviously displeased at leaving that now out-of-sight wife of wives that we all had taken with our eyes, he led us off and to the right along another trail, well-worn and smooth, through woods that looked like fall at home and where you might expect to flush a grouse and have him whirr off to the other hill or pitch down in the valley.

So, sure enough we put up partridges and, watching them fly, I was thinking all the country in the world is the same country and all hunters are the same people. Then we saw a fresh kudu track beside the trail and then, as we moved through the early morning woods, no undergrowth now, the first sun coming through the tops of the trees, we came on the ever miracle of elephant tracks, each one as big around as the circle you make with your arms putting your hands together, and sunk a foot deep in the loam of the forest floor, where some bull had passed, travelling after rain. Looking at the way the tracks graded down through the pleasant forest I thought that we had the mammoths too, a long time ago, and when they travelled through the hills in southern Illinois they made these same tracks. It was just that we were an older country in America and the biggest game was gone.

We kept along the face of this hill on a pleasant sort of jutting plateau and then came out to the edge of the hill where there was a valley and a long open meadow with timber on the far side and a circle of hills at its upper end where another valley went off to the left. We stood in the edge of the timber on the face of this hill looking across the meadow valley which extended to the open out in a steep sort of grassy basin at the upper end where it was backed by the hills. To our left there were steep, rounded, wooded hills, with outcroppings of limestone rock that ran, from where we stood, up to the very head of the valley and there formed part of the other range of hills that headed it. Below us, to the right, the country was rough and broken in hills and stretches of meadow and then a steep fall of timber that ran to the blue hills we had seen to the westward beyond the huts where the Roman and his family lived. I judged camp to be straight down below us and about five miles to the northwest through the timber.

The husband was standing, talking to the brother and gesturing and pointing out that he had seen the sable feeding on the opposite side of the meadow valley and that they must have fed either up or down the valley. We sat in the shelter of the trees and sent the Wanderobo-Masai down into the valley to look for tracks. He came back and reported there were no tracks leading down the valley below us and to the westward, so we knew they had fed on up the meadow valley.

Now the problem was to so use the terrain that we might locate them, and get up and into range of them without being seen. The sun was coming over the hills at the head of the valley and shone on us while everything at the head of the valley was in heavy shadow. I told the outfit to stay where they were in the woods, except for M'Cola and the husband who would go with me, we keeping in the timber and grading up our side of the valley until we could be above and see into the pocket of the curve at the upper end to glass it for the sable.

You ask how this was discussed, worked out, and understood with the bar of language, and I say it was as freely discussed and clearly understood as though we were a cavalry patrol all speaking the same language. We were all hunters except, possibly, Garrick, and the whole thing could be worked out, understood, and agreed to without using anything but a forefinger to signal and a hand to caution. We left them and worked very carefully ahead, well back in the timber to get height. Then, when we were far enough up and along, we crawled out onto a rocky place and, being behind rock, shielding the glasses with my hat so they would not reflect the sun, M'Cola nodding and grunting as he saw the practicability of that, we glassed the opposite side of the meadow around the edge of the timber, and up into the pocket at the head of the valley; and there they were. M'Cola saw them just before I did and pulled my sleeve.

"N'Dio," I said. Then held my breath to watch them. All looked very black, big necked, and heavy. All had the back-curving horns. They were a long way away. Some were lying down. One was standing. We could see seven.

"Where's the bull?" I whispered.

M'Cola motioned with his left hand and counted four fingers. It was one of those lying down in the tall grass and the animal did look much bigger and the horns much more sweeping. But we were looking into the morning sun and it was hard to see well. Behind them a sort of gully ran up into the hill that blocked the end of the valley.

Now we knew what we had to do. We must go back, cross the meadow far enough down so we were out of sight, get into the timber on the far side and work along through the timber to get above the sable. First we must try to make sure there were no more of them in the timber or the meadow that we must work through before we made our stalk.

I wet my finger and put it up. From the cool side it seemed as though the breeze came down the valley. M'Cola took some dead leaves and crumpled them and tossed them up. They fell a little toward us. The wind was all right and now we must glass the edge of the timber and check on it.

"Hapana," M'Cola said finally. I had seen nothing either and my eyes ached from the pull of the eight-power glasses. We could take a chance on the timber. We might jump something and spook the sable but we had to take that chance to get around and above them.

We made our way back and down and told the others. From where they were we could cross the valley out of sight of its upper end and bending low, me with my hat off, we headed down into

the high meadow grass and across the deeply cut watercourse
that ran down through the center of the meadow, across its rocky
shelf, and up the grassy bank on the other side, keeping under the
edge of a fold of the valley into the shelter of the woods. Then
we headed up through the woods, crouched, in single file, to try to
get above the sable.

We went forward making as good time as we could and still
move quietly. I had made too many stalks on big horn sheep only
to find them fed away and out of sight when you came round the
shoulder of the mountain to trust these sable to stay where they
were and, since once we were in the timber we could no longer see
them, I thought it was important that we come up above them as
fast as we could without getting me too blown and shaky for the
shooting.

M'Cola's water bottle made a noise against the cartridges in
his pocket and I stopped and had him pass it to the Wanderobo-
Masai. It seemed too many people to be hunting with, but they all
moved quietly as snakes, and I was over-confident anyway. I was
sure the sable could not see us in the forest, nor wind us.

Finally I was certain we were above them and that they must
be ahead of us, and past where the sun was shining in a thinning
of the forest, and below us, under the edge of the hill. I checked
on the aperture in the sight being clean, cleaned my glasses and
wiped the sweat from my forehead remembering to put the used
handkerchief in my left pocket so I would not fog my glasses wiping them with it again. M'Cola and I and the husband started to
work our way to the edge of the timber; finally crawling almost to
the edge of the ridge. There were still some trees between us and
the open meadow below and we were behind a small bush and
a fallen tree when, raising our heads, we could see them in the
grassy open, about three hundred yards away, showing big and
very dark in the shadow. Between us was scattered open timber
full of sunlight and the openness of the gulch. As we watched two
got to their feet and seemed to be standing looking at us. The shot
was possible but it was too bloody long to be certain and as I
lay, watching, I felt somebody touch me on the arm and Garrick,
who had crawled up, whispered throatily, "Piga! Piga, B'wana!
Doumi! Doumi!" saying to shoot, that it was a bull. I glanced

back and there were the whole outfit on their bellies or hands and knees, the Wanderobo-Masai shaking like a bird dog. I was furious and motioned them all down.

So that was a bull, eh, well there was a much bigger bull that M'Cola and I had seen lying down. The two sable were watching us and I dropped my head, I thought they might be getting a flash from my glasses. When I looked up again, very slowly, I shaded my eyes with my hand. The two sable had stopped looking and were feeding. But one looked up again nervously and I saw the dark, heavy-built antelope with scimitar-like horns swung back staring at us.

I had never seen a sable. I knew nothing about them, neither whether their eyesight was keen, like a ram who sees you at whatever distance you see him, or like a bull elk who cannot see you at two hundred yards unless you move. I was not sure of their size either, but I judged the range to be all of three hundred yards. I knew I could hit one if I shot from a sitting position or prone, but I could not say where I would hit him.

Then Garrick again, "Piga B'wana Piga!" I turned on him as though to slug him in the mouth. It would have been a great comfort to do it. I truly was not nervous when I first saw the sable, but Garrick was making me nervous.

"Far," I whispered to M'Cola who had crawled up and was lying by me.

"Yes."

"Shoot?"

"No. Glasses."

We both watched, using the glasses guardedly. I could only see four. There had been seven. If that was a bull that Garrick pointed out, then they were all bulls. They all looked the same color in the shadow. Their horns all looked big to me. I knew that with mountain sheep the rams all kept together in bunches until late in the winter when they went with the ewes; that in the late summer you found bull elk in bunches too, before the rutting season, and that later they herded up together again. We had seen as many as twenty impala rams together up on the Serenea. All right, then, they could all be bulls, but I wanted a good one, the best one, and I tried to remember having read something about them, but all I could remember was a silly story of some man seeing the same bull every morning in the same place and never getting up on him. All I could remember was the wonderful pair of horns we had seen in the Game Warden's office in Arusha. And here were sable now, and I must play it right and get the best one. It never occurred to me that Garrick had never seen a sable and that he knew no more about them than M'Cola or I.

"Too far," I said to M'Cola.

"Yes."

"Come on," I said, then waved the others down, and we started crawling up to reach the edge of the hill.

Finally we lay behind a tree and I looked around it. Now we could see their horns clearly with the glasses and could see the other three. One, lying down, was certainly much the biggest and the horns, as I caught them in silhouette, seemed to curve much higher and farther back. I was studying them, too excited to be happy as I watched them, when I heard M'Cola whisper "B'wana."

I lowered the glasses and looked and there was Garrick, taking no advantage of the cover, crawling on his hands and knees out to join us. I put my hand out, palm toward him, and waved him down but he paid no attention and came crawling on, as conspicuous as a man walking down a city street on hands and knees. I saw one sable looking toward us, toward him, rather. Then three more got to their feet. Then the big one got up and stood broadside with head turned toward us as Garrick came up whispering, "Piga, B'wana! Piga! Doumi! Doumi! Kubwa Sana."

There was no choice now. They were definitely spooked and I lay out flat on my belly, put my arm through the sling, got my elbows settled and my right toe pushing the ground and squeezed off on the center of the bull's shoulder. But at the roar I knew it was bad. I was over him. They all jumped and stood looking, not knowing where the noise came from. I shot again at the bull and threw dirt all over him and they were off. I was on my feet and hit him as he ran and he was down. Then he was up and I hit him again and he took it and was in the bunch. They passed him and I shot and was behind him. Then I hit him again and he was trailing slowly and I knew I had him. M'Cola was handing me cartridges and I was shoving shells down into the damned-to-hell, lousy, staggered, Springfield magazine watching the sable making heavy weather of it crossing the watercourse. We had him all right. I could see he was very sick. The others were trailing up into the timber. In the sunlight on the other side they looked much lighter and the one I'd shot looked lighter, too. They looked a dark chestnut and the one I had shot was almost black. But he was not black and I felt there was something wrong. I shoved the last shell in and Garrick was trying to grab my hand to congratu-late me when, below us across the open space where the gully that we could not see opened onto the head of the valley, sable started to pass at a running stampede.

"Good God," I thought. They all looked like the one I had shot and I was trying to pick a big one. They all looked about the same and they were crowding running and then came the bull. Even in the shadow he was a dead black and shiny as he hit the sun, and his horns swept up high, then back, huge and dark, in two great curves nearly touching the middle of his back. He was a bull all right. God, what a bull.

"Doumi," said M'Cola in my ear. "Doumi!"

I hit him and at the roar he was down. I saw him up, the oth-ers passing, spreading out, then bunching. I missed him. Then I saw him going almost straight away up the valley in the tall grass and I hit him again and he went out of sight. The sable now were going up the hill at the head of the valley, up the hill at our right, up the hill in the timber across the valley, spread out and travel-ling fast. Now that I had seen a bull I knew they all were cows including the first one I had shot. The bull never showed and I was absolutely sure that we would find him where I had seen him go down in the long grass.

The outfit were all up and I shook off handshaking and thumb pulling before we started down through the trees and over the edge of the gully and to the meadow on a dead run. My eyes, my mind, and all inside of me were full of the blackness of that sable bull and the sweep of those horns and I was thanking God I had the rifle reloaded before he came out. But it was excited shooting, all of it, and I was not proud of it. I had gotten excited and shot at the whole animal instead of the right place and I was ashamed;

but the outfit now were drunk excited. I would have walked but you could not hold them, they were like a pack of dogs as we ran. As we crossed the meadow opening where we had first seen the seven and went beyond where the bull had gone out of sight, the grass suddenly was high and over our heads and every one slowed down. There were two washed-out concealed ravines ten or twelve feet deep that ran down to the watercourse and what had looked a smooth grass-filled basin was very broken, tricky country with grass that was from waist-high to well above our heads. We found blood at once and it led off to the left, across the watercourse and up the hillside on the left toward the head of the valley. I thought that was the first sable but it seemed a wider swing than he had seemed to make when we watched him going from above in the timber. I made a circle to look for the big bull but I could not pick his track from the mass of tracks and in the high grass and the broken terrain it was difficult to figure just where he had gone.

They were all for the blood spoor and it was like trying to make badly-trained bird dogs hunt a dead bird when they are crazy to be off after the rest of the covey.

"Doumi! Doumi!" I said. "Kubwa Sana! The bull. The big bull."

"Yes," everybody agreed. "Here! Here!" The blood spoor that crossed the watercourse.

Finally I took that trail thinking we must get them one at a time, and knowing this one was hard hit and the other would keep. Then, too, I might be wrong and this might be the big bull, he might possibly have turned in the high grass and crossed here as we were running down. I had been wrong before, I remembered.

We trailed fast up the hillside, into the timber, the blood was splashed freely; made a turn toward the right, climbing steeply, and at the head of the valley in some large rocks jumped a sable. It went scrambling and bounding off through the rocks. I saw in an instant that it was not hit and knew that, in spite of the back-swung dark horns, it was a cow from the dark chestnut color. But I saw this just in time to keep from shooting. I had started to pull when I lowered the rifle.

"Manamouki," I said. "It's a cow."

M'Cola and the two Roman guides agreed. I had very nearly shot. We went on perhaps five yards and another sable jumped. But this one was swaying its head wildly and could not clear the rocks. It was hard hit and I took my time, shot carefully, and broke its neck.

We came up to it, lying in the rocks, a large, deep chestnut-brown animal, almost black, the horns black and curving handsomely back, there was a white patch on the muzzle and back from the eye, there was a white belly; but it was no bull.

M'Cola, still in doubt, verified this and feeling of the short, rudimentary teats said "Manamouki," and shook his head sadly.

It was the first big bull that Garrick had pointed out.

"Bull down there," I pointed.

"Yes," said M'Cola.

I thought that we would give him time to get sick, if he were only wounded, and then go down and find him. So I had M'Cola make the cuts for taking off the head skin and we would leave the old man to skin out the head while we went down after the bull.

I drank some water from the canteen. I was thirsty after the run and the climb and the sun was up now and it was getting hot. Then we went down the opposite side of the valley from that we had just come up trailing the wounded cow, and below, in the tall grass, casting in circles, commenced to hunt for the trail of the bull. We could not find it.

The sable had been running in a bunch as they came out and any individual track was confused or obliterated. We found some blood on the grass stems where I had first hit him, then lost it, then found it again where the other blood spoor turned off. Then the tracks had all split up as they had gone, fan-wise, up the valley and the hills and we could not find it again. Finally I found blood on a grass blade about fifty yards up the valley and I plucked it and held it up. This was a mistake. I should have brought them to it. Already every one but M'Cola was losing faith in the bull.

He was not there. He had disappeared. He had vanished. Perhaps he had never existed. Who could say he was a real bull? If I had not plucked the grass with the blood on it I might have held them. Growing there with blood on it, it was evidence. Plucked, it meant nothing except to me and to M'Cola. But I could find no more blood and they were all hunting half-heartedly now. The only possible way was to quarter every foot of the high grass and trace every foot of the gullies. It was very hot now and they were only making a pretense of hunting.

Garrick came up. "All cows," he said. "No bull. Just biggest cow. You killed biggest cow. We found her. Smaller cow get away."

"You wind-blown son of a bitch," I said, then, using my fingers. "Listen. Seven cows. Then fifteen cows and one bull. Bull hit. Here."

"All cows," said Garrick.

"One big cow hit. One bull hit."

I was so sure sounding that they agreed to this and searched for a while but I could see they were losing belief in the bull.

"If I had one good dog," I thought. "Just one good dog."

Then Garrick came up. "All cows," he said. "Very big cows."

"You're a cow," I said. "Very big cow."

This got a laugh from the Wanderobo-Masai, who was getting to look a picture of sick misery. The brother half believed in the bull, I could see. Husband, by now, did not believe in any of us. I didn't think he even believed in the kudu of the night before. Well, after this shooting, I did not blame him.

M'Cola came up. "Hapana," he said glumly. Then, "B'wana, you shot that bull?"

"Yes," I said. For a minute I began to doubt whether there ever was a bull. Then I saw again his heavy, high-withered blackness and the high rise of his horns before they swept back, him running with the bunch, shoulder higher than them and black as hell and as I saw it, M'Cola saw it again too through the rising mist of the savage's unbelief in what he can no longer see.

"Yes," M'Cola agreed. "I see him. You shoot him."

I told it again. "Seven cows. Shoot biggest. Fifteen cows, one bull. Hit that bull."

They all believed it now for a moment and circled, searching, but the faith died at once in the heat of the sun and the tall grass blowing.

"All cows," Garrick said. The Wanderobo-Masai nodded, his mouth open. I could feel the comfortable lack of faith coming over me too. It was a damned sight easier not to hunt in that sun in that shadeless pocket and in the sun on that steep hillside. I told M'Cola we would hunt up the valley on both sides, finish skinning out the head, and he and I would come down alone and find the bull. You could not hunt them against that unbelief. I had had no chance to train them; no power to discipline. If there had been no law I would have shot Garrick and they would all have hunted or cleared out. I think they would have hunted. Garrick was not popular. He was simply poison.

M'Cola and I came back down the valley, quartered it like bird dogs, circled and followed and checked track after track. I was hot and very thirsty. The sun was something serious by now.

"Hapana," M'Cola said. We could not find him. Whatever he was, we had lost him.

"Maybe he was a cow. Maybe it was all goofy," I thought, letting the unbelief come in as a comfort. We were going to hunt up the side hill to the right and then we would have checked it all and would take the cow head into camp and see what the Roman had located. I was dead thirsty and drained the canteen. We would get water in camp.

We started up the hill and I jumped a sable in some brush. I almost loosed off at it before I saw it was a cow. That showed how one could be hidden, I thought. We would have to get the men and go over it all again; and then, from the old man, came a wild shouting.

"Doumi! Doumi!" in a high, screaming shout.

"Where?" I shouted, running across the hill toward him.

"There! There!" he shouted, pointing into the timber on the other side of the head of the valley. "There! There! There he goes! There!"

We came on a dead run but the bull was out of sight in the timber on the hillside. The old man said he was huge, he was black, he had great horns, and he came by him ten yards away, hit in two places, in the gut and high up in the rump, hard hit but going fast, crossing the valley, through the boulders and going up the hillside.

I gut-shot him, I thought. Then as he was going away I laid

that one on his stern. He lay down and was sick and we missed him. Then, when we were past, he jumped.

"Come on," I said. Every one was excited and ready to go now and the old man was chattering about the bull as he folded the head skin and put the head up on his own head and we started across through the rocks and up, quartering up onto the hillside. There, where the old man had pointed, was a very big sable track, the hoof marks spread wide, the tracks grading up into the timber and there was blood, plenty of it.

We trailed him fast, hoping to jump him and have a shot, and it was easy trailing in the shade of the trees with plenty of blood to follow. But he kept climbing, grading up around the hill, and he was travelling fast. We kept the blood bright and wet but we could not come up on him. I did not track but kept watching ahead thinking I might see him as he looked back, or see him down, or cutting down across the hill through the timber, and M'Cola and Garrick were tracking, aided by every one but the old man who staggered along with the sable skull and head skin held on his own gray head. M'Cola had hung the empty water bottle on him, and Garrick had loaded him with the cinema camera. It was hard going for the old man.

Once we came on a place where the bull had rested and watched his back track, there was a little pool of blood on a rock where he had stood, behind some bushes, and I cursed the wind that blew our scent on ahead of us. There was a big breeze blowing now and I was certain we had no chance of surprising him, our scent would keep everything moving out of the way ahead of us as long as anything could move. I thought of trying to circle ahead with M'Cola and let them track but we were moving fast, the blood was still bright on the stones and on the fallen leaves and grass and the hills were too steep for us to make a circle. I did not see how we could lose him.

Then he took us up and into a rocky, ravine-cut country where the trailing was slow and the climbing difficult. Here, I thought, we would jump him in a gully but the spatters of blood, not so bright now, went on around the boulders, over the rocks and up and up and left us on a rim-rock ledge. He must have gone down from there. It was too steep above for him to have gone over the top of the hill. There was no other way to go but down, but how had he gone, and down which ravine? I sent them looking down three possible ways and got out on the rim to try to sight him. They could not find any spoor, and then the Wanderobo-Masai called from below and to the right that he had blood and, climbing down, we saw it on a rock and then followed it in occasional drying splatters down through a steep descent to the meadow below. I was encouraged when he started down hill and in the knee-high, heavy grass of the meadow trailing was easy again, because the grass brushed against his belly and while you could not see tracks clearly without stooping double and parting the grass to look, yet the blood spoor was plain on the grass blades. But it was dry now and dully shiny and I knew we had lost much time on him when he rim-rocked us on the hill.

Finally his trail crossed the dry watercourse about where we had first come in sight of the meadow in the morning and led away into the sloping, sparsely-wooded country on the far side. There were no clouds and I could feel the sun now, not just as heat but as a heavy deadly weight on my head and I was very thirsty. It was very hot but it was not the heat that bothered. It was the weight of the sun.

Garrick had given up tracking seriously and was only contributing theatrical successes of discovering blood when M'Cola and I were checked. He would do no routine tracking any more, but would rest and then track in irritating spurts. The Wanderobo-Masai was useless as a blue-jay and I had M'Cola give him the big rifle to carry so that we would get some use out of him. The Roman's brother was obviously not a hunter and the husband was not very interested. He did not seem to be a hunter either. As we trailed, slowly, the ground, hard now as the sun had baked it, the blood only black spots and splatters on the short grass, one by one the brother, Garrick, and the Wanderobo-Masai dropped out and sat in the shade of the scattered trees.

The sun was terrific and as it was necessary to track with heads bent down and stooping, in spite of a handkerchief spread over my neck I had a pounding ache in my head.

M'Cola was tracking slowly, steadily, and absolutely absorbed in the problem. His bare, bald head gleamed with sweat and when it ran down in his eyes he would pluck a grass stem, hold it with each hand and shave the sweat off his forehead and bald black crown with the stem.

We went on slowly. I had always sworn to Pop that I could out-track M'Cola but I realized now that in the past I had been giving a sort of Garrick performance in picking up the spoor when it was lost and that in straight, steady trailing, now in the heat, with the sun really bad, truly bad so that you could feel what it was doing to your head, cooking it to hell, trailing in short grass on hard ground where a blood spot was a dry, black blister on a grass blade, difficult to see; that you must find the next little black spot perhaps twenty yards away, one holding the last blood while the other found the next, then going on, one on each side of the trail; pointing with a grass stem at the spots to save talking, until it ran out again and you marked the last blood with your eye and both made casts to pick it up again, signalling with a hand up, my mouth too dry to talk, a heat shimmer over the ground now when you straightened up to let your neck stop aching and looked ahead, I knew M'Cola was immeasurably the better man and the better tracker. Have to tell Pop, I thought.

At this point M'Cola made a joke. My mouth was so dry that it was hard to talk.

"B'wana," M'Cola said, looking at me when I had straightened up and was leaning my neck back to get the crick out of it.

"Yes?"

"Whiskey?" and he offered me the flask.

"You bastard," I said in English and he chuckled and shook his head.

"Hapana whiskey?"

"You savage," I said in Swahili.

We started tracking again, M'Cola shaking his head and very amused, and in a little while the grass was longer and it was easier again. We crossed all that semi-open country we had seen from the hillside in the morning and going down a slope the tracks swung back into high grass. In this higher grass I found that by half shutting my eyes I could see his trail where he had shouldered through the grass and I went ahead fast without trailing by the blood, to M'Cola's amazement, but then we came out on very short grass and rock again and now the trailing was the hardest yet.

He was not bleeding much now; the sun and the heat must have dried the wounds and we found only an occasional small starry splatter on the rocky ground.

Garrick came up and made a couple of brilliant discoveries of blood spots, then sat down under a tree.

Under another tree I could see the poor old Wanderobo-Masai holding his first and last job as gun bearer. Under another was the old man, the sable head beside him like some black-mass symbol, his equipment hanging from his shoulders. M'Cola and I went on trailing very slowly and laboriously across the long stony slope and back and up into another tree-scattered meadow, and through it, and into a long field with piled up boulders at the end. In the middle of this field we lost the trail completely and circled and hunted for nearly two hours before we found blood again.

The old man found it for us below the boulders and to the right a half a mile away. He had gone ahead down there on his own idea of what the bull would have done. The old man was a hunter.

Then we trailed him very slowly, onto hard stony ground a mile away. But we could not trail from there. The ground was too hard to leave a track and we never found blood again. Then we hunted on our various theories of where the bull would go, but the country was too big and we had no luck.

"No good," M'Cola said.

I straightened up and went over to the shade of a big tree. It felt cool as water and the breeze cooled my skin through the wet shirt. I was thinking about the bull and wishing to God I had never hit him. Now I had wounded him and lost him. I believe he kept right on travelling and went out of that country. He never showed any tendency to circle back. Tonight he would die and the hyenas would eat him, or, worse, they would get him before he died, hamstringing him and pulling his guts out while he was alive. The first one that hit that blood spoor would stay with it until he found him. Then he would call up the others. I felt a son of a bitch to have hit him and not killed him. I did not mind killing anything, any animal, if I killed it cleanly, they all had to die and my interference with the nightly and the seasonal killing that went on all the time was very minute and I had no guilty feeling at all. We ate the meat and kept the hides and horns. But I felt rotten sick over this sable bull. Besides, I wanted him. I wanted him damned badly, I wanted him more than I would admit. Well, we had played our string out with him. Our chance was at the start when he was down and we missed him. We had lost that. No, our best chance, the only chance a rifleman should ever ask, was when I had a shot and shot at the whole animal instead of calling the shot. It was my own lousy fault. I was a son of a bitch to have gut-shot him. It came from over-confidence in being able to do a thing and then omitting one of the steps in how it is done. Well, we had lost him. I doubted if there was a dog in the world could trail him now in that heat. Still that was the only chance. I got out the dictionary and asked the old man if there were any dogs at the Roman's place.

"No," said the old man. "Hapana."

We made a very wide circle and I sent the brother and the husband out in another circle. We found nothing, no trace, no tracks, no blood, and I told M'Cola we would start for camp. The Roman's brother and the husband went up the valley to get the meat of the sable cow we had shot. We were beaten.

M'Cola and I ahead, the others following, we went across the long heat haze of the open country, down to cross the dry watercourse, and up and into the grateful shade of the trail through the woods. As we were going along through the broken sunlight and shadow, the floor of the forest smooth and springy where we cut across to save distance from the trail, we saw, less than a hundred yards away, a herd of sable standing in the timber looking at us. I pulled back the bolt and looked for the best pair of horns.

"Doumi," Garrick whispered. "Doumi kubwa sana!"

I looked where he pointed. It was a very big cow sable, dark chestnut, white marks on the face, white belly, heavy built and with a fine curving pair of horns. She was standing broadside to us with her head turned, looking. I looked carefully at the whole lot. They were all cows; evidently the bunch whose bull I had wounded and lost, and they had come over the hill and herded up again together here.

"We go to camp," I said to M'Cola.

As we started forward the sable jumped and ran past us, crossing the trail ahead. At every good pair of cow horns Garrick said, "Bull, B'wana. Big, big bull. Shoot, B'wana. Shoot, oh, shoot!"

"All cows," I said to M'Cola when they were past, running in a panic through the sun-splashed timber.

"Yes," he agreed.

"Old man," I said. The old man came up.

"Let the guide carry that," I said.

The old man lowered the cow sable head.

"No," said Garrick.

"Yes," I said. "Bloody well yes."

We went on through the woods toward camp. I was feeling better, much better. All through the day I had never thought once of the kudu. Now we were coming home to where they were waiting.

It seemed much longer coming home although, usually, the return over a new trail is shorter. I was tired all the way into my bones, my head felt cooked, and I was thirstier than I had ever been in my life. But suddenly, walking through the woods, it was much cooler. A cloud had come over the sun.

We came out of the timber and down onto the flat and in sight of the thorn fence. The sun was behind a bank of clouds now and then in a little while the sky was covered completely and the clouds looked heavy and threatening. I thought perhaps this had been the last clear hot day; unusual heat before the rains. First I thought: if it had only rained, so that the ground would hold a track, we could have stayed with that bull forever; then, looking at the heavy, woolly clouds that so quickly had covered all the sky, I thought that if we were going to join the outfit, and get the car across that ten-mile stretch of black cotton road on the way to Handeni, we had better start. I pointed to the sky.

"Bad," M'Cola agreed.

"Go to the camp of B'wana M'Kubwa?"

"Better." Then, vigorously, accepting the decision, "N'Dio. N'Dio."

"We go," I said.

Arrived at the thorn fence and the hut, we broke camp fast.

There was a runner there from our last camp who had brought a note, written before P. O. M. and Pop had left, and bringing my mosquito net. There was nothing in the note, only good luck and that they were starting. I drank some water from one of our canvas bags, sat on a petrol tin and looked at the sky. I could not, conscientiously, chance staying. If it rained here we might not even be able to get out to the road. If it rained heavily on the road, we would never get out to the coast that season. Both the Austrian and Pop had said that. I had to go.

That was settled so there was no use to think how much I wanted to stay. The day's fatigue helped make the decision easy. Everything was being loaded into the car and they were all gathering up their meat from the sticks around the ashes of the fire.

"Don't you want to eat, B'wana?" Kamau asked me.

"No," I said. Then in English, "Too bloody tired."

"Eat. You are hungry."

"Later, in the car."

M'Cola went by with a load, his big, flat face completely blank again. It only came alive about hunting or some joke. I found a tin cup by the fire and called to him to bring the whiskey, and the blank face cracked at the eyes and mouth into a smile as he took the flask out of his pocket.

"With water better," he said.

"You black Chinaman."

They were all working fast and the Roman's women came over and stood a little way away watching the carrying and the packing of the car. There were two of them, good-looking, well built, and shy, but interested. The Roman was not back yet. I felt very badly to go off like this with no explanation to him. I liked the Roman very much and had a high regard for him.

I took a drink of the whiskey and water and looked at the two pairs of kudu horns that leaned against the wall of the chicken coop hut. From the white, cleanly picked skulls the horns rose in slow spirals that spreading made a turn, another turn, and then curved delicately in to those smooth, ivory-like points. One pair was narrower and taller against the side of the hut. The other was almost as tall but wider in spread and heavier in beam. They were the color of black walnut meats and they were beautiful to see. I went over and stood the Springfield against the hut between them and the tips reached past the muzzle of the rifle. As Kamau came back from carrying a load to the car I told him to bring the camera and then had him stand beside them while I took a picture. Then he picked them up, each head a load, and carried them over to the car.

Garrick was talking loudly and in a roostery way to the Roman's women. As near as I could make out he was offering them the empty petrol boxes in exchange for a piece of something.

"Come here," I called to him. He came over still feeling smart.

"Listen," I told him in English. "If I get through this safari without socking you it's going to be a bloody marvel. And if I ever hit you I'll break your mucking jaw. That's all."

He did not understand the words but the tone made it clearer than if I had gotten something out of the dictionary to tell him. I stood up and motioned to the women that they could have the petrol tins and the cases. I was damned if I could not have anything to do with them if I would let Garrick make any passes.

"Get in the car," I told him. "No," as he started to make delivery of one of the petrol tins, "in the car." He went over to the car.

We were all packed now and ready to go. The horns were curling out the back of the car, tied onto the loads. I left some money for the Roman and one of the kudu hides with the boy. Then we got in the car. I got in the front seat with the Wanderobo-Masai. In back were M'Cola, Garrick, and the runner, who was a man from the old man's village by the road. The old man was crouched on top of the loads in back, close under the roof.

We waved and started, passing more of the Roman's household, the older and uglier part, roasting up piles of meat by a log fire beside the trail that came up from the river through the maize field. We made the crossing all right, the creek was down and the banks had dried and I looked back at the field, the Roman's huts, and the stockade where we had camped, and the blue hills, dark under the heavy sky, and I felt very badly not to have seen the Roman and explain why we had gone off like this.

Then we were going through the woods, following our trail and trying to make time to get out before dark. We had trouble, twice, at boggy places and Garrick seemed to be in a state of great hysteria, ordering people about when we were cutting brush and shovelling until I was certain I would have to hit him. He called for corporal punishment the way a showing-off child does for a spanking. Kamau and M'Cola were both laughing at him. He was playing the victorious leader home from the chase now. I thought it was really a shame that he could not have his ostrich plumes.

Once when we were stuck and I was shovelling and he was stooping over in a frenzy of advice and command-giving, I brought the handle of the shovel, with manifest un-intention, up hard into his belly, and he sat down backwards. I never looked toward him, and M'Cola, Kamau, and I could not look at each other for fear we would laugh.

"I am hurt," he said in astonishment, getting to his feet.

"Never get near a man shovelling," I said in English. "Damned dangerous."

"I am hurt," said Garrick holding his belly.

"Rub it," I told him and rubbed mine to show him how. We all got in the car again and I began to feel sorry for the poor, bloody, useless, theatrical bastard, so I told M'Cola I would drink a bottle of beer. He got one out from under the loads in back, we were going through the deer-park-looking country now, opened it, and I drank it slowly. I looked around and saw Garrick was all right now, letting his mouth run freely again. He rubbed his belly and seemed to be telling them what a hell of a man he was and how he had never felt it. I could feel the old man watching me from up under the roof as I drank the beer.

"Old man," I said.

"Yes, B'wana."

"A present," and I handed what was left in the bottle back. There wasn't much left but the foam and a very little beer.

"Beer?" asked M'Cola.

"By God, yes," I said. I was thinking about beer and in my mind was back to that year in the spring when we walked on the mountain road to the Bains de Alliez and the beer-drinking contest where we failed to win the calf and came home that night around the mountain with the moonlight on the fields of narcissus that grew on the meadows and how we were drunk and talked about how you would describe that light on that paleness, and the brown beer sitting at the wood tables under the wisteria vine at

Aigle when we came in across the Rhone Valley from fishing the Stockalper with the horse chestnut trees in bloom and Chink and I again discussing writing and whether you could call them waxen candelabras. God, what bloody literary discussions we had; we were literary as hell then just after the war, and later there was the good beer at Lipp's at midnight after Mascart-Ledoux at the Cirque de Paris or Routis-Ledoux, or after any other great fight where you lost your voice and were still too excited to turn in; but beer was mostly those years just after the war with Chink and in the mountains. Flags for the Fusilier, crags for the Mountaineer, for English poets beer, strong beer for me. That was Chink then, quoting Robert Graves, then. We outgrew some countries and we went to others but beer was still a bloody marvel. The old man knew it too. I had seen it in his eye the first time he saw me take a drink.

"Beer," said M'Cola. He had it open, and I looked out at that park-like country, the engine hot under my boots, the Wanderobo-Masai as strong as ever beside me, Kamau watching the grooves of the tire tracks in the green turf, and I hung my booted legs over the side to let my feet cool and drank the beer and wished old Chink was along. Captain Eric Edward Dorman-Smith, M.C. of His Majesty's Fifth Fusiliers. Now if he were there we could discuss how to describe this deer park country and whether deer park was enough to call it. Pop and Chink were much alike. Pop was older and more tolerant for his years and the same sort of company. I was learning under Pop, while Chink and I had discovered a big part of the world together and then our ways had gone a long way apart.

But that damned sable bull. I should have killed him; but it was a running shot. To hit him at all I had to use him all as a target. Yes, you bastard, but what about the cow you missed twice, prone, standing broadside? Was that a running shot? No. If I'd gone to bed last night I would not have done that. Or if I'd wiped out the bore to get the oil out she would not have thrown high the first time. Then I would not have pulled down and shot under her the second shot. Every damned thing is your own fault if you're any good. I thought I could shoot a shot-gun better than I could and I had lost plenty of money backing my opinion but I knew, coldly and outside myself, that I could shoot a rifle on game as

well as any son of a bitch that ever lived. Like hell I could. So
what? So I gut-shot a sable bull and let him get away. Could I
shoot as well as I thought I could? Sure. Then why did I miss on
that cow? Hell, everybody is off sometime. You've got no bloody
business to be off. Who the hell are you? My conscience? Listen,
I'm all right with my conscience. I know just what kind of a son
of a bitch I am and I know what I can do well. If I hadn't had to
leave and pull out I would have got a sable bull. You know the
Roman was a hunter. There was another herd. Why did I have to
make a one night stand? Was that any way to hunt? Hell, no. I'd
make some money some way and when we came back we would
come to the old man's village in trucks, then pack in with porters
so there wouldn't be any damned car to worry about, send the
porters back, and make a camp in the timber up the stream above
the Roman's and hunt that country slowly, living there and hunting out each day, sometimes laying off and writing for a week, or
writing half the day, or every other day, and get to know it as I
knew the country around the lake where we were brought up. I'd
see the buffalo feeding where they lived, and when the elephants
came through the hills we would see them and watch them breaking branches and not have to shoot, and I would lie in the fallen
leaves and watch the kudu feed out and never fire a shot unless
I saw a better head than this one in back, and instead of trailing that sable bull, gut-shot to hell, all day, I'd lie behind a rock
and watch them on the hillside and see them long enough so they
belonged to me forever. Sure, if Garrick didn't take his B'wana
Simba back in there and shoot the country out. But if he did I'd go
on down beyond those hills and there would be another country
where a man could live and hunt if he had time to live and hunt.
They'd gone in wherever a car could go. But there must be pockets like this all over, that no one knows of, that the cars pass all
along the road. They all hunt the same places.

"Beer?" asked M'Cola.

"Yes," I said.

Sure, you couldn't make a living. Every one had explained
that. The locusts came and ate your crops and the monsoon failed,
and the rains did not come, and everything dried up and died.
There were ticks and fly to kill the stock, and the mosquitoes gave

you fever and maybe you got blackwater. Your cattle would die and you would get no price for your coffee. It took an Indian to make money from sisal and on the coast every coconut plantation meant a man ruined by the idea or making money from copra. A white hunter worked three months out of the year and drank for twelve and the Government was ruining the country for the benefit of the Hindu and the natives. That was what they told you. Sure. But I did not want to make money. All I wanted was to live in it and have time to hunt. Already I had had one of the diseases and had experienced the necessity of washing a three-inch bit of my large intestine with soap and water and tucking it back where it belonged an unnumbered amount of times a day. There were remedies which cured this and it was well worth going through for what I had seen and where I had been. Besides I caught that on the dirty boat out from Marseilles. P. O. M. hadn't been ill a day. Neither had Karl. I loved this country and I felt at home and where a man feels at home, outside of where he's born, is where he's meant to go. Then, in my grandfather's time, Michigan was a malaria ridden state. They called it fever and ague. And in Tortugas, where I'd spent months, a thousand men once died of yellow fever. New continents and islands try to frighten you with disease as a snake hisses. The snake may be poisonous too. You kill them off. Hell, what I had a month ago would have killed me in the old days before they invented the remedies. Maybe it would and maybe I would have gotten well.

It is easier to keep well in a good country by taking simple precautions than to pretend that a country which is finished is still good.

A continent ages quickly once we come. The natives live in harmony with it. But the foreigner destroys, cuts down the trees, drains the water, so that the water supply is altered and in a short time the soil, once the sod is turned under, is cropped out and, next, it starts to blow away as it has blown away in every old country and as I had seen it start to blow in Canada. The earth gets tired of being exploited. A country wears out quickly unless man puts back in it all his residue and that of all his beasts. When he quits using beasts and uses machines, the earth defeats him quickly. The machine can't reproduce, nor does it fertilize the soil, and it eats what he cannot raise. A country was made to be as we found it. We are the intruders and after we are dead we may have ruined it but it will still be there and we don't know what the next changes are. I suppose they all end up like Mongolia.

I would come back to Africa but not to make a living from it. I could do that with two pencils and a few hundred sheets of the cheapest paper. But I would come back to where it pleased me to live; to really live. Not just let my life pass. Our people went to America because that was the place to go then. It had been a good country and we had made a bloody mess of it and I would go, now, somewhere else as we had always had the right to go somewhere else and as we had always gone. You could always come back. Let the others come to America who did not know that they had come too late. Our people had seen it at its best and fought for it when it was well worth fighting for. Now I would go somewhere else. We always went in the old days and there were still good places to go.

I knew a good country when I saw one. Here there was game, plenty of birds, and I liked the natives. Here I could shoot and fish. That, and writing, and reading, and seeing pictures was all I cared about doing. And I could remember all the pictures. Other things I liked to watch but they were what I liked to do. That and ski-ing. But my legs were bad now and it was not worth the time you spent hunting good snow any more. You saw too many people, ski-ing now.

Now, the car making a turn around a bank and crossing a green, grassy field, we came in sight of the Masai village.

When the Masai saw us they started running out and we stopped, surrounded by them, just below the stockade. There were the young warriors who had run with us, and now their women and the children all came out to see us. The children were all quite young and the men and women all seemed the same age. There were no old people. They all seemed to be our great friends and we gave a very successful party with refreshments in the shape of our bread which they all ate with much laughing, the men first, then the women. Then I had M'Cola open the two cans of mince meat and the plum pudding and I cut these into rations and passed them out. I had heard and read that the Masai subsisted only on the blood of their cattle mixed with milk, drawing the blood off from a wound in a vein of the neck made by shooting an arrow at close range. These Masai, however, ate bread, cold mince meat and plum pudding with great relish and much laughter and joking. One very tall and handsome one kept asking me something that I did not understand and then five or six more joined in. Whatever this was they wanted it very badly. Finally the tallest one made a very strange face and emitted a sound like a dying pig. I understood finally; he was asking if we had one of those, and I pressed the button of the klaxon. The children ran screaming, the warriors laughed and laughed, and then as Kamau, in response to popular demand, pressed the klaxon again and again, I watched the look of utter rapture and ecstasy on the women's faces and knew that with that klaxon he could have had any woman in the tribe.

Finally we had to go and after distributing the empty beer bottles, the labels from the bottles, and finally the bottle caps, picked up by M'Cola from the floor, we left, klaxoning the women into ecstasy, the children into panic, and the warriors into delight. The warriors ran with us for a good way but we had to make time, the going was good through the park-like country and, in a little while, we waved to the last of them standing straight and tall, in their brown skin garments, their clubbed pig-tails hanging, their faces stained a red-brown, leaning on their spears, looking after us and smiling.

The sun was almost down and as I did not know the road I had the runner get up in front to sit with the Wanderobo-Masai and help direct Kamau and I sat in the back with M'Cola and Garrick. We were out of the park country and onto the dry bush-spattered plain before the sun went down and I had another bottle of the German beer and, watching the country, saw, suddenly, that all the trees were full of white storks. I did not know whether they were there in migration or were following the locusts but, in the twilight, they were lovely to see and, deeply moved by them, I gave the old man a good two fingers of beer that was left in the bottom of the bottle.

On the next bottle I forgot and drank it all before I remembered the old man. (There were still storks in the trees and we saw some Grant's gazelles feeding off to the right. A jackal, like a gray fox, trotted across the road.) So I told M'Cola to open another bottle and we were through the plain and climbing the long slope toward the road and the village, the two mountains in sight now, and it almost dark and quite cold when I handed the bottle to the old man, who took it where he was crouched up under the roof, and nursed it tenderly.

At the village we stopped in the road in the dark, and I paid the runner the amount it said to give him in the note he had brought. I paid the old man the amount Pop said to pay him and a bonus. Then there was a big dispute among them all. Garrick was to go to the main camp to get his money. Abdullah insisted upon going along. He did not trust Garrick. The Wanderobo-Masai insisted pitifully that he go. He was sure the others would cheat him out of his share and I was fairly sure they would, too. There was petrol that had been left for us to use in case we were short and for us to bring in any event. We were overloaded and I did not know how the road was ahead. But I thought we might carry Abdullah and Garrick and squeeze in the Wanderobo-Masai. There was no question of the old man going. He had been paid off and had agreed to the amount, but now he would not leave the car. He crouched on top of the load and hung onto the ropes saying, "I am going with B'wana."

M'Cola and Kamau had to break his handholds and pull him off to re-load, him shouting, "I want to go with B'wana!"

While they were loading in the dark he held onto my arm and talked very quietly in a language that I could not understand.

"You have the shillings," I said.

"Yes, B'wana," he said. That was not what it was about. The money was all right.

Then, when we started to get in the car he broke away and started to climb up through the back and onto the loads. Garrick and Abdullah pulled him down.

"You can't go. There isn't room."

He talked to me softly again, begging and pleading.

"No, there is no room."

I remembered I had a small penknife and I got it out of my pocket and put it in his hand. He pushed it back in my hand.

"No," he said. "No."

He was quiet then and stood by the road. But when we started, he started to run after the car and I could hear him in the dark screaming, "B'wana! I want to go with B'wana!"

We went on up the road, the headlights making it seem like a boulevard after where we had been. We drove fifty-five miles on that road in the dark night without incident. I stayed awake until after we were through the bad part, a long plain of deeply rutted black cotton where the headlights picked out the trail through bushes and then, when the road was better, I went to sleep, waking occasionally to see the headlights shining on a wall of tall trees, or a naked bank, or when we ground in low gear up a steep place the light slanting up ahead.

Finally, when the speedometer showed fifty miles, we stopped and woke a native in his hut and M'Cola asked about the camp. I slept again and then woke as we were turning off the road and on a track through trees with the fires of the camp showing ahead. Then as we came to where our lights shone on the green tents I shouted and we all commenced to shout and blew the klaxon and I let the gun off, the flame cutting up into the dark and it making a great noise. Then we were stopped and out from Pop's tent I saw him coming, thick and heavy in his dressing gown, and then he had his arms around my shoulders and said, "You god damned bull fighter," and I was clapping him on the back.

And I said, "Look at them, Pop."

"I saw them," he said. "The whole back of the car's full of them."

Then I was holding P. O. M. tight, she feeling very small inside the quilted bigness of the dressing gown, and we were saying things to each other.

Then Karl came out and I said, "Hi, Karl."

"I'm so damned glad," he said. "They're marvellous."

M'Cola had the horns down by now and he and Kamau were holding them so they could all see them in the light of the fire.

"What did you get?" I asked Karl.

"Just another one of those. What do you call them? Tendalla."

"Swell," I said. I knew I had one no one could beat and I hoped he had a good one too. "How big was he?"

"Oh, fifty-seven," Karl said.

"Let's see him," I said, cold in the pit of my stomach.

"He's over there," Pop said, and we went over. They were the biggest, widest, darkest, longest-curling, heaviest, most unbelievable pair of kudu horns in the world. Suddenly, poisoned with envy, I did not want to see mine again; never, never.

"That's great," I said, the words coming out as cheerfully as a croak. I tried it again. "That's swell. How did you get him?"

"There were three," Karl said. "They were all as big as that. I couldn't tell which was the biggest. We had a hell of a time. I hit him four or five times."

"He's a wonder," I said. I was getting so I could do it a little better but it would not fool anybody yet.

"I'm awfully glad you got yours," Karl said. "They're beauties. I want to hear all about them in the morning. I know you're tired tonight. Good night."

He went off, delicate as always, so we could talk about it if we wanted to.

"Come on over and have a drink," I called.

"No thanks, I think I better go to bed. I've got a sort of headache."

"Good night, Karl."

"Good night. Good night, Poor Old Mamma."

"Good night," we all said.

By the fire, with whiskey and soda, we talked and I told them about it all.

"Perhaps they'll find the bull," Pop said. "We'll offer a reward for the horns. Have them sent to the Game Department. How big is your biggest one?"

"Fifty-two."

"Over the curve?"

"Yes. Maybe he's a little better."

"Inches don't mean anything," Pop said. "They're damned wonderful kudu."

"Sure. But why does he have to beat me so bloody badly?"

"He's got the luck," Pop said. "God, what a kudu. I've only seen one head killed over fifty in my life before. That was up on Kalal."

"We knew he had it when we left the other camp. The truck came in and told us," P. O. M. said. "I've spent all my time praying for you. Ask Mr. J. P."

"You'll never know what it meant to see that car come into

the firelight with those damned horns sticking out," Pop said. "You old bastard."

"It's wonderful," P. O. M. said. "Let's go and look at them again."

"You can always remember how you shot them. That's what you really get out of it," Pop said. "They're damned wonderful kudu."

But I was bitter and I was bitter all night long. In the morning, though, it was gone. It was all gone and I have never had it again.

Pop and I were up and looking at the heads before breakfast. It was a gray, overcast morning and cold. The rains were coming.

"They're three marvellous kudu," he said.

"They look all right with the big one this morning," I said. They did, too, strangely enough. I had accepted the big one now and was happy to see him and that Karl had him. When you put them side by side they looked all right. They really did. They all were big.

"I'm glad you're feeling better," Pop said. "I'm feeling better myself."

"I'm really glad he has him," I said truly. "Mine'll hold me."

"We have very primitive emotions," he said. "It's impossible not to be competitive. Spoils everything, though."

"I'm all through with that," I said. "I'm all right again. I had quite a trip, you know."

"Did you not," said Pop.

"Pop, what does it mean when they shake hands and get hold of your thumb and pull it?"

"It's on the order of blood brotherhood but a little less formal. Who's been doing that to you?"

"Everybody but Kamau."

"You're getting to be a hell of a fellow," Pop said. "You must be an old timer out here. Tell me, are you much of a tracker and bird shot?"

"Go to hell."

"M'Cola has been doing that with you too?"

"Yes."

"Well, well," said Pop. "Let's get the little Memsahib and have some breakfast. Not that I'm feeling up to it."

"I am," I said. "I haven't eaten anything since day before yesterday."

"Drank some beer though, didn't you?"

"Ah, yes."

"Beer's a food," Pop said.

We got the little Memsahib and old Karl and had a very jolly breakfast.

A month later P. O. M., Karl, and Karl's wife who had come out and joined us at Haifa, were sitting in the sun against a stone wall by the Sea of Galilee eating some lunch and drinking a bottle of wine and watching the grebes out on the lake. The hills made shadows on the water, which was flat calm and rather stagnant looking. There were many grebes, making spreading wakes in the water as they swam, and I was counting them and wondering why they never were mentioned in the Bible. I decided that those people were not naturalists.

"I'm not going to walk on it," Karl said, looking out at the dreary lake. "It's been done already."

"You know," P. O. M. said, "I can't remember it. I can't remember Mr. J. P.'s face. And he's beautiful. I think about him and think about him and I can't see him. It's terrible. He isn't the way he looks in a photograph. In a little while I won't be able to remember him at all. Already I can't see him."

"You must remember him," Karl said to her.

"I can remember him," I said. "I'll write you a piece some time and put him in."

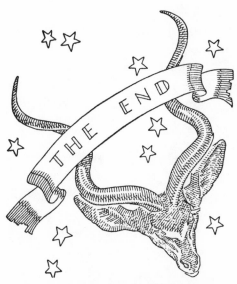

Figure 1. Pauline Pfeiffer Hemingway just prior to departing for the African safari, 1933. Ernest Hemingway Collection, John F. Kennedy Library and Museum, Boston.

Figure 2. Ernest Hemingway with his lion on the Serengeti Plain.
Ernest Hemingway Collection, John F. Kennedy Library and Museum, Boston.

Figure 3. Lion with a zebra kill on the Serengeti Plain. Photo by Ernest Hemingway.
Ernest Hemingway Collection, John F. Kennedy Library and Museum, Boston.

Figure 4. Pauline Pfeiffer Hemingway (P.O.M.) with her lion on the Serengeti Plain. Ernest Hemingway Collection, John F. Kennedy Library and Museum, Boston.

Figure 5. Pauline Pfeiffer Hemingway (P.O.M.) holding her Mannlicher rifle with a Thomson's gazelle. Ernest Hemingway Collection, John F. Kennedy Library and Museum, Boston.

Figure 6. Ernest Hemingway with a Cape buffalo, his Springfield rifle resting on its belly. Ernest Hemingway Collection, John F. Kennedy Library and Museum, Boston.

Figure 7. Ernest Hemingway with Cape buffalo, close up.
Ernest Hemingway Collection, John F. Kennedy Library and Museum, Boston.

Figure 8. Ernest Hemingway with safari crew and rhino.
Ernest Hemingway Collection, John F. Kennedy Library and Museum, Boston.

Figure 9. Pauline Pfeiffer Hemingway (P.O.M.) with Ernest's rhino.
Ernest Hemingway Collection, John F. Kennedy Library and Museum, Boston.

Figure 10. Left to right: Ben Fourie, Charles Thompson (obscured), Philip Percival, and Ernest Hemingway at the end of the kudu hunt.
Ernest Hemingway Collection, John F. Kennedy Library and Museum, Boston.

Figure 11. Ernest Hemingway with his kudu and roan antelope trophies.
Ernest Hemingway Collection, John F. Kennedy Library and Museum, Boston.

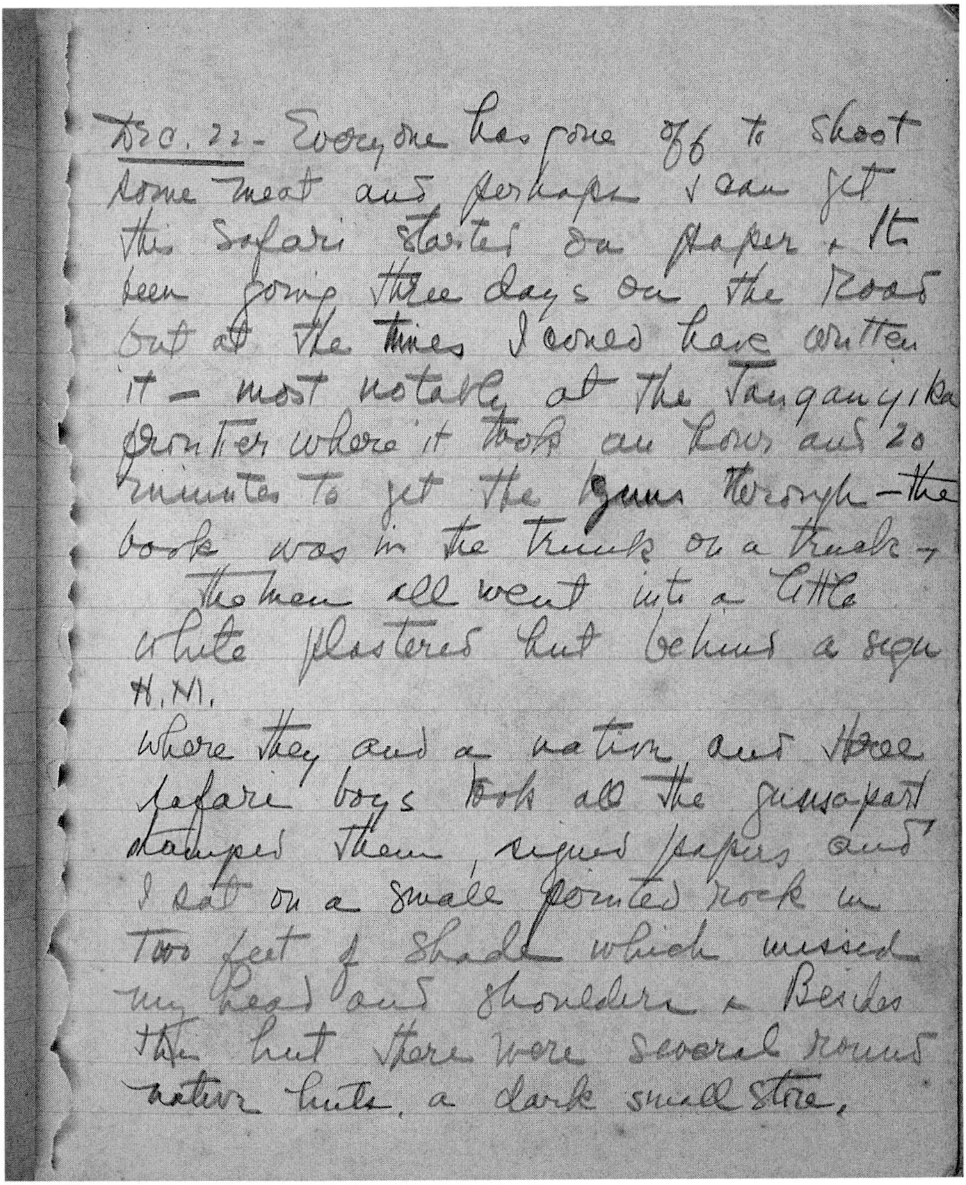

Dec. 22 - Everyone has gone off to shoot
some meat and perhaps I can get
this Safari started on paper. It's
been going three days on the Road
but at the times I could have written
it — most notably at the Tanganyika
frontier where it took an hour and 20
minutes to get the guns through — the
book was in the trunk on a truck —
The men all went into a little
white plastered hut behind a sign
H.M.
Where they and a nation and three
safari boys took all the guns apart
stamped them, signed papers and
I sat on a small pointed rock in
two feet of shade which missed
my head and shoulders. Besides
this hut there were several round
native huts, a dark small store,

Figure 12. First page of Pauline's safari journal. Handwritten pencil manuscript,
Item M1344, p. 2, Department of Special Collections and University Archives,
Stanford University Libraries. Image courtesy of Stanford University Libraries.

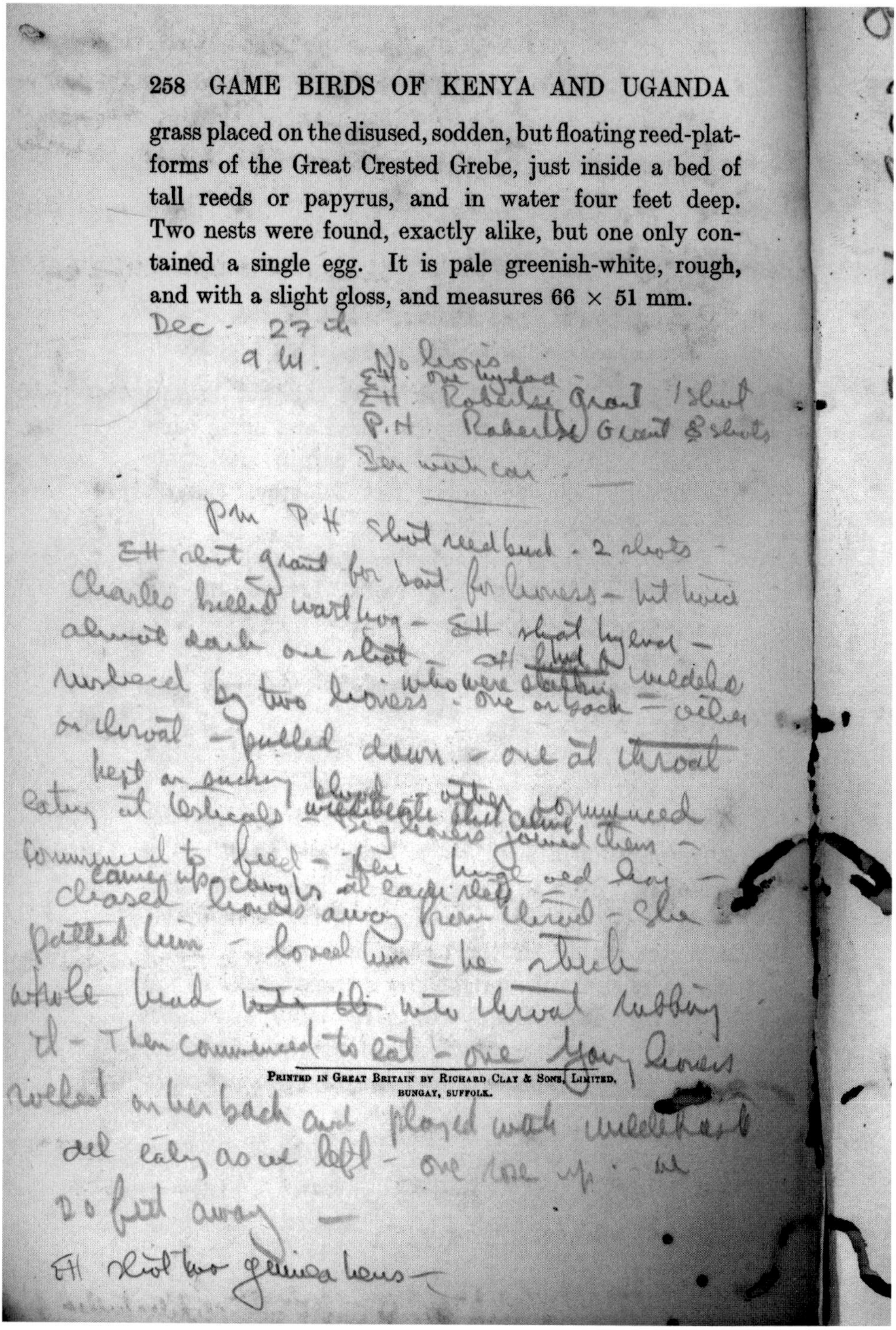

258 GAME BIRDS OF KENYA AND UGANDA

grass placed on the disused, sodden, but floating reed-platforms of the Great Crested Grebe, just inside a bed of tall reeds or papyrus, and in water four feet deep. Two nests were found, exactly alike, but one only contained a single egg. It is pale greenish-white, rough, and with a slight gloss, and measures 66 × 51 mm.

Dec. 27th
9 AM. No lions
EH one hyena
EH Roberts Grant 1 shot
P.H. Roberts Grant 2 shots
Ben with car —

pm P.H. shot reedbuck - 2 shots -
EH shot grant for bait for lioness - but [illegible]
Charles killed wart hog - EH shot hyena -
almost dark one shot - [illegible]
watched by two lioness who were stalking wildebeeste
- one on back - other
on throat - pulled down - one at throat
kept on sucking blood - other commenced
eating at testicals while beast still alive
big lions joined them -
commenced to feed - then huge old boy
came up - caught at [illegible]
chased lioness away from throat - she
patted him - loved him - he stuck
whole head into throat rubbing
it - Then commenced to eat - one young lioness
rolled on her back and played with wildebeest
all [illegible] as we left - one rose up - we
drove away —
EH shot two guinea hens —

PRINTED IN GREAT BRITAIN BY RICHARD CLAY & SONS, LIMITED,
BUNGAY, SUFFOLK.

Figure 13. Ernest Hemingway's safari notes from December 27, 1933, written on page 258 of Sir Frederick J. Jackson, *Notes on the Game Birds of Kenya and Uganda (Including the Sand-Grouse, Pigeons, Snipe, Bustards, Geese, and Ducks)* (London: Williams & Norgate, Ltd., 1926).
Ernest Hemingway Collection, John F. Kennedy Library and Museum, Boston.

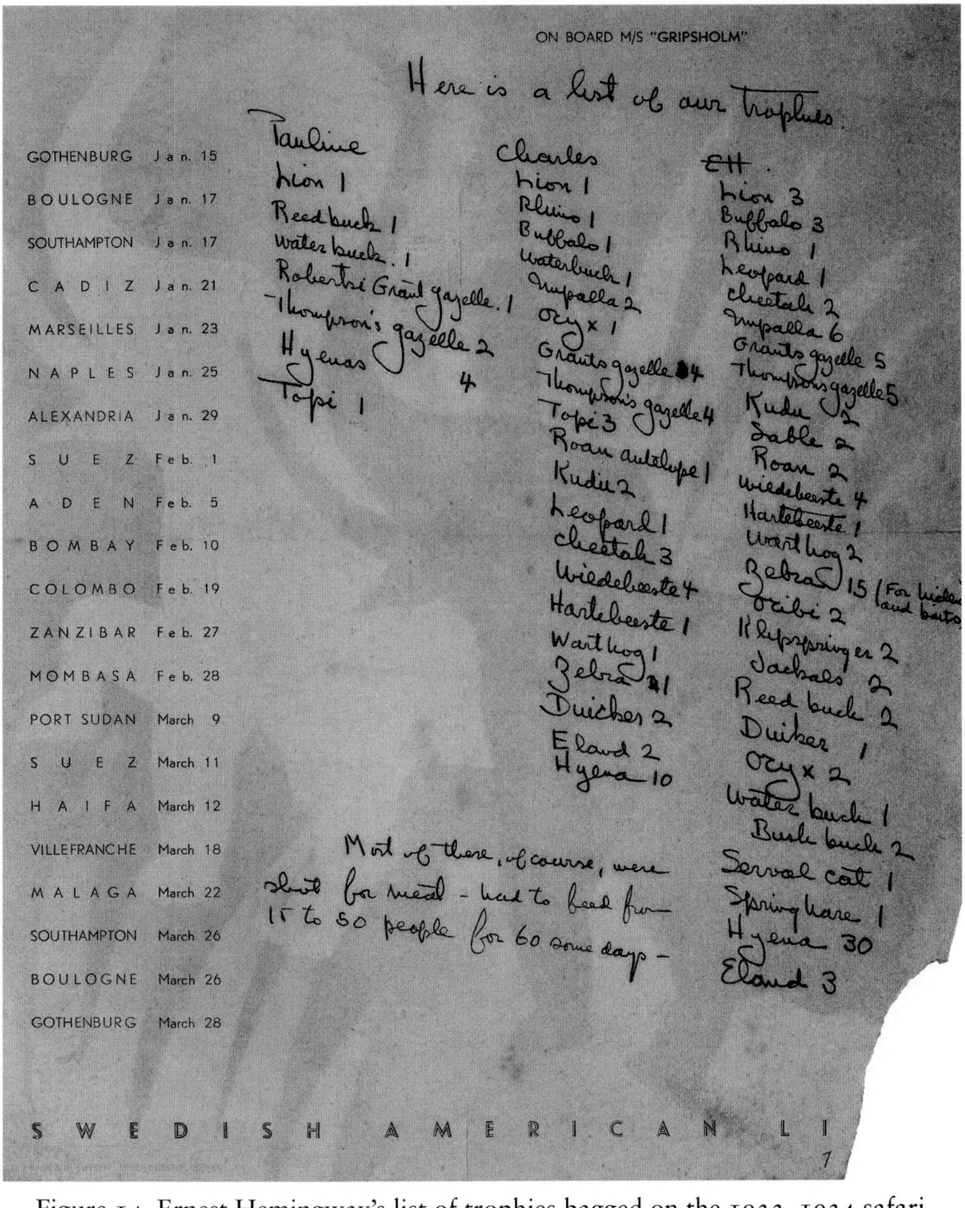
ON BOARD M/S "GRIPSHOLM"

Here is a list of our trophies:

GOTHENBURG	Jan. 15
BOULOGNE	Jan. 17
SOUTHAMPTON	Jan. 17
CADIZ	Jan. 21
MARSEILLES	Jan. 23
NAPLES	Jan. 25
ALEXANDRIA	Jan. 29
SUEZ	Feb. 1
ADEN	Feb. 5
BOMBAY	Feb. 10
COLOMBO	Feb. 19
ZANZIBAR	Feb. 27
MOMBASA	Feb. 28
PORT SUDAN	March 9
SUEZ	March 11
HAIFA	March 12
VILLEFRANCHE	March 18
MALAGA	March 22
SOUTHAMPTON	March 26
BOULOGNE	March 26
GOTHENBURG	March 28

Pauline
Lion 1
Reedbuck 1
Waterbuck. 1
Roberts Grant gazelle. 1
Thompson's gazelle 2
Hyenas 4
Topi 1

Charles
Lion 1
Rhino 1
Buffalo 1
Waterbuck 1
Impalla 2
Oryx 1
Grants gazelle 4
Thompson's gazelle 4
Topi 3
Roan antelope 1
Kudu 2
Leopard 1
Cheetah 3
Wiedebeeste 4
Hartebeeste 1
Wart hog 1
Zebra 1
Duicker 2
Eland 2
Hyena 10

EH.
Lion 3
Buffalo 3
Rhino 1
Leopard 1
Cheetah 2
Impalla 6
Grants gazelle 5
Thompsons gazelle 5
Kudu 2
Sable 2
Roan 2
Wiedebeeste 4
Hartebeeste 1
Wart hog 2
Zebra 15 (For hides and baits)
Oribi 2
Klipspringer 2
Jackals 2
Reed buck 2
Duiker 1
Oryx 2
Water buck 1
Bush buck 2
Serval cat 1
Spring hare 1
Hyena 30
Eland 3

Most of these, of course, were shot for meat - had to feed from 15 to 50 people for 60 some days -

SWEDISH AMERICAN LI

7

Figure 14. Ernest Hemingway's list of trophies bagged on the 1933–1934 safari. Made after the safari while on board the M/S *Gripsholm* en route to Europe.

Ernest Hemingway Collection, John F. Kennedy Library and Museum, Boston.

Figure 15. Newspaper clipping. Ernest Hemingway Collection, John F. Kennedy Library and Museum, Boston.

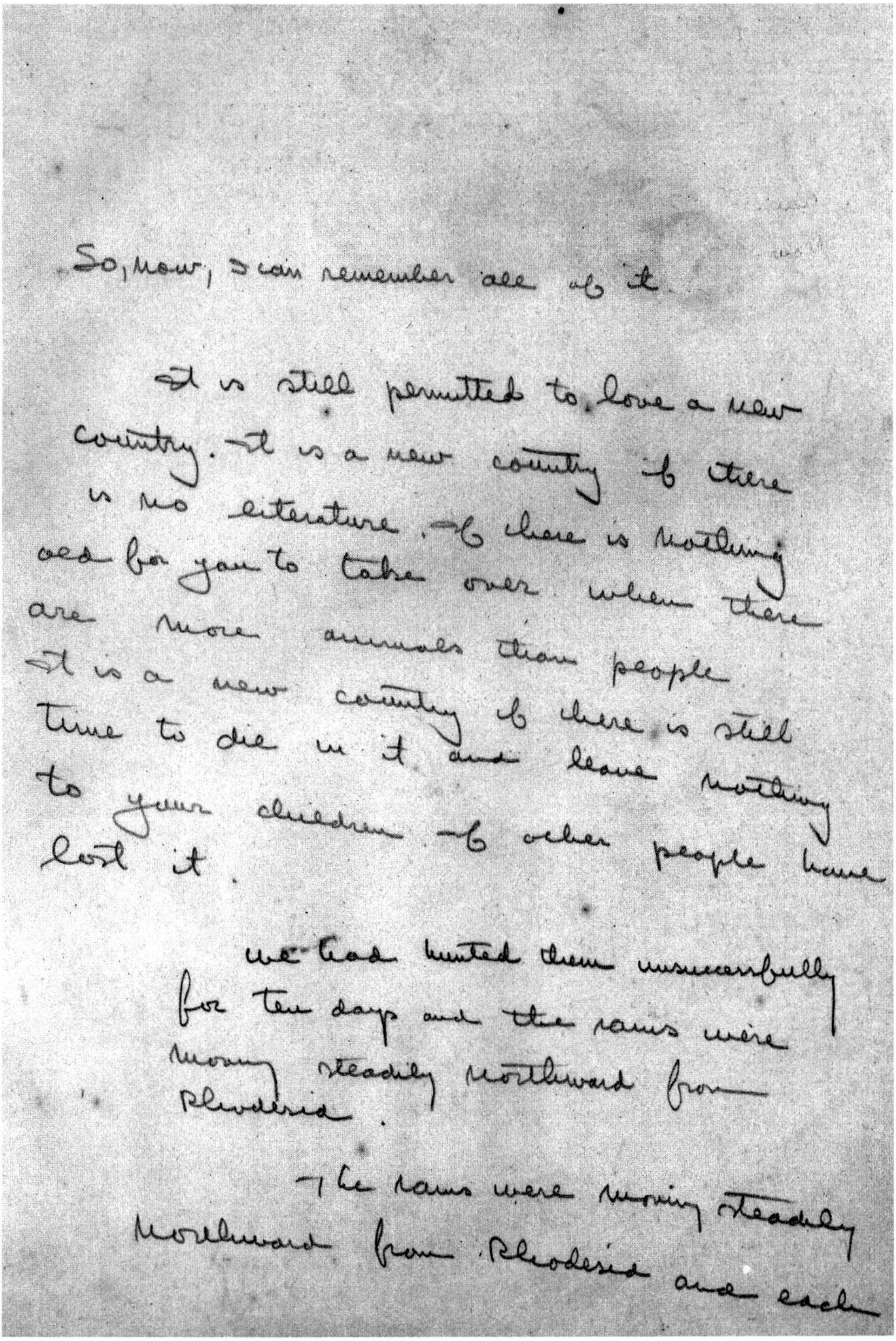

So, now, I can remember all of it.

It is still permitted to love a new
country. It is a new country if there
is no literature, if there is nothing
old for you to take over when there
are more animals than people
It is a new country if there is still
time to die in it and leave nothing
to your children if other people have
lost it.

We had hunted them unsuccessfully
for ten days and the rains were
moving steadily northward from
Rhodesia.

The rains were moving steadily
northward from Rhodesia and each

Figure 16. Early handwritten draft of the beginning of *Green Hills of Africa*.
Ernest Hemingway Collection, John F. Kennedy Library and Museum, Boston.

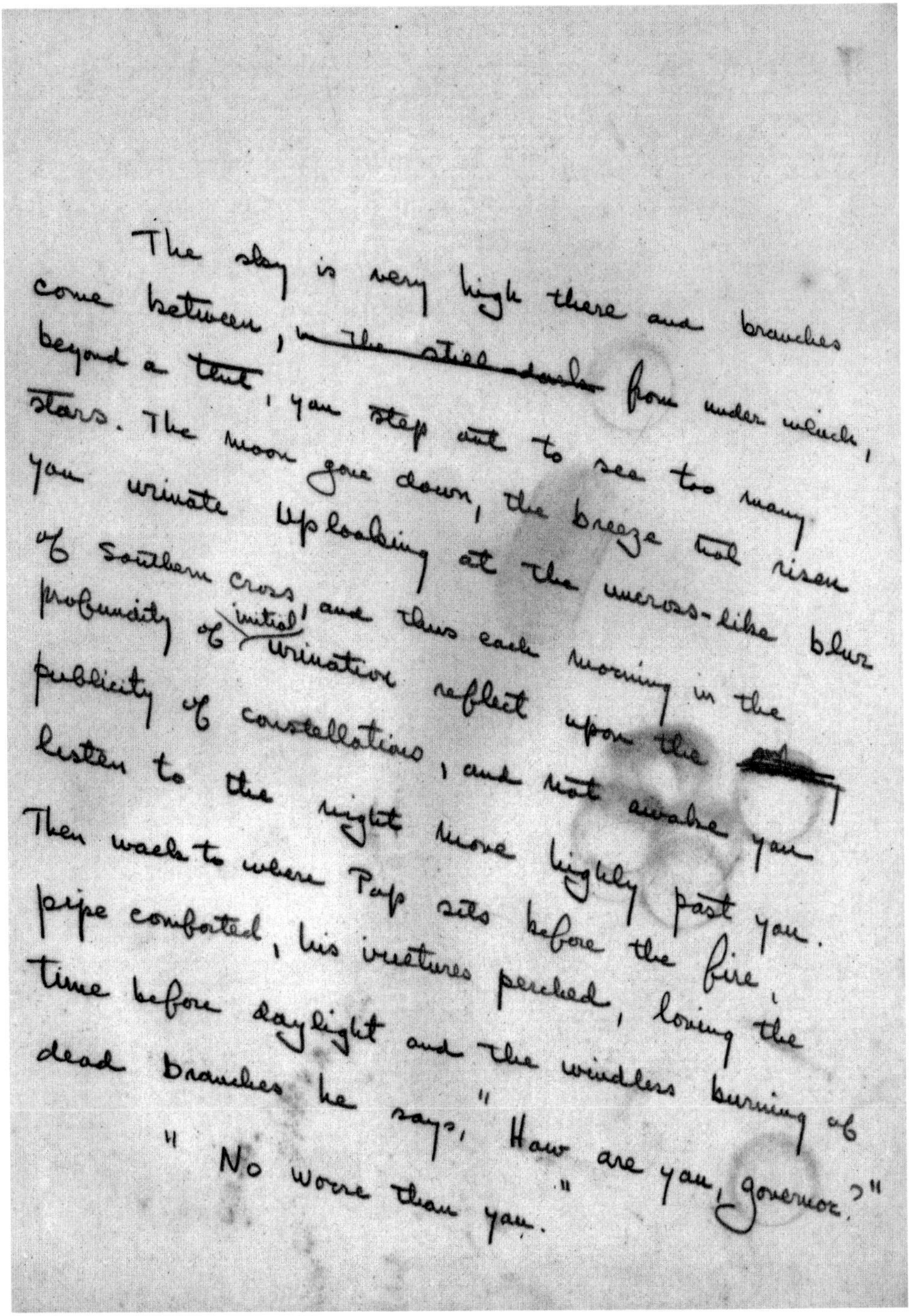

The sky is very high there and branches come between, ~~the still dark~~ from under which, beyond a tent, you step out to see too many stars. The moon gone down, the breeze that risen you urinate Up looking at the ~~uncross~~-like blur of Southern cross *initial* and thus each morning in the profundity of urination reflect upon the publicity of constellations, and not awake you listen to the night move lightly past you. Then walk to where Pop sits before the fire, pipe comforted, his vultures perched, loving the time before daylight and the windless burning of dead branches he says, "How are you, governor?"

"No worse than you."

Figure 17. Manuscript fragment: "The sky is very high there . . ."
Ernest Hemingway Collection, John F. Kennedy Library and Museum, Boston.

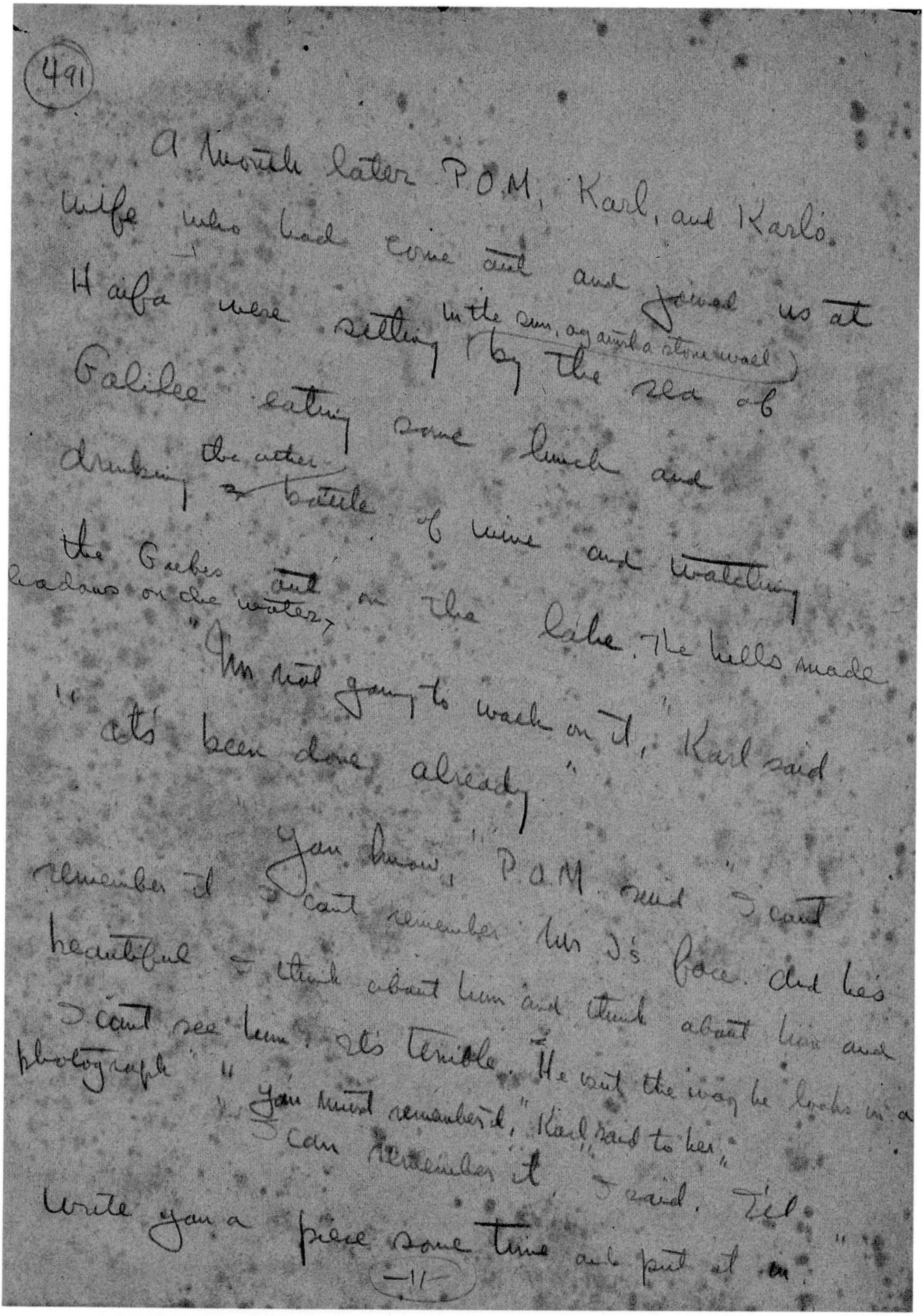

(491)

A month later P.O.M., Karl, and Karl's wife who had come out and joined us at Haifa were sitting (in the sun, against a stone wall) by the sea of Galilee eating some lunch and drinking the other bottle of wine and watching the Grebes out on the lake. The hills made shadows on the water.

"I'm not going to wash on it," Karl said.

"It's been done already."

"You know," P.O.M. said, "I can't remember his face. And he's beautiful. I think about him and think about him and I can't see him. It's terrible. He isn't the way he looks in a photograph."

"You must remember it," Karl said to her.

"I can remember it," I said. "I'll write you a piece some time and put it in."

—//—

Figure 18. Last page of the handwritten holograph manuscript of *Green Hills of Africa*. Ernest Hemingway Papers, 1925–1966, Accession #6250, etc., Clifton Waller Barrett Library of American Literature, Albert and Shirley Small Special Collections Library, University of Virginia, Charlottesville, VA. Image courtesy of the University of Virginia Library.

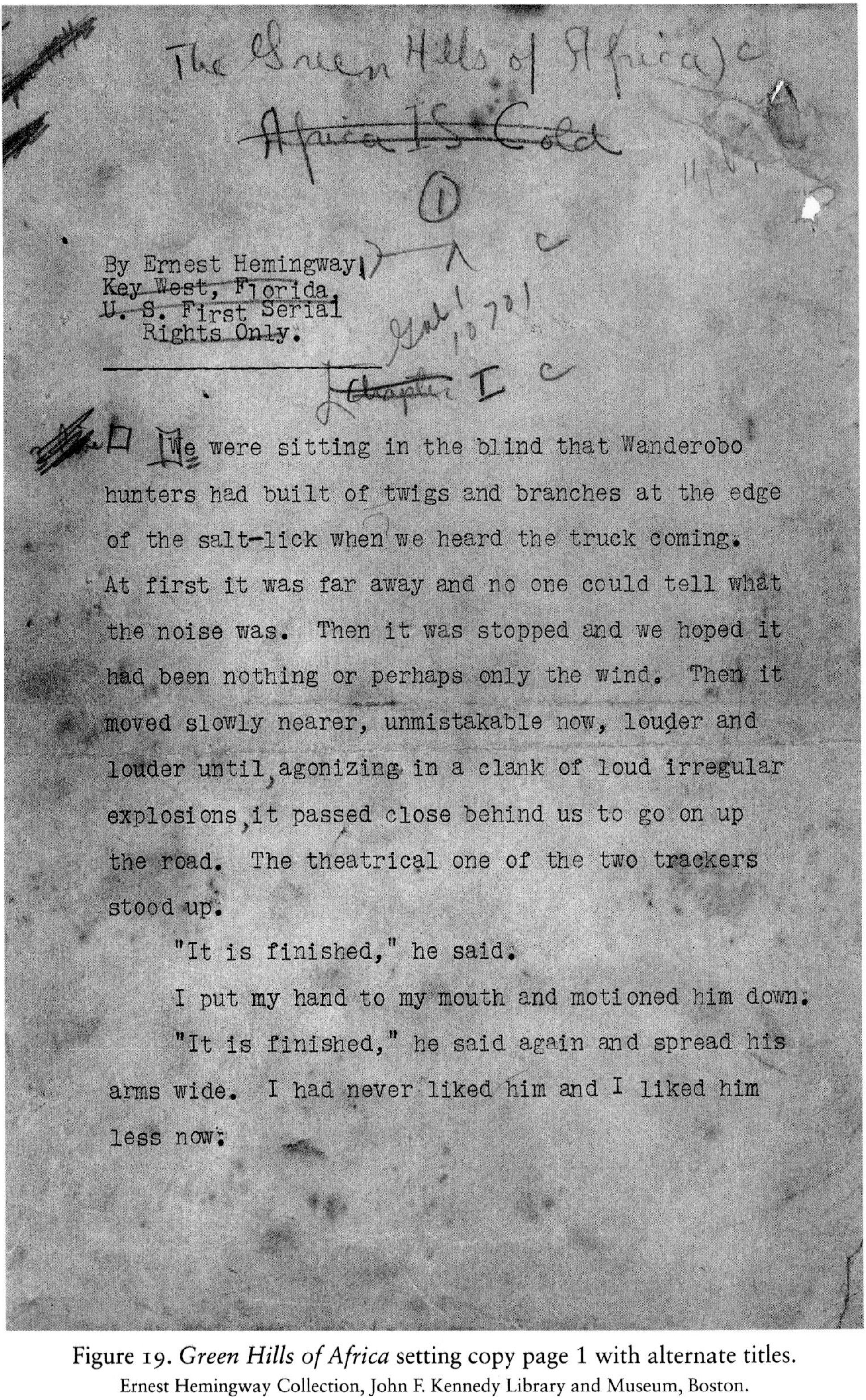

The Green Hills of Africa)c

~~Africa Is Cold~~

①

By Ernest Hemingway)
Key West, Florida.
U. S. First Serial
Rights Only.

Chapter I c

We were sitting in the blind that Wanderobo
hunters had built of twigs and branches at the edge
of the salt-lick when we heard the truck coming.
At first it was far away and no one could tell what
the noise was. Then it was stopped and we hoped it
had been nothing or perhaps only the wind. Then it
moved slowly nearer, unmistakable now, louder and
louder until agonizing in a clank of loud irregular
explosions it passed close behind us to go on up
the road. The theatrical one of the two trackers
stood up.

"It is finished," he said.

I put my hand to my mouth and motioned him down.

"It is finished," he said again and spread his
arms wide. I had never liked him and I liked him
less now.

Figure 19. *Green Hills of Africa* setting copy page 1 with alternate titles.
Ernest Hemingway Collection, John F. Kennedy Library and Museum, Boston.

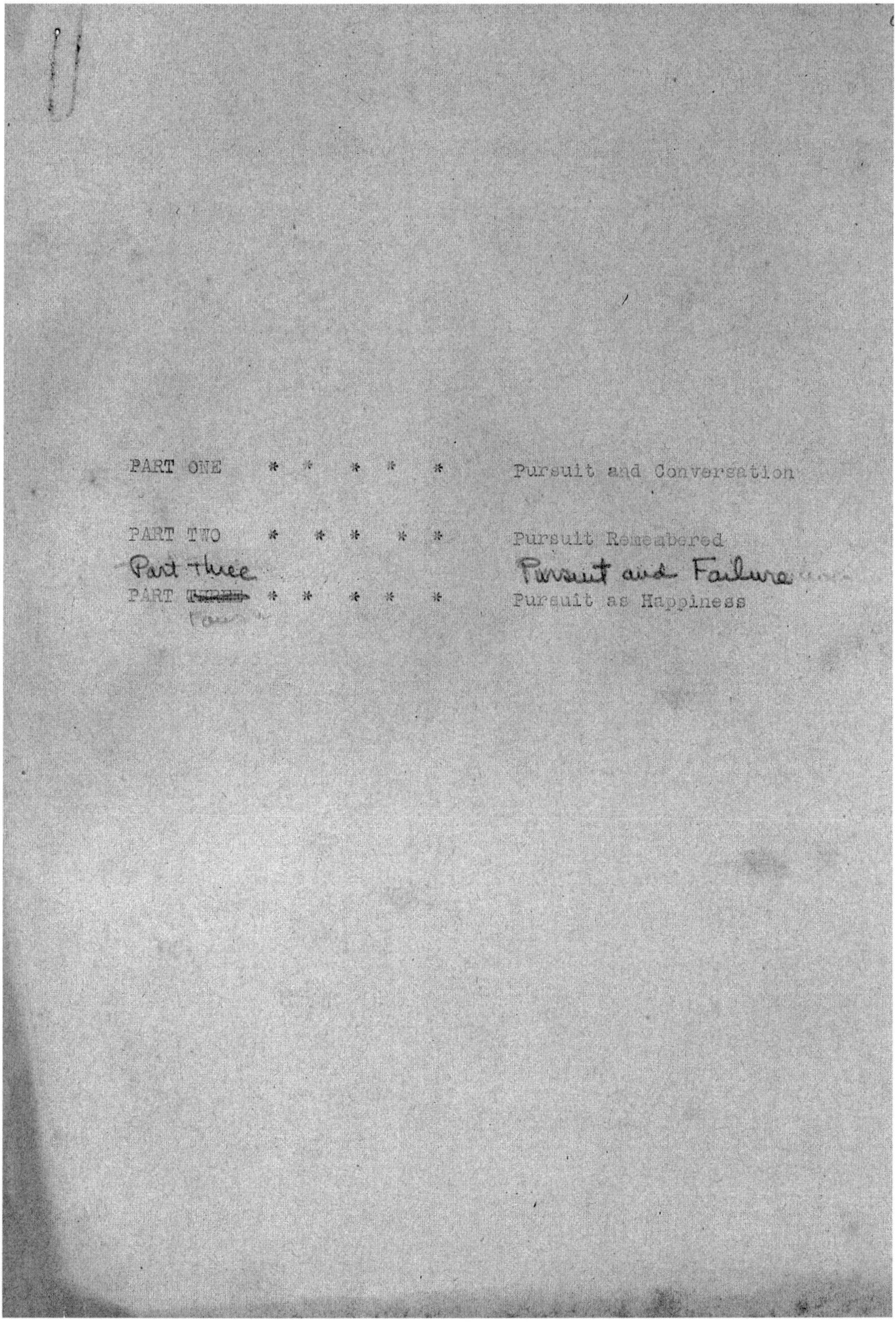

PART ONE * * * * * Pursuit and Conversation

PART TWO * * * * * Pursuit Remembered

Part three

PART ~~THREE~~ * * * * * Pursuit as Happiness

Pursuit and Failure

Figure 20. *Green Hills of Africa* carbon typescript with typed divisions and part three, "Pursuit and Failure," added by hand. Ernest Hemingway Collection, John F. Kennedy Library and Museum, Boston.

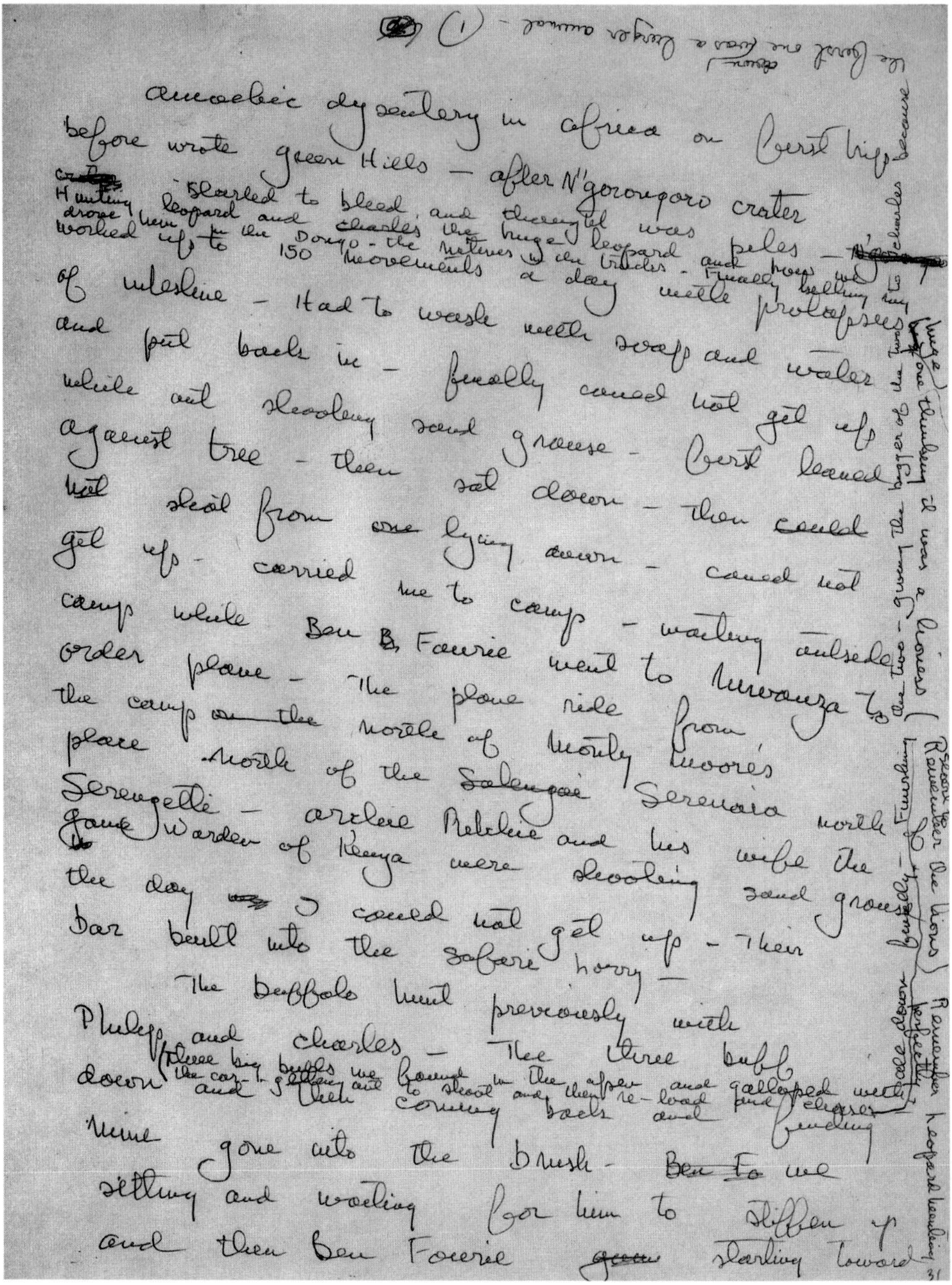

Figure 21. A page of Ernest Hemingway's handwritten notes in ink about his experiences on the 1933–1934 safari written while on his second safari of 1953–1954. Ernest Hemingway Collection, John F. Kennedy Library and Museum, Boston.

Appendix I:
Pauline Pfeiffer Hemingway's
1933–1934 Safari Journal

Handwritten pencil manuscript, Item M1344 in the Department of Special Collections and University Archives of the Stanford University Libraries. Minor editing of misspellings and punctuation has been made to this transcription. Editorial comments appear in brackets in the text or as footnotes.

Dec 22

Everyone has gone off to shoot some meat and perhaps I can get this safari started on paper. It's been going three days on the road, but at the times I could have written it—most notably at the Tanganyika frontier where it took an hour and twenty minutes to get the guns through—the book was in the trunk on a truck.

The men all went into a little white plastered hut behind a sign "H.M." where they and a native and three safari boys took all the guns apart, stamped them, signed papers and I sat on a small pointed rock in two feet of shade which missed my head and shoulders. Besides the hut there were several round native huts, a dark small store, two or three goats and four born dead geraniums. I watched the native life, two quite handsome females and a tall male in khaki. One of the women was old and she went off, maybe to the fields, and the other two stood around laughing and sort of wrestling until finally he picked her up and carried her into the hut with sounds of more laughing and wrestling. It seems the natives are a very moral people. They certainly have no anatomical self-consciousness, as they work naked in the field, and the

skins and cloths they wrap themselves in are wrapped according to
the needs of the weather. The Maasai are particularly handsome,
coal black, shiny and shapely. They are supposed to be the snooty
tribe. Yesterday, some time after going through customs, we were
stopped on the road by a man carrying a spear with a letter on the
end of it and a key in his hand, and a little group of people. He
wanted us to take them all to town because one of their warriors
had killed a man, and he pointed with the key at the warrior, a
little unfortunate black boy with handcuffs on, who looked about
13 or 14 years old. Ernest wanted to photograph him, but I cried
out no, because he looked so young and his mouth was working
so. But it turned out he was chewing —— and that a warrior must
be at least —— years old. But I only found out these things when
we were well on the way without the picture.

However, we started on this safari Dec. 20 around eleven
o'clock after a lot of waiting and beer. We went through the most
lovely country, plains then rolling country, then light bush, all
beautifully green after the rains. This day we really saw a lot of
game, flocks of wildebeest, Grant's gazelles, impala, Tommies,
giraffe, zebra, guinea fowl, a large warthog, a big black and white
bird with a long tail called a Plantenia [Secretary bird?], a red
legged and red billed hornbill, many greater bustard, a stork in a
group of vultures. The giraffe were at the side of the road, a large
herd, and we saw many more at a distance as we went along.

We spent the night at a rest camp in plastered huts with two
windows, large mosquito nets and no air. Never slept so deli-
ciously and, as a matter of fact, never needed it so much, for the
next day, Dec 21, was a long day though. We started at eight and
got to Arusha, our destination and the exact center of something,
about 1:30. But we went through hot, dusty country over quite
bumpy roads. The only time it was really exciting was when two
large and united herds of wildebeest and zebra wanted to cross in
front of our car. They would race along slightly in front of the car
at the side of the road at a fast pace, frequently slipping, one by
one daring to go in front of the car and cross the road at impossible speed and then gallop off apparently very satisfied. The fat
rumps of the zebras looked particularly satisfied, though the wildebeest appeared to have worked harder. There was a great feel-

ing of jest and freedom in this game on a completely open hot plain.

Another thing, Kilimanjaro kept appearing and disappearing high in the air like the Cheshire Cat all day.

We had a late lunch, a quiet afternoon and a swim, and dinner at the Hotel Arusha, very comfortable. When I came to lunch the dining room was all decorated from the ceiling with those festoons that unpleat in cutouts—big round ones in all colors. Mr. Percival was sitting at a table with a reddish saffron colored young man with a reddish saffron colored beard that went around his chin from ear to ear finishing in long hair of the same color and big round blue eyes.

I said, "Is all this for Christmas?"

And he said, "I'm sure I don't know. I wouldn't know you know because I'm a Mohammedan," and he smiled in a not very smart but very friendly way.

"Have you been here long?" he said.

I thought it was rather plain that we had just come, and hesitated and then he said, "Will you be here long?"

And I hesitated again because he seemed to want yes or no, and then Mr. Percival said the table was too small for all of us and Ernest and Charles and I went to another table. I said to Ernest that young man is a goofy, and he said he's cockeyed. It turned out he's a little of both and Lord Lovelace, England's best, and so far, save for a sister who looked very nice, the end of his line.

The swimming pool was quite wide, about 40 feet, surrounded by rough garden. This country is a very nice combination of comfort, sophistication and primitive life and country. This hotel was extremely comfortable, and the rest of the town, allowing for difference in architectural material—both have the same veranda effect—might be pioneer days along the Mississippi, general store, tiny bank, primitive post office, but a well-stocked grocery store with many darn good things to eat for people who know what they want. We left reasonably early and had lunch at our first campsite. At first we had thought to push on to Ngorongoro Crater because of the Christmas holidays, but finally decided to chance it. The trucks came up about an hour and a half later; at least one of them did—the other had a vital break and had to be repaired from Arusha so it was just as well we planned camp there.

Dec 23

Yesterday around four, after tea, Ernest, Charles and Mr. Percival went out to hunt. They came back around 6:30 with two spurfowl and a Tommy, all shot by Ernest. The Tommy was shot down once from considerable distance. He got up and started off and was finished on the run with one shot. Everyone was very impressed. Drinks, baths, more drinks, dinner in pajamas. It is warm here, even in early morning, and quite hot in the middle of the day. The sun takes the color out of my nail polish in a few hours. The altitude is about 3000 feet. We are right in the shadow of the Rift—that ridge formation that runs the whole length of Africa.

This morning Ernest, Mr. P. and I went out in a car, and Charles went with his gun bearer in a truck. We spent the morning from 7:30 until one pursuing an enormous Grant's gazelle with a really fine head. Ernest must have fired 30 shots—I never saw him miss so completely and he behaved beautifully—and he stalked him on foot and in the car until finally the whole herd was jittering. The Grant's gazelle left the herd and we gave chase but he got away, so Ernest took after another one—smaller—wounded it after five or six shots, re-wounded it and finally got him down.

Mr. Percival says everyone misses when they first come out here.

We came back in the car in full sun and in a whirlwind of dust. Found a truck from Alfred Vanderbilt's safari there with his trophies. I haven't seen them but Charles says they are fine.

Charles got three sand grouse and a wildebeest that turned out to be a cow in four shots, also a Grant's gazelle.

We had Tommy chops for lunch and now we are languishing until teatime—quite hot, and I'm quite tired. Don't care much for car hunting.

Dec 24

Here I am sitting all alone on top of Ngorongoro Crater in the rain. Mr. Percival is worried about the trucks getting up the grades and perhaps everyone has gone to see about them. The crater is very beautiful, about twelve miles across and blue, gray and green, all flat from this height, but you can see grass and trees and thousands of wildebeest. Ernest could see zebra but I couldn't. It is a game reserve, and in the hands of the Maasai. We are spending Christmas Eve here, and it will be very cold at night—maybe before with this rain and wind. We climbed all morning, a native driving at great speed up the one-car road. About two-thirds up the jungle started, the first we had seen, and very beautiful and tangled with roots and overhanging branches—pretty awful to get lost in. Saw three beautiful birds with long legs and soft topknots faintly pink [Kavirondo cranes]. Ernest said they were a kind of stork. When we got here Ernest told me to go away while he went to the bathroom. I said why can't you go away, and he said he was afraid of snakes. The grass is about three feet high, and all the other vegetation is piled on that. When you step on it, it sinks about two feet. The crater is supposed to be full of lions too.

Yesterday afternoon Ernest shot and hit four times a wildebeest that turned into a cow—he thought Mr. Percival referred to one head and he was looking at another. We came home late with much difficulty making the road over a stony rolling plain. The gun bearer went ahead and pointed the way. He was soon joined by Mr. P. and some time later by the two native car drivers, and they all cleared the way of stones. We got in without mishap. I almost forgot that I shot once at a wildebeest and three times at another—my characteristic good shot, just a l-i-t-t-l-e high, or low or right or left. I have shot so far ten of these splendid shots. Everyone seems satisfied with my shooting, but I have a faintly disappointed feeling.

Charles got a wildebeest in the neck with one standing shot at 290 yards. Called it a great piece of luck.

When Ernest shot the wildebeest cow several of the Maasai came over and one was henna'd all over—looked very handsome.

It seems they all use henna the year they are circumcised. Sort of like their college year Ernest says.

Dec 26

Christmas all over; big day of travel down from the crater, very hot, with dust and glare. The first view of the Serengeti was very fine, *full* of game moving in all directions, and when we got near our camp site we ran into great herds of wildebeest, unbelievable— ten thousand in sight, also zebra, Tommies, Grant's gazelles, Topis and innumerable birds. We shot fifteen sand grouse and a bustard (I shot five of the sand grouse, two on the wing) and we saw spurfowl, secretary birds, doves, plover, etc. We have a lovely camp here in front of a stony hill, with trees in front. All very tired for Christmas dinner, presents and to bed. I got a fine waterproof dustproof wristwatch from Ernest, which I've wanted for some time.

The afternoon at the crater, the 24th, was by far the most exciting time we've had. Ernest, Mr. P. and I went out in the car and Charles went alone on foot with his gun bearer. We hadn't gone far when we ran into a flock of guinea, so E and I went after them; they flew some distance and we pursued them. Ernest went one way and I the other and Ernest ran and drove them over toward me. Suddenly I saw what I thought was an animal like a leopard and rushed around over to Ernest losing the guinea and greatly displeasing my husband, as the animal turned out to be a jackal.

We went back to the car and drove along. Suddenly on a large rock about three hundred yards away Mr. Percival saw what he at first thought was a leopard but which turned out to be the most beautiful lioness. She was crouched down on the rock but as we watched her she moved out to the side and sat down.

Suddenly both Mr. P. & E. thought they saw two lion on the plain to the left and we went for them guns all ready, but they turned out to be zebra. So Ernest shot two zebra for bait (he only meant to shoot one, but another got it on a shot he didn't think went home) for the lioness and a possible lurking lion. Then we went back to watch the lioness who by this time had started down the rock and slope and came straight for the road. We went toward her, me for one very excited, and got to see her very well indeed. She was magnificent—large and with a beautiful coat. When she got to within fifty yards of the car she turned off the road and I was pleased as she was on my side and I never want to get too close to these large animals that kill cows but won't hurt you.

As we were going back to watch the lioness there was a terrific gun report beside Ernest's head and I thought he was killed. After shooting the zebras he had put the gun uncocked on top of the car and it fell off stock first on the ground beside the car and went off. We were pretty shaken.

When we got back, very tired, excited and a bit shaky we found Charles who was so full of his own excitement he could hardly listen to ours. He had seen a male rhino, and a female and baby (*mtoto**) rhino, a waterbuck and a bushbuck.

Dec 27

Yesterday morning went out looking for lion. Started at seven and came upon five that rose out of the grass before us at 10:10. They were smaller and less impressive than the Crater lioness, and Mr. P. said they were too young for our purposes—none of them was maned.

I shot a Tommy with one shot through the back and Ernest shot a wildebeest with a single shot and a hyena. I know now that it is very bad to call anyone a hyena.

I rested in the afternoon and the rest went out. They found no lions, but when Ernest shot a hyena three lionesses came out for meat. Charles shot an eland with 27 inch horns.

This morning we went lion hunting again, but had very little luck. Ernest shot a grant with a single shot; I shot another with eight shots. Ernest shot a hyena. Came back around noon to find Bai with the new car, a large blue Dodge built like a bus with a space for the gun bearers at the back. No mail but two telegrams,

---

**Mtoto* is Swahili for "little one" or "baby."

one from Leicester and one from Harry Burton saying he wanted the story for the *Cosmopolitan* and a lot more like it.

We went out in the afternoon and saw five lions—only one really a lion. We came on the three lionesses and a lion under a tree, the lion very old, all very formidable. Mr. P. said the lionesses were the same that came out after meat the other day. We circled round them in the car and they lay there in the shade, very calm and peaceful. Mr. P. said the lion was good enough but we could do better so we went on—I felt rather wobbly. Am not brave with wild animals. We hunted for a considerable time in beautiful bush country with giraffe looking out of the trees, or rather over them, and baboons playing on the slopes, and herds of zebra running about and a series of pairs of reedbuck. I shot one twice—missed the first time, broke his back the second. He is not a very impressive trophy, very small, undistinguished horns, but pretty. Sometime after that one of the gun bearers spotted a lioness under a tree. We went by her and Mr. Percival suggested killing a Grant's gazelle for her, which Ernest did with one—or was it two—shots. This was then put on the car and we drove over to the lion. Mr. P. tossed it off but she didn't take any notice of it, so it was put back on the car and we drove closer. Mr. P. cast it off again and we drove on a bit to see what she would do. While we were sitting there she got up and glided over to the track of the blood, followed it and pounced on the Grant and took it under a tree. As she was eating, we saw a pig that Mr. P. said had enough tusks to shoot. Ernest and Charles drew lots and Charles won. He shot several times. At first shot the lioness jumped up and ran with the grant in her mouth, but she settled down again.

The warthog is a strange looking animal close, has I should say, a little crocodile blood. Has a long flat snout, small pig eyes, double tusks on each side. These were not very long.

On our way home Ernest shot a hyena before we came on the same three lionesses, all separated about fifty feet with their eyes on a wildebeest standing alone in an open space. A lion was some distance from all this. Mr. P. and Bai decided, and Ernest, that this was a family, lion, lioness and two young ones. Ernest shot the wildebeest and he went down, but was not dead. He struggled to get up and like a flash the two young lions were on him, one at his throat and one playing him like a cat. They all struggled a little and then the wildebeest went down. They both started sucking his blood, one at the throat, the other at the hind quarter. Then the old lioness came softly out and over and a great sucking sound was made by all. When this was in full progress the lion joined them, pushed aside the lioness at the throat and took his place there. All together they really made a pretty awful sound. We watched for a little and then came home. Big afternoon.

Dec 28

I didn't go out as I was too damn sleepy. Ernest shot 4 hyenas, Charles 1, Ernest shot a cobra, and one shot at a cheetah. Thought it was dead, but it got up soon and ran so fast it got away. Ernest also shot a warthog running, 5 shots, killed with the fifth at three hundred yards. Charles got a robertsi Grant's gazelle, a nice one, single shot. They also got six ducks and some covies. But when they came to reload the camera found that there hadn't been a film in it.

We had a visit right after lunch from a white hunter named Lucy and his charges, Colonel and Mrs. Philips. She's a writer and I think wanted to commune with other writers, but Ernest sat with his chin on his chest staring out. Said afterward he didn't like the woman. Neither did Mr. P. Mr. P. is a darling—most attractive man on African continent. Seeing a white hunter of the Lucy sort brings this strongly home.

This is now the rest hour and I had intended to write a little description of the camp, but what with the visitors and helping Charles or rather watching him light Ernest's Christmas present, and sleepiness don't think I can do it.

Dec 29

Yesterday afternoon after shooting at a waterbuck we found a lion that Mr. P. said would do to shoot, a light lion, old, with not too bad a mane. I shot first, once, very excited and missed and Ernest killed it with a single shot, though he shot another afterward. Very fine lion, very impressive. Despite my miss, the word went round the camp by way of M'Cola that Mama had shot a *Simba*, so I was greeted by all the boys clapping and chanting and carried on their shoulders to my tent. Very splendid; wished I had shot the lion. Gave everybody a shilling. This morning we changed camp—a long hot drive. Four lions for whom E. killed a zebra, and 19 others in a big school in a very pretty place like a park helped pass the morning. There was one handsome old lion, very wary. Hunted waterbuck and called on the game warden, Monty Moore, and his new wife. Both nice, he very handsome, full of hidden something—maybe sex appeal, maybe more. Then we had lunch and went on to camp to find no boys, though the trucks had passed us sometime before. It was very hot, dusty and disappointing, but we pushed on from 3 to 5:30 wondering if we should find the boys by following some tracks. When we got to the next camp there they were, tents up, drinks waiting.

Dec 30

We changed camp this morning. Are in a lovely place near water and palms, like a little park. Our tents are laid out neatly in a row—ours, Charles', Mr. P.'s and Bai's, with the dining tent in front of them, and the cook's quarters way round to the right and in front. On the way here Charles shot a waterbuck amid great excitement—his excitement. Once we were within four feet of him in the car. He was a lovely creature, rich chocolate brown and light brown. The waterbuck is the roundest and plumpest of all the bucks. The afternoon for the first time was without action—though I believe an impala was shot at once.

Dec 31

The morning was a chronicle of shoot and miss. First a roan by Ernest, then we jumped a leopard that was stalking a pig and three young. He loped off into the brush, fast, Ernest firing three shots, Charles once, all rather close. A little later Ernest wounded a cheetah and E., Mr. P., C. and the gun bearers followed him for nearly an hour up and over a hill but finally lost him.

In the afternoon Charles shot a beautiful impala. It was a big stalking event, with Charles quite nervous as he already had some unfortunate experience with impala. He fired six or seven shots with the last three out of four telling. Lovely animal. Mr. P. went with C. to stalk and lost his pipe.

Jan 1

I felt quite tired so didn't go out this morning and this is what happened:

E. wounded a warthog that got away

E. killed a nice impala with a single shot

E. hit another warthog

E. killed a cheetah and two klipspringers. Then what should appear in the distance on the plains but three buffalo, looking black and big and powerful. E. & C. had a wonderful time killing them <u>all</u>, one of which got up when they thought it dead and charged Bai, who so far was moved as to say Sonofabitch. Ben came after me to see them at eleven, and it took us an hour and a half to drive back and find the place. The buffalo looked pretty impressive. We got back to camp around two and didn't go out in the afternoon. As it passed I got gloomier and gloomier and finally so tired and gloomy had dinner in bed.

Jan 2

Woke up gloomy but pushed myself up and everyone was <u>so</u> nice finally got over being gloomy. We went first to the buffalo left on the plain to see if the lion had come to feed on them. He hadn't though the one we left open was picked by the birds; the one under the bush was considerably picked—there were droves of mournful birds all about; and the one under the bush with the toilet paper spotted about untouched. Ernest shot a beautiful roan, large heavy horns, and then we all fired at five cheetahs, E., C., and I, a regular bombardment. E. got one; Charles thought he nicked one, and I knew I didn't, as the bead was jittering in the air. Don't know why I was so excited. The cheetahs are very beautiful. Mr. P. says they make fine pets, a cross between a cat and a dog.

In the afternoon Ernest shot an impala for bait and we hid it in a tree for a possible leopard. Afterwards I shot a waterbuck, wounding it, then hit it again and it went off. So Mr. P. and I stalked it, starting up hill after it. Then Mr. P. said he rather thought we'd find it downhill, which I doubted, but sure enough there it was standing below us, a fine shot. But as we looked it sat down and the grass was so high it hardly showed. I fired and missed. Then shot again and it disappeared in the donga. We crept into the donga and there was the waterbuck in the water at the bottom. Finished him off with two shots. Waterbuck always go to water when wounded, if possible. Hence (perhaps) waterbuck.

Jan 3

Broke camp and went first to see the impala bait. Nothing had hit it. On the way to the next camp Ernest shot a senile old eland that appeared quite close. He was large and beautiful and very silver gray, but his horns were worn away. We left him and went on to the campsite and had lunch. Waited some time for the trucks and then went back to where the eland and Chiaro had been left. Found the trucks there hacking up the eland; said they were late because Molo forgot bwana H's hat and they had to return for it.

As we started back Chiaro mentioned that while he was there watching the eland, two leopards came out towards the eland. So we waited on the road at a little distance from the eland for about half an hour. Then we rode up and as we approached saw all the birds gathered a little away from the eland, which was a fine sign. And then we saw the leopard. C. and E. poured out of the car. I tried to. They both shot and Charles hit it, knocking it down. Then it struggled up and started slowly, but gaining momentum, off. They both shot again and Charles cracked it down. That's certainly your leopard, Charles, I said. It was good shooting. And it was very exciting to finally have a leopard.

After tea in the afternoon we went out and saw a leopard just as he disappeared into the brush. Ben and I went home to get the truck, leaving E. and C. stationed at one end of the donga, and Mr. P. and M'Cola to watch. We came back with the truck full of boys and guns and it was rather like an Irish raid. We drove along the donga, Ben firing into it at intervals. Suddenly we heard a shot and found the leopard had started out and Ernest had shot it. It went back into the donga and the female (which it seems was there all the time and I didn't know it) ran down the donga and the fearless Mr. P. shot it. It crashed down but we paid no attention to it. Then there was more shooting into the green bush where E. said the leopard disappeared and suddenly Ben saw it through the leaves. E. gave it what we hoped was a finishing shot and we went around to the other side of the donga for a better view. There he lay, apparently dead. I fired, hit him with the twenty-eight, and he didn't move. So he was fished out of the donga, very large and orange and beautiful—I thought more beautiful than Charles' was, and his was lovely. Everyone very pleased.

Jan 4

We went out for eland and Ernest had one nicely wounded when two lions were spied on an opposite hill. After mending a puncture and Ernest going to the bathroom (Diarrhea) we went over to the lions, which turned out to be a lioness and a super lion. We went toward them but instead of retreating they advanced inquiringly on the car, the lioness going to one side, the lion to the other. It had been agreed that I was to shoot at this lion and I was pushed out in the face of the advancing super lion.

I took aim and was about to fire when my dear Mr. P. said for Christ's sake don't shoot the lioness. Can I be shooting the lioness, I thought, and turned to look at the lioness, which really was a lioness; then resumed beading of lion. While this was going on Charles was trying to get out of the car in full view of the lions, which certainly would have spooked them and E. was in the car unable to aid his wife should the lion charge. I shot standing up—think I squeezed off—and missed, but of course it was a very fine shot and considerable difference of opinion was had whether or not I had hit the lion, which disappeared into the donga, and was never heard of again although we got the truck and beat both sides of the donga. Came home and had despair again. Everyone seemed to feel he had lost his head.

The afternoon was quiet. Ernest killed a bushbuck (lovely looking creature) with a single shot and shot twice late in the afternoon at an eland without wounding it.

Jan 5

We went out after eland and Ernest shot one at a great distance in the herd, and it went down greatly to the surprise of all. Nice head. The truck brought home a lot of the meat, which is very good, while we walked about two and a half miles, me very constipated and I'm sure people could have been kind enough to say quite disagreeable. Everyone tired by walk but happy.

Eland marrow and buffalo marrow are delicious, so is buffalo steak, and the greater part of eland.

In the afternoon we went out in nice wild country, saw a lot of game, but none suited to our purposes, i.e. lion and buffalo.

Jan 6

We moved camp again which took about all day what with the trucks not appearing and our having to go after them back to the old camp and not finding them until about five in a place they'd picked for themselves. However in the morning E. and C. both shot impalas with single shots and Ernest shot a beautiful big eland with very spread horns. Also a hyena; makes 10 hyenas. We had no lunch and a sardine tea about five, with everyone pretty tired. Ernest's diarrhea holding up very well. Can't sit down any too well now.

Jan 7

We moved camp again and everyone was very stiff from sitting in the car all the day before. Old story of the phantom trucks. We waited until one for them at the new site and then Ben and Mr. P went after them. While waiting Monty Moore and wife and Mr. Ritchie, wife and friend came by out photographing and gave us a gin drink. Finally trucks came. While going along in the morning Ernest shot the biggest and most lovely impala to date. Also, very early in the morning we saw a lioness run down and kill a wildebeest calf. She seemed to knock it over. Very exciting. We saw three other lions and E shot a Serval cat, a very pretty animal with a head just like a cat and skin rather like a cheetah but softer.

Jan 8

We were out at seven o'clock, Ernest with diarrhea and piles on one side of me, Charles with piles on other and all very bitten by tsetse fly, but cheerful. We had gone scarcely out of sight of the camp when Ernest saw two lionesses. Then we came upon a super lion and lioness (turned out were two lionesses afterwards) and Charles got out and shot him four times. The last two times with the lion on the run. Then he disappeared in the tall grass. Sent for truck, which couldn't get across the donga, so we set out on foot after an hour of waiting, all of us with the two gun bearers tracking; agreed that anyone who saw the lion was to shoot it; Charles feeling very low at not getting his lion. We had gone about twenty yards when Mr. Percival gave a shout and there was the lion at our feet, stone dead in the grass. He was a beauty; don't make them any better, Mr. P. and Ben both said. Lion skinned and beheaded and all of us back in camp by 9:30. We had tea where Ernest's malady was discussed in detail and he took more salts. Very sore but seems to think he's a little better.

Lunch; rain; mug; brought this diary up to date.

In the afternoon Ernest didn't feel well so he stayed at home while we went over to find Warden Ritchie and have a sundowner with him. But no Ritchie at the place he was supposed to be. So we came home. Charles killed a Tommy for meat.

Jan 9

On the way out breaking camp we ran into the Ritchies shooting birds (sand grouse) that flew back and forth from one lake to another. Ernest shot a while. Ritchie very good bird shot. We then came upon two lions and five lionesses, then one lion. Brought the hyena figure up from eighteen to twenty-three. We reached camp and had lunch, Ernest feeling none too good. We went out in the afternoon to find the stream risen and the game to hell and gone. Saw seven cheetah.

Jan 10

Ernest suffered considerably as we went on long rough ride to lion hill to scout out the game—didn't get back until nearly 1:30—no traces of lion. On the way up in the morning we came on some ponds with ducks, so we got out and shot. E got four—one *pas trouvé* and I with Mr. P's help (not sure he didn't shoot this bird) wounded a lovely black duck. Shot at him repeatedly but never passed him out. Too bad. Got home and found the trucks, which hadn't gone off the road had seen a nice lion over a hill.

Jan 11

E.'s diarrhea very bad—taking chlorine all day. This morning broke camp and decided to go back to the Ritchie camp where the bird shooting was so good and E. could rest a bit. Hunted on the way up and brought the hyena total to 33. Saw eight of them worrying a wildebeest in the middle of the lake out from Moro. Then we looked for lion and about forty-five minutes from this camp we found two lions, large, lovely, though light in color, and a lioness. One lion was more or less out in the open, but the other and the lioness went into a donga and refused to come out, even when E. killed a zebra for them. We got fine pictures of the other lion; and finally by driving the car into the edge of the donga got the lion and lioness out, even got them slightly separated. Then Mr. P. said if Ernest could get the lion with one shot he might take him, while he watched the lioness, which Ernest did. Handsome lion—didn't smell so bad as Charles's lion, which smelled like a vampire. Noble beast, the lion, though.

Jan 12

The Ritchies came by for drinks last night and on the advice of Mrs. R. decided to put Ernest on a milk diet. He was feeling very bad and drank a bottle of champagne for his diarrhea. Ernest didn't go out today and it was rather dull. We went out for lion and found two lions and one lioness, now 82 lions, none suited to our purposes. I shot a spurfowl and a guinea greatly to everyone's surprise. Charles shot two hyenas bringing total to 35. Charles went out alone with his boys later and shot a Tommy and a Grant's gazelle. E. shot a Tommy from his bed.

Jan 13

E. felt very bad but we went out for sand grouse. He got six and two *pas trouvé*, C. four and I got four, very good for me; seemed to greatly surprise Mr. P. Mr. P. very splendid man, very handsome. We met the Moores on our way home. They had papers for us and returned books and stayed for tea. Both very nice. We looked for lion in the afternoon and saw one, bringing the total to 84 lions. As we were going along in the car Charles happened to look down a large hole and saw a pig sticking out. We got out and Ben stomped on the back of the hole without success and pig had disappeared from the front of the hole. Then suddenly like a cannon shot out came the pig, grey and shedding dust. Was very amazed and unbalanced by this. He ran off fast on his short legs. Mr. P. told C. to shoot it out. By the time he gathered his forces together the pig was well on his way and C missed it three times, which seemed to please him as he didn't want the pig anyway. Charles killed a Topi alone with his boys for meat, and saved the skin, which Mr. P. says is very nice.

Jan 14

We went after sand grouse although E. felt very bad and couldn't sit in the car, but stood outside. The birds were slow in coming and E. was very miserable. Killed 10 when they did come, but I think the long standing up in the cold did him harm rather than good. C shot four birds and I missed them all. Finally prevailed on Mr. P to take the gun, which he did protesting that he couldn't shoot anything. Three birds came along and he shot them all with one shot. No more birds came after that. We drove home, E. in great pain and went to bed. It was decided to get a plane to take him in to Arusha instead of going in the car—three days over rough roads. The plane does it in two hours and he must do something about his fatal-combination malady (piles-diarrhea). Ben went off to nearest station (on Lake Victoria 115 miles) to send the wire and Mr. P. went as far as Monty Moore's to be sure a wire could be sent from there. Ben will get there tonight—should get there tonight and the plane will be here in the morning. E. stayed in bed all day—no alcohol as no good for diarrhea, bad for piles. He moved out to the campfire at sundown and had some mashed potatoes while we had drinks. Poor Ernest. I killed a Topi out with Charles.

Jan 15

A very noisy night with wind and rain and some animal bit my toe through the covers, maybe a pack rat. Awake much of the time and alarmed, but E. slept through and thought himself much better until he began to move around. Ben got back at two this morning driving straight through because afraid of the roads with the rain. The plane is expected around two—don't know why two particularly. E. is all packed and lying in bed reading the English magazines Mrs. Moore brought—*Time, Punch, Field, Daily Sketch*, etc.

We waited all afternoon but no plane; a very dull day. Charles and I went after birds about five but found none. I shot at a mongoose but missed although Charles declared he saw him go over backwards. E. feeling maybe a bit better. More mashed potatoes. Ben got a message from Manley over the radio. No plane available Monday, but one would come Tuesday morning.

Jan 16

And so it did around 10 o'clock. While we had tea there was much discussion whether E should go to Nairobi or Arusha—mail at Arusha but less comforts—on other hand could fix up fishing but horrible nursing home yawning in Nairobi and big gip doctor. Gov. doctor at Arusha. Last decision for Arusha. Ernest went off very gay and handsome (partly due to extreme thinness) in a small silver plane with a tiny pilot belonging to the weasel family.

After he left we broke camp and came up here, having lunch on the way. Beautiful camp with yellow tree trunks, not far from the big soda lake. We came across the Serengeti to get here, and in the afternoon about a mile before we got to lion hill two big— very big and beautiful—lions rose up, right along the road. I got under Ben's wing to shoot and just as I got down on my knees to shoot the gun went off. I then shot nine times without hitting once and the lions made off. We got back in the car and went after them. Fortunately, there was no carcass anywhere. Then I got out again and shot two times hitting him both times. Then Charles shot him in the shoulder knocking him over. Then everyone shot and poor fellow was dead. The other lion then behaved very well from the point of view of a lion, but annoyingly from ours. He refused to leave his dead comrade and took to snarling. So it was decided, we having our quota of lions, to take the other on Ben's. So Ben shot three beautiful shots at the lion down on all fours looking toward him. The first shot greatly surprised the lion and completely changed his expression from one of defiance to amazement. They were lovely lions. I think mine is the best of all the 85 we've seen and I'm very happy to have it. Wish my performance could have been a little more brilliant.

Charles shot two hyenas and I did too.

We got to camp around 4:30, got a little cockeyed at sundown. Mr. P. has indigestion—probably nervous, over E. and I have a little too. Slept fitfully without Ernest and at two thought the tent was surrounded by a hyena cracking bones, but it turned out to be a super beetle bug—big as a small bird walking on the mosquito net, unfortunately, inside. Hit him many times with the searchlight but like native he was unstunable, but he finally dropped and I put him out.

Jan 17

Now that Ernest has been gone a day and Mr. P. has his indigestion hunting has become rather sorry affair. We went out this morning to get two Topi—like that—and about twenty-eight shots were fired before one Topi was brought down. Charles fired and fired and then asked me to shoot, which I did three times without a hit. Very unfortunate affair but Topi finally defeated by tireless tracking and shooting by Charles. We came home after that and poor Mr. P. went to bed.

In the afternoon Charles killed a Topi with two shots, and we each killed a hyena. Saw a fine cow rhino and calf on the plains coming home. Remarkable looking creatures. The cow had two fine fiery red (from rooting) horns and the year-old baby had one about an inch and a half. They're grey and prehistoric and cumbersome and stupid looking, and they can't see very well, but will charge a car.

Charles and I got two guinea fowl around 6:30. Shot them out of a tree in the dusk—very sporting.

Jan 18

We broke camp and came up to the crater. Mr. P. feeling pretty feverish. Nursed the trucks to the top then Mr. P. went to bed. Charles went out in the evening after bushbuck.

Jan 19

Mr. P. still in fever's hollow palm. Charles and I went out alone with our boys (one carrying rhino gun, one carrying my gun, one carrying small water jug). We saw two (or the same one twice) doe bushbuck. We came home, then went down to glass the crater.* Very little game. Coming home we picked some flowers and I fell down in a thorn bush. Very painful taking out thorns from fatty part of anatomy. Put flowers on the table in a tooth mug where they fell over twice, wetting everything.

In the afternoon we went out with Chiaro and two rhino guides. One of them (droopy lids and a very fine specimen) is a wonder tracker. Think Ernest is to have him; hope so. We went into the bamboo, very fascinating cool overhung place, very jungle like and tracked a rhino. Could hear it chewing but couldn't see it. Suddenly there was a crashing sound and we thought he was charging us but he went in the other direction and we tried to trace him in vain. It sounded as though the whole forest was crashing down. Came home and found a rather shaky Mr. P.

Jan 20

Around 7:30 we broke camp and descended from the Ngorongoro Crater and at the bottom Charles and Ben waited for the truck to make camp where Charles will hunt kudu, and Mr. P. and I (Mr. P. very seedy) went on the hot dusty road to Arusha to surprise Ernest. The dust and the heat were always with us and we

---

* To "glass" is to sweep with binoculars in search of game.

got to Arusha about 3:30 (4 by Arusha time) very dirty, dashed (mildly) into the hotel and asked for Mr. Hemingway from the Hindu clerk. Mr. Hemingway not here, he said. Had never heard of Mr. H. It developed when we saw the proprietor's wife who said that Ernest had come here in a plane in high spirits, had collected everyone's mail and gone on to Nairobi. Don't know who was more crushed, but think I was if possible. Mr. P. took to drink and I took to bed. Mr. P. looked a trifle better by whiskey light.

Jan 21

Today is Sunday and I heard several church bells. Feel very guilty I didn't go to church, if any, but had no stockings. Only alternative was wearing trousers. Had doubts about trousers. Mr. P. doesn't look any worse this morning but is quite subdued. Think maybe he's a little worried about his malady, which seems to be more complicated than appears on the surface, from dropped remarks. Also may be sort of overwhelmed at thought of me to look after though I have said I didn't need looking after and am trying to keep out of his way. Am going now to try to send a telegram to Ernest. Mr. P. and I stayed up quite late (10:45 pm) and drank beer, which I don't think was any too good for Mr. P.

Jan 22

Telegrams from E. this morning. One before I was dressed brought by Mr. P. saying arrive Monday 11:30 all cured Love, and the second at breakfast and which threw us into consternation by saying waiting until tomorrow for mail until we realized it was sent the day before and in answer to my telegram.

Went out to the air field, 5 miles out which is being put in shape for the expected visit of the Secretary of State and there came Ernest, all cured but looking a little peaked. He really seemed well, only weak. He and Mr. P. had a fine time drinking gin and whiskey and beer. Fine social time; talked about the war.

We went to Luigi's for drinks. Luigi told a lot of fine practically unintelligible tales, but fortunately didn't get on the subject of Mussolini when he talked so convincingly as to get Mr. P. to say that he'd heard he was a fine chap. Nevertheless though the Luigis very nice and Mrs. Luigi very handsome and kind. Two nice children with exotic pink and pale orange skins.

Jan 23

Couldn't leave this morning on account of a mysterious Ford part in one of the trucks breaking down. And the truck couldn't start until the next day. So we killed the day with drinks and letters and E and I took a fast rather hilly little walk and ended at the German hotel Seibert for beer. Very good. Came back late for a sundowner to find Mr. P. pretty sunk again. He is getting better, I suppose, but he certainly has his downs. Comes out of it beautifully with a few whiskies.

Jan 24

Set out quite early. Truck not fixed but we got another—ours to follow. Report of rain ahead and bad roads. Got stuck three times. No lunch until 2, and then sardine sandwiches in the rain. Ernest feeling fine with big appetite, though got tired hunting a Grant's gazelle in the morning. Mr. P. in grip of sore stomach.

"I go now to save my Lord from the water closet."

Saw oryx in the afternoon, which Ernest went after and missed at 400 or more yards. Mr. P took a nap, or rather laid down across the road. We stopped in front of a native road gang's hut, where there were two fine looking native girls. Camped at Mosquito river.

Jan 25

Ernest and I went out after a wildebeest and Ernest hit one on the dead run. The first shot maddened him, and at the second he fell over. Also got a spurfowl on the way out. Mr. P. rested in camp, which broke and started for the base camp in the hope of running into Ben, which we did. Had lunch there and then came over here to look for rhino with old droopy lids. We ascended a steep hill about four-thirty and stayed until 6:15 and saw . . . [sentence left unfinished.]

[Diary continues two pages later:]

Jan 28

We decided to invade the rhino country so we broke camp and moved it by porter (no trucks possible) to the side of the river in the Mbulombulo district.* It looked fine to see the porters coming along, wrapped in old curtains below the chest (with trousers underneath) and boxes on their heads. We hunted all the way over but saw nothing save a couple of reedbuck. Ernest got one of these.

In the afternoon we went out to the highest point available at 4:30 and stayed there until sundown, with scouts in the surrounding country, without success. Came home, had sundowners. E. and Mr. P. talked about the war.

Jan 29

Called in what seemed to be the middle of the night (but which turned out to be a little after 5) by lantern light. Ernest got up in bed and said, "I think maybe I won't go," but he finally got up, and it's a darn good thing he did because we went up the hill back of the camp after breakfast about 6 and stayed there a little while on Mr. P.'s advice, the scouts going up on the surrounding hills, and suddenly M'Cola said, "huh, huh," and along came a rhino down the hill very fast like a locomotive toward the water and the forest. Mr. P said he's not awfully good, but we'll shoot him, and sent the boys for the guns. Ernest shot him three times with the Springfield and we thought hit him once (he snorted), though

* The actual name of this area is the Mbulu District.

the old rhino went crashing on. When he came out again from under cover E. shot him again 2 times, but the range was too far. The range was long to start and we went running along without hope of finding him. Droopy Lids and friends went to track him, and finally found blood, which was most encouraging. We finally caught up with Droopy and heard the old rhino breathing heavily (what turned out to be his death rattle) and finally came upon him, feet in the air, dead. E. shot twice more to be sure and then there was the celebration. Even the cook came out and innumerable pictures were taken. The rhino is a nice clean animal. His hide cuts through white like coconut. Came home and had beer to celebrate. Then rested. Mr. P. much impressed; said longest away he'd ever seen a rhino shot (first shot about 250 meters away) and said it was best shooting he had seen E. do. Ernest has now shot all the so-called dangerous game with the Springfield.

Charles shot Tommy, Grant's gazelle and wildebeest yesterday, but no oryx, which he and Ben were after. They are at our last camp.

Jan 30

We went out in the afternoon and sat on the hill back of the camp but without success. Not one rhino.

Jan 31

We broke camp and hoofed back to Charles and Ben. Saw no rhino on the way. Ernest killed a reedbuck. It was a nice two-hour walk. We came in to find Charles with very bloody hands and trousers putting a new film in his camera.

"Did you get something, Charles?" I asked.

He'd been out alone with his boys for a rather dismal (I think) unsuccessful time.

"Yes," he said, "a rhino, and it turned out to be a beauty with about a 23 inch horn." (E.'s is 17 in.)

He was very pleased. We all had a fine lunch together and

then parted company, Charles going to Mosquito River after oryx and we went with Droopy for a possible four days on rhino and buffalo. Got over there in time to go to the highest mountain and glass the country. I thought the outlook rather dismal with what looked like hellish country to hunt. Nobody very cheerful. No rhino sign.

Feb 1

Nevertheless we were called before dawn by lantern light and started at 6:00 on our longest and most exciting day on foot. Took lunch. We went at what I thought was a brisk trot up and down hills and finally reached the principal riverbed where we followed rhino tracks for some time, suddenly spying in the tall grass along the water a rhino and her calf. In the same place was a buffalo, and another rhino which I never saw and which got away. The boys threw sticks into the grass and the buffalo jumped out and started up the hill on the opposite bank. Ernest shot twice, or maybe three times and hit it the first time. He tore up the hill and we didn't go after him as we were really on a rhino hunt. We saw one rhino high upon the hill within easy shooting distance, but the horn wasn't worth taking and later 4 buffalo on a hill on its other side. In the meantime it was getting late so we rested under a tree, had early lunch and a little nap. At 1:30 E. and Mr. P. went out to track a rhino herd and were gone until 3—sweating out alcohol they said later—and I joined them up the stream where we had tea on Droopy's advice while the scouts were busy trying to locate rhino. Not finding any we started to try to pick up the trail of the buffalo E wounded in the morning. Mr. P. found the first sign—a bloody shrub, and for a time the blood trail was vigorous and clear. As we went on it got to be drop by drop and a few chawed leaves. We went sharply up hill and then down to the tall grass of the river, finally coming to a place Mr. P. said was too dangerous to venture into. So just as we were abandoning this trail, Mr. P. saw two buffalo high on the hill. Ernest ran out and fired very quickly his Springfield at the larger one. He thought he hit it, and very excited but (personally speaking) a little dashed by tracking another wounded animal straight up an enormous hill and feet hurting, we went galloping up the hill puffing and panting. (We had planned to take this hill at our own pace and that a slow one). Two-thirds up we saw the buffalo above us stretched out cold. We got there and found a beautiful bull with forty inch horns with handsome curve. E. and Mr. P were very pleased and Mr. P said it was a marvelous shot—general congratulations and compliments. We left the boys at 6 to skin and butcher, much against their inclination as no native likes to be out alone after dark in a rhino buffalo country, and we faltered wearily home in the dark, getting in at eight—14 hours in the saddle.

Feb 2

We were up early and rather subdued to go out again for rhino. Fortunately, my feet healed in the night. I'd expected to have to wrap them in swaddling clothes. We had a pleasant trek down the stream and then up on a high cool hill, Droopy tracking beautifully and looking marvelous, but finally losing the trail. We took a council and to everyone's relief (I think) decided it wasn't much use going on so back to camp around 11. We had lunch and broke camp to join the others about 6:30.

Feb 3

We went out after a few of the twelve zebra for friends. We shot seven (E. 6, C. 1) and afterwards went after oryx in a cloud of dust. Ernest got one, the biggest in the herd with a single shot, and it was a beauty, a cow, 33 in. with a lovely curve. He was very pleased, both with the shot and the trophy, which is in the record class. While this was going on Charles and Ben went off and got another, a bull with a nice horn. The cow oryx is a simply dazzling animal. Then we came home in the heat and dust perfectly filthy.

In the afternoon we went to Manyara Lake to see the rose flamingoes—a beautiful place, and eight literally pink miles of flamingoes but far away and found duck and geese flying. Ernest got two teal and a curlew by wading to his hips. We decided to come back there the next evening earlier and try for the duck.

Feb 3 [second time] 4 zebra in the morning. I didn't go on account of the dust and Mr. P. on account of his eyes hurting.

About 4:30 we went to the lake and took up three strategic positions—C., E., and Mr. P and I. I was feeling rather dreary and men ridden, and Mr. P. and I sat in the marsh and waited rather leisurely for shots. We could hear the others shooting but thought their birds were probably as much out of range as the ones that came near us. Finally, Mr. P. shot with the Mannlicher at some ducks on a pool, getting two teal. In the end he left me and wading to his waist got three more. Then C. and E. came in, Ernest with 15 and Charles with five, very tired from wading. Then E. got two more in a passing flock, so we went home with twenty-seven. And I got over my gloom. A nice ride home through jungle land with a fine whiskey glow.

Feb 4

Move to Babati had beer and ducks for lunch with a view of the lake and up to Dick Cooper's place. It is a charming place, high and cool and swimming in flowers and vines, with a lovely view of Lake Manyara. It also has slow running water and rather uncertain electric lights. We played the gramophone and drank on the veranda until 9:15 waiting the ducks that finally came on the last truck. Margaux and Midor with them and brandy and Mr. P. in his stark dressing gown and Dick Cooper's manager (nice boy with nice manners) and so to bed in a big double bed. Think Jane* would like this place.

Feb 5

Left Dick Cooper's place, went through Babati and had a lovely ride with no dust to our present camp, which was up with lunch

* Jane Mason.

by one. More ducks. Galipo is a nice camp with kudu in back of us and a mission up the road. E. & C. went out for the kudu and Mr. P and I went to the mission with avocados in the back of our mind. The resident priests were on leave, and we found a rather lonesome young American one just arrived from America and not liking it at all. We had cigarettes and coffee and avocados and brown bread and saw the English cemetery. One of the mission buildings is very pretty. There are about 30 native children there. Nice walk coming home—hot going.

Feb 6

Charles went out and got a beautiful roan. No kudu. Both Charles and Ernest and I went out in the afternoon, but no kudu. Shot a roan cow through guide's error.

Feb 7

Out early with Ernest after kudu started at 6 and got back at 11:45, going almost a steady trot. We saw impala, waterbuck, roan, heard a lion cough (and E. went after it alone with his boys) and finally climaxed the morning by shooting a roan cow. Much feeling about the guide's walking too fast, going the wrong places and pointing out the wrong sex to shoot. Got in very exhausted and perpetualized it by drinking a whole bottle of beer. Too tired to go out in the afternoon or even to go walking with Mr. P, who went out to come back in the truck with Charles and brought home the missionary bearing 4 avocados, all there were left and they green. Stayed for two lime juices and told us about getting up to within twenty yards of a sleeping rhino—thought it was a rock.

Charles came home without a kudu, and pretty tired after a whole day alone with his mattress and his boys on the mountain top.

Feb 8

Ernest got a bushbuck, very nice. No kudu.

Feb 9

We broke camp and drove the whole day until 4:30. Ernest and Charles hunted about an hour. I stretched prone in bed.

Feb 10

We broke camp again to get to the new kudu country and got there for lunch. Kijungu is a pretty camp and reports are that there are many kudu about. Charles went hunting down the road and Ernest and I went to the salt lake—many tracks but we saw no kudu from the blind where we drank a bottle of beer. Mr. P's daughter Joyce got home today.

Feb 11

I stayed in bed and heard some altercation over who was to go to the salt-lick and who to the hills. Distinctly heard 4-letter word and Charles went to the salt-lick, E. to the hills. About 9 I heard the car in bed, and then Charles' voice very calm, so I didn't go out and then I heard Charles say what do you think he'd measure, so I leapt over and there was a beautiful kudu, shot at the salt-lick, measuring 38 inches with a spread of 35 1/2 inches—very massive. Everyone very pleased. Ernest got back at 10:45—no kudu. Saw 2 cows and a calf.

About three o'clock with Ernest sound asleep, Mr. P. (wakened from profound sleep) came and said the guides whetted by Charles' guides wanted to take Ernest to a wonderland of kudu a long way off. So he got up and set out with flash and flask. Stayed till well after dark and got back at 9:15, but with no kudu, very hungry and sleepy.

Mr. P., Charles and I took a short stroll after birds, but raised none. Charles had a headache and salts.

Feb 12

Ernest left before dawn (I could see a very sad figure sitting up through the mosquito net at 4:45) for the salt lick where Charles got his kudu and Charles went to the far sable camp. Only 5 more hunting days after today.

Ernest came back around ten—no kudu. He went out again around four and found the kudu had already been there. Got back around 7:30 very tired, but not discouraged and planned to leave at 4:30 am tomorrow and stay until ten. In the meantime Mr. P. and I sit in camp and wait for shots—wearing procedure. The tedium was lifted by the arrival of a short round little man, the spirit of the Tyrol, who was practically laid on our doorsteps by the complete breakdown of his truck. All engines are against me, he says. He works for an Indian and his name is Mr. Koritschoner, and he is very amusing and nice and dictatorial and worries about his truck. Our lovely Mr. P. has very kindly offered to tow the truck to Dodoma. Ernest met him first on the road and introduced himself. Hemingway, the little man said, Hemingway—what does that mean to me. Ah, yes, it is the name of a good writer that I read in German. After such an auspicious statement he was naturally well received. It is now 9:30 and we are all three sitting— Mr. P. and I waiting for a possible gun report. This kudu business is a waiting game—and another of the five hunting days is gone.

Feb 14

Ernest came in around 11:30 yesterday. No kudu. They got there before daylight and spooked three kudu at the lick and then they stayed there 6 hours. No more came. Mr. Koritschoner for lunch full of ideas. Ernest had a long nap after lunch and went again with his boys, flask, citronella, quinine, mattress to the far salt lick. He is going to try to get there at least a lesser kudu, getting back sometime tomorrow.

Mr. P. and I went out in the afternoon after the rain. It rained yesterday, too, in the afternoon and Mr. P. and Mr. K. both think it is time to be getting to the good roads as the rains are in the making. It seems there is a bad stretch of road between us and Handeni that is impossible in rain.

On our walk Mr. P. hit two dik-dik with the twenty-two but they went into the bush and we never found them.

Home to dinner with Mr. K. who talked much and very tolerantly. His rheumatic shoulder pained him considerably and he is of the opinion that now he will always have this shoulder. He seemed quite relieved when I said it might leave him like a shot.

Feb 14
[a second entry, probably written on February 15]

Got up early intending to go out with Mr. P. and shoot some meat for the pot after getting off Mr. K. who left at 6:30 with his big butter pot and his shoulder greatly improved. Sorry to see the old thing go. He's to be towed into Handeni where at least he can telephone his wife.

Turned out to be no game for us to shoot so here we are at 9:20 waiting for—what do you think—kudu news! A lot of cows are mooing at the side of the camp, sounding exactly how I feel. Should have stayed in bed longer. 2 1/2 more hunting days after today. Alas that all good things must come to an end.

Ernest got back from the far kudu salt lick around 11:30 to report that one salt lick was under water and a Wanderobo had stampeded the kudu off the other. Not very encouraging. Went in the hills in the afternoon but saw nothing. Time's winged chariot hurrying near.

Feb 15

Got up around 7:30 and had breakfast with Mr. P. Ernest left early in time to get to the salt lick by 5:40. Nothing. In the afternoon he went again into the hills. Followed two steaming tracks, which turned out to be cows. Ernest very merry at dinner despite all this. Mr. P. and I finally got a walk in the afternoon after being stopped once by the rain. Rain certainly on the make.

Feb 16

Ernest and I both got up early, he to the salt lick and I out with Mr. P. to kill meat for the pot. Mr. P. got a guinea and 3 Grant's gazelles. Uncertain shooting at first but very good towards last. Came back around 10 to find no E. Bad sign. He came in around 11:30 having seen NOTHING and pretty discouraged. We all were, for the rains are certainly with us and the kudu are not. Rather dismal lunch.

We were just going to shuteye when in came a guide to say that scouts had seen not only a fine kudu bull in a herd but also two herds of sable about 2 hours walk away. There was immediately rejoicing where there had been gloom and consternation and Ernest started out again with mattress, food, citronella, whiskey, beer, *tout ce qu'il faut* to be gone the night and maybe the day. Do hope he gets something, maybe both.

And Mr. P. and I are left to our now too familiar occupation of waiting. Both very restless. Weather gloomy.

Feb 17

We broke camp this morning and started in truck to join Charles and Ben. Met Ben about 5 miles on the way, who said Charles had got an enormous kudu 2 days before (57 inches!). Saw it when we got to camp and it is a beauty—like a cathedral. I went out in the afternoon with Charles after sable but we saw nothing. Feeling rather sad about Ernest not getting a kudu and I'm afraid none too glad about Charles getting one. We had an early dinner and were in bed by 9:30. At 10 there was a fearful noise, which woke me up, and I wondered why Mr. P. let a noise like that go on. Then I thought I heard Ernest's voice and I dashed out of bed. There he was with two kudu 46–51 1/4 inches and a sable cow. The natives were shouting and singing and there was general rejoicing. Mr. P. said he was reading in his tent when he saw the car lights and then a car with enormous horns sticking out all over. Food and drinks were had by all and the story of the chase. Very fine ending to the safari.

Appendix II:
Ernest Hemingway's
Introductory Letter and Safari Notes

1. Letter of November 6, 1933, from Ernest Hemingway to
   J. F. Manley, Esq., business manager for the Tanganyika
   Guide Service. Letter in the Ernest Hemingway Collection
   at the John F. Kennedy Library and Museum, Boston.

[Ernest Hemingway]
Care Guaranty Trust Co. of N.Y.
4 Place de la Concorde
Paris—France
Cable Address—Garritus Paris

November 6, 1933

J. F. Manley, Esq.
Machakos
Kenya

Dear Sir:
 Thank you for your letter of August seventh. I have delayed
answering for various reasons. Will not bore you with them but
outline the present situation.
 My wife, myself and a friend, Mr. Charles Thompson, are sail-
ing on the General Metzinger of the Messageries Maritime from
Marseille for Mombasa on Nov. 22—Due Mombasa December
9—
 We want to hunt in Tanganyika and do a general safari Lion,
Rhino, Buffalo etc. and try to get good heads of what we kill in

general. Naturally would like to get better things if we could but this is a first shoot. We will be bringing our .30-06 Springfields and my wife's 6.5 Mannlicher and two shotguns. Will be counting on getting all tropical equipment in Nairobi and will need 3 or 4 days there for that. Major Cooper has very kindly invited us to use his place in Tanganyika. (This data seems rather un-related but is intended to give you all information.)

My wife plans to go on safari for only a month and stay somewhere, possibly at Coopers, the rest of the time while we are out. Thompson and I would like to shoot as much as possible. We can be out until the first of March.

My wife plans to take only a fortnight license—but might take out a full license.

We have all hunted mountain sheep etc. in the West of U.S. and are used to working hard and living rather roughly in the field.

One of the principle reasons I have delayed writing you has been the steady fall of the dollar and the fact that we have now almost exactly £2000 to spend on the shoot—exclusive of licenses etc. Have bought the necessary pounds and they are now unaffected by what the dollar does.

I am very reluctant to write about this (i.e. finances) and understand perfectly if your terms are quite rigid.

The things which might make us less expensive than an ordinary safari are that my wife has no desire to make a bag of any kind but merely for us to be together for a part of the trip. That she will go out with me when she goes out to shoot. That I have no objection to hunting with a native hunter so that we will only need one white hunter for the three of us. That we are used to shooting in the west and do not need much luxury.

Charles Curtis of Boston gave me a letter to Mr. Philip Percival several years ago when we first planned to come out and I have always hoped to be able to hunt with him. A letter from Major Cooper said that he might be free now to go out.

If you think we could make a general shoot in Tanganyika with you for 2000 pounds, my wife to go for a month, Thompson and I for two months with Philip Percival as white hunter would you cable me care of <u>Garritus, Paris</u>? Whatever your answer I will be very glad to pay the cable charges. Please let me know, too, if it is impossible. The word "impossible" would do! In case you reply favorably I will consider the matter as arranged and will hope to hear from you at Mombasa.

Will try to get this off now by the Wednesday plane. Please cable me whenever you get this as I will arrange for the Bank to relay it in case we have sailed.

Thanking you for your letter and regretting my delay in answering.

Yours very truly,

Ernest Hemingway

2. Ernest Hemingway's safari notes from December 14–28, 1933, in the endpapers of Sir Frederick J. Jackson, *Notes on the Game Birds of Kenya and Uganda (Including the Sand-Grouse, Pigeons, Snipe, Bustards, Geese, and Ducks)* (London: Williams & Norgate, Ltd., 1926). Item EHPP-BK01-056 in the Ernest Hemingway Collection at the John F. Kennedy Library and Museum, Boston. Hemingway may have stopped writing these notes because he began to run out of room in the book or on account of his amoebic dysentery worsening by late December, or perhaps a combination of both events.

First endpaper
1.
Birds Dec 14
EH—   1 guinea
        2 partridge
CT 1 partridge (*pas trouvé*)
        1 partridge (doubled Jim)
        1 buck
Pauline   1 partridge (doubled Jim)
              1 pigeon
Jim   2 partridge (doubled)

Dec 15
EH—   1 partridge (doubled Charles) 1 steinbuck
CT   1 guinea
Kapiti P.M. EH Grant (1)   Bustard (0)

Kapiti P.M.   EH Kongoni (1)
               Charles   Bustard (1)

Dec 17
Lion Hill—   EH   Tommy (1)
                      Impala (1)
              CT   Tommy (1)
                      Grant (1)

Dec 18
EH—1 Jackal
[First endpaper continued bottom right]
Dec 19 Nairobi
Dec 20 ?Eruati Tanganyika
Dec 21 Arusha
Dec 22 camped under escarpment
        EH   1 Tommy (2 shots)
                2 spurfowl
        Charles 1 wildebeest

Second endpaper (opposite first endpaper)
at night heard flamingoes flighting—
Dec 23—EH 1 grant (finally/hunted big Grant all morning—
saw many spurfowl—possibly 150—found crashed plane—saw
big eland—bad head—flabby—saw 3 big Grant rams—distant
Oryx—spooked with giraffes—saw one herd of wildebeest—
no good heads—saw one bustard—EH missed about 10 shots
at Grant—running—walking and distant—missed 2 good
shots—About noon—then hit small Grant for meat but through
shoulder—got up and went off about 200 yards—stood there and
I missed him at least 8 or 9 times—he started to run and I lay
down and hit him—worst shooting I ever did.

    Charles shot another wildebeest and a very good Grant/Truck
arrived with Alfred V's heads.

P.M. after rain squall went down rift—tracks of truck—back to main road—EH hit wildebeest bull—went off lost in Maasai herds—big herds—shot at another wildebeest—hit in neck—down—up hit again—down—up and away—shot through ribs forward into heart and lungs.

Pauline missed big bull 4 times shooting very close to him—got back to camp cross country through stones of all sizes—trucks and Charles came out finally.

Third endpaper

3.

[December 23 continued] Got in late—Pauline went to bed before supper.

Found Charles had killed good bull with shot at 290 yards—hit him in the neck—whiskeys; bath—supper—Tommy chops—delicious as good or better than tender cut of sheep or elk.

Dec 24—up before sunrise to break camp and leave for Ngorongoro Crater.

    Hunted guineas

Dec 24 P.M. saw lioness—EH shot 3 zebra for bait—

    Charles missed bush buck and waterbuck—saw big rhino—and cow rhino with calf.

Dec 24—Ngorongoro Crater to first Serengeti camp

Hundreds of thousands of wildebeest and zebra—Tommies—

EH   5 sand grouse—2 spurfowl

Pauline   5 sand grouse—greater bustard—

Charles   5 sand grouse

Dec 26   saw 5 lion

EH   2 hyena—1 wildebeest buck—1 lesser bustard

Pauline   1 Tommy ram

Saw Egyptian geese—plover—teal—Demoiselle cranes—1 white spoonbill

Hundreds of 1000s game

Saw 3 lion p.m.—Charles killed a hyena

Page 258
Dec 27th
AM No lions
EH one hyena
EH robertsi Grant 1 shot
PH robertsi Grant 8 shots
With car

PM PH shot reedbuck—2 shots
EH shot Grant for bait for lioness—hit twice
Charles killed warthog—EH shot hyena—
almost dark one shot—EH hit wildebeest
rushed by two lioness who were stalking one on back—other on
throat—pulled down—one at throat kept sucking blood, other
commenced eating at testicles. Wildebeest still alive—big lioness
joined them—commenced to feed—then huge old lion—came
up—coughs at each step—chased lioness away from throat—she
patted him—loved him—he stuck whole head into throat rubbing
it—then commenced to eat—one young lioness rolled on her back
and played with wildebeest.
All eating as we left—one rose up 20 feet away
EH shot two guinea hens—

Page 256
Saw 2 male lions mile from camp
Dec 28—AM—EH hit cheetah—told not to shoot it again.
Walked up to it—it jumped and away like a flash—EH shot 4
hyenas—one wildebeest for a bunch of five lioness
Saw two big male lions in donga—then two male lions—one very
old—no mane—one young

Page 257
Dec 28—am Lions seen 17
10 lioness—7 males
Hyena shot 12—
Charles shot fine Robertsi Grant—one hyena eating his own
entrails—while hit five times—
Found hyena shot day before dead in donga—shot 4 teal—2 large
ducks—

EH killed big cobra—7 feet—

3. Ernest Hemingway's list of trophies bagged on the 1933–1934 safari. Made after the safari while on board the M/S *Gripsholm* en route back to Europe. Handwritten list on *Gripsholm* India Cruise 1934 stationary, which lists the route and dates of the ship's ports of call. Ernest Hemingway Papers, Ernest Hemingway Collection at the John F. Kennedy Library and Museum, Boston.

Here is a list of our trophies.

Pauline: Lion 1; Reedbuck 1; Waterbuck 1; robertsi Grant's gazelle 1; Thompson's gazelle 2; Hyenas 4; Topi 1

Charles: Lion 1; Rhino 1; Buffalo 1; Waterbuck 1; Impala 2; Oryx 1; Grant's gazelle 4; Thompson's gazelle 4; Topi 3; Roan antelope 1; Kudu 2; Leopard 1; Cheetah 3; Wildebeest 4; Hartebeest 1; Warthog 1; Zebra 1; Duiker 2; Eland 2; Hyena 10

EH: Lion 3; Buffalo 3; Rhino 1; Leopard 1; Cheetah 2; Impala 6; Grant's gazelle 5; Thompson's gazelle 5; Kudu 2; Sable 2; Roan 2; Wildebeest 4; Hartebeest 1; Warthog 2; Zebra 15 (for hides and baits); Oribi 2; Klipspringer 2; Jackals 2; Reedbuck 2; Duiker 1; Oryx 2; Waterbuck 1; Bushbuck 2; Serval cat 1; Springhare 1; Hyena 30; Eland 3.

Most of these, of course, were shot for meat—had to feed from 15 to 50 people for 60 some days.

4. Three pages of handwritten notes in ink about Hemingway's experiences on the 1933–1934 safari. Ernest Hemingway Papers, Ernest Hemingway Collection at the John F. Kennedy Library and Museum, Boston. These notes are reminiscences that were likely made during Hemingway's second safari to East Africa in 1953–1954. Note how Hemingway mixes the names Charles (Thompson) and Karl, his

personification in *Green Hills of Africa*, and also discusses real-life influences for his short stories "The Short Happy Life of Francis Macomber" and "The Snows of Kilimanjaro."

Amoebic dysentery in Africa on first trip before wrote *Green Hills*—after Ngorongoro Crater.

(Hunting leopard and the huge leopard and how we drove him in the donga—the natives in the trucks—finally killing it. Remember the lions—Remember leopard hunting)

Started to bleed and thought was piles—worked up to 150 movements a day with prolapsus of intestine—Had to wash with soap and water and put back in—finally could not get up while out shooting sand grouse—first leaned against tree—then sat down—then ~~could not~~ shot from ~~one~~ lying down—could not get up—carried me to camp—waiting outside camp while Ben Fourie went to Mwanza to order plane—the plane ride from the camp ~~on the~~ north of ~~Salengai~~ Serenea north Serengeti—Archie Ritchie and his wife the game warden of Kenya were shooting sand grouse the day I could not get up—Their bar built into the safari lorry—

The buffalo hunt previously with Philip and Charles—the three buff down (three big bulls we found in the open and galloped with the car) getting out to shoot and then re-load and chase all down finally—finishing the two—giving the bigger of the two to Charles because the first one was a larger animal—and then coming back and finding mine gone into the brush and waiting for him to stiffen up and then Ben Fourie starting toward [p. 2] the patch of brush and running wildly and the buff coming—Charles standing and shooting and me seeing the bits of horn flying from the boss like chips from a slate roof and I sitting and shooting for the sticking place—the buff coming with his head high—I shot all six 220 grain .30-06 into a patch of hide you could cover with the palm of your hand and the bull died with his head in my lap—truly—used some of it and wrote part of the action for Francis Macomber—

invented all that story—gave white hunter the appearance of Philip but the habits of von Blixen—it was Blix who carried the double—Philip never fired—was covering Pauline when the buff came out and not for fear of hitting us, enjoying the spectacle.—then the bull's head was not beautiful—only massive—the tips worn down—the boss flaked and splintered by Karl's shots—ticks crawling on him—the hide worn and bare—hair sparse and in patches—gray and scabby—my trousers wet with the blood when I stood up (Philip helped me up)—the bull's eyes glazing—we hunted leopard after that—I was up to close to 60–70 movements then—losing blood all the time—In Nairobi after the flight from Serenea that I wrote in "The Snows of Kilimanjaro" the good doctor—1st emetine injections—then carbasone—did not go to hospital—Remember him filling me with emetine—syringe—typed instructions and carbasone pills with instructions—like big gray black buckshot or artificial black pearls. [p. 3] Telling me that no matter what I ever had wrong with bowels or liver never to let anyone operate but remember it was amoebic—that it could re-appear or do damage under every form of disguise—what the Institute of Tropical Medicine had learned about it then—Rejoining the safari at Dick Cooper's place in Babati—they had come out of the lower end of the Serengeti and down through the Mbulu hills and Pauline had gotten her beautiful lion when I had not been there—she had really shot him but it had been un-satisfactory too as when had helped in the *Green Hills of Africa*—started the action after the amoebic dysentery interlude after we had left the Mbulu country and gone down toward Handeni for kudu and then put in flashbacks as I needed them—such as the hyena—Pauline's first lion that I really killed—

Appendix III:
The Tanganyika Letters

"A.D. in Africa: A Tanganyika Letter"
Esquire, January 1934

To write this sort of thing you need a typewriter. To describe, to narrate, to make funny cracks you need a typewriter. To fake along, to stall, to make light reading, to write a good piece, you need luck, two or more drinks and a typewriter. Gentlemen, there is no typewriter.

The air-mail leaves tomorrow night. Your amoebic dysentery correspondent is in bed, fully injected with emetine, having flown four hundred miles to Nairobi via Arusha from where the outfit is camped on the Serenea River on the far side of the Serengeti Plain. Cause of flight, a.d. Cause of a.d. unknown. Symptoms of a.d. run from weakly insidious through spectacular to phenomenal. I believe the record is held by a Mr. McDonald with 232 movements in the twenty-four hours although many old a.d. men claim the McDonald record was never properly audited.

According to Dr. Anderson the difficulty about a.d. is to diagnose it. My own diagnosis was certainly faulty. Leaning against a tree two days ago shooting flighting sand-grouse as they came into a water hole near camp after ten days of what Dr. Anderson says was a.d. all the time, I became convinced that though an unbeliever I had been chosen as the one to bear our Lord Buddha when he should be born again on earth. While flattered at this, and wondering how much Buddha at that age would resemble Gertrude Stein, I found the imminence of the event made it difficult to take high incoming birds and finally compromised by reclining against the tree and only accepting crossing shots. This, the coming of Buddha symptom, Dr. Anderson describes as prolapsus.

Anyway, no matter how you get it, it is very easily cured. You feel the good effects of the emetine within six hours and the remedy, continued, kills the amoeba the way quinine kills the malarial parasite. Three days from now we'll fly back to join the outfit in the country to the south of Ngorongoro where we are going to hunt greater kudu. But, as stated, there is no typewriter; they won't let you drink with this; and if the reader finds this letter more dysenteric than the usual flow, lay it to the combination of circumstances.

The general run of this highland country is the finest that I have ever seen. When there has been rain the plains roll green against the blue hills the way the western end of Nebraska lifts as you approach Wyoming when it has gone too long without rain. It is a brown land like Wyoming and Montana but with greater roll and distance. Much of the upland bush country that you hunt through looks exactly like an abandoned New England orchard until you top a hill and see the orchard runs on for fifty miles. Nothing that I have ever read has given any idea of the beauty of the country or the still remaining quantity of game.

On the Serengeti we struck the great migration of the wildebeest. Where they were grazing the plain was green after a nine months' drought and it was black with the bison shaped antelope as far as you could see in all directions during a full day in the truck. The Game Department of Tanganyika estimates the herd at three million. Following them and living on the fringe of the herd were the lions, the spotted hyenas and the jackals.

Going out at sunrise every morning we would locate lions by the vultures circling above a kill. Approaching you would see the jackals trotting away and hyenas going off in that drag belly obscene gallop, looking back as they ran. If the birds were on the ground you knew the lions were gone.

Sometimes we met them in the open plain on their way toward a gully or shallow water course to lie up for the day. Sometimes we saw them on a high knoll in the plain with the herd grazing not half a mile away, lying sleepy and contemptuous looking over the country. More often we saw them under the shade of a tree or saw their great round heads lift up out of the grass of a shallow donga as they heard the noise of the truck. In two weeks and three days in lion country we saw 84 lions and lionesses. Of these twenty were maned lions.

We shot the twenty-third, the forty-seventh, the sixty-fourth and the seventy-ninth. All were shot on foot, three were killed in bush country to the west of the Serengeti and one on the plain itself. Three were full-maned lions and one was a lioness. She was in heat and when the big lion she was with was hit and had gotten into cover the lioness took up her position outside the thick bush. She wanted to charge and it was impossible to go after the lion without killing her first. I broke her neck with a 220 grain .30-06 solid at thirty yards.

At this point Dr. Anderson just came in and administered another injection of emetine and offered the information that when you take emetine you can't think coherently. So this may be a good place to knock off. Had been feeling that too for some time.

In the next letter I will attempt to discuss whether lion shooting in Tanganyika is a sport or not; go into the difference between lion and leopard hunting, have a few remarks on the buffalo and try to get in a lot of facts. This letter has been pretty well emetined.

As far as bag goes, if anyone is interested, we have good heads of Eland, Waterbuck, Grant robertsi, and other gazelles. A fine roan antelope, two big leopard, and excellent, if not record, impala; also the limit all around on cheetah. They are much too nice an animal to shoot and I will never kill another.

On the other hand we shot thirty-five hyena out of the lot that follow the wildebeest migration to keep the cows that are about to calve and wish we had ammunition to kill a hundred.

In three days we start out for rhino, buffalo again, lesser and greater kudu, and sable antelope.

Dr. Anderson, a little emetine, please.

"Shootism vs. Sport: The Second Tanganyika Letter"
Esquire, June 1934

There are two ways to murder a lion. One is to shoot him from a motor car, the other, to shoot him at night with a flashlight from a platform or the shelter of a thorn boma, or blind, as he comes to feed on a bait placed by the shootist or his guide. (Tourists who shoot in Africa are called shootists to distinguish them from sportsmen.) These two ways to murder lion rank, as sport, with dynamiting trout or harpooning swordfish. Yet many men who go to Africa return to think of themselves as sportsmen and big game hunters, have killed lions from motor cars or from blinds.

The Serengeti plain is the great lion country of present day Africa and the Serengeti is a motor car proposition. The distances between water are too great for it to have been reached and hunted on foot in the old foot safari days, and that was what preserved it. The game migrations, which are determined by the food which is produced by an often casual and unpredictable rainfall, are movements over hundreds of miles, and you may drive seventy-five or a hundred miles over a brown dry, parched, dusty waste without seeing a herd of game, to come suddenly onto a rise of green horizon broken and edged with the black of wildebeest as far as you can see. It is because of these distances that you must use the motor car in hunting the Serengeti, since your camp must be on a water hole and the game may be over half a day's march away on the plain.

Now a lion, when you locate him in the morning after he has fed, will have only one idea if he sees a man, to get away into cover where the man will not trouble him. Until he is wounded, that lion will not be dangerous unless you come on him unexpectedly, so closely that you startle him, or unless he is on a kill and does not want to leave it.

If you approach the lion in a motor car, the lion will not see you. His eyes can only distinguish the outline or silhouette of objects, and, because it is illegal to shoot from a motor car, this object means nothing to him. If anything, since the practice of shooting a zebra and dragging it on a rope behind the motor car as a bait for lion in order to take photographs, the motor car may seem a friendly object. For a man to shoot at a lion from the protection of a motor car, where the lion may not even see what it is that is attacking him, is not only illegal but is a cowardly way to assassinate one of the finest of all game animals.

But supposing, unexpectedly, as you are crossing the country, you see a lion and lioness say a hundred yards from the car. They are under a thorn tree and a hundred yards behind them is a deep donga, or dry, reed-filled water course, that winds across the plain for perhaps ten miles and gives perfect cover in the daytime to all the beasts of prey that follow the game herds.

You sight the lions from the car; you look the male over and decide he is shootable. You have never killed a lion. You are allowed to kill only two lions on the Serengeti and you want a lion with a full mane, as black as possible. The white hunter says quietly:

"I believe I'd take him. We might beat him but he's a damned fine lion."

You look at the lion under the tree. He looks very close, very calm, very, very big and proudly beautiful. The lioness has flattened down on the yellow grass and is swinging her tail parallel to the ground.

"All right," says the white hunter.

You step out of the car from beside the driver on the side away from the lion, and the white hunter gets out on the same side from the seat behind you.

"Better sit down," he says. You both sit down and the car drives away. As the car starts to move off you have a very different feeling about lions than you have ever had when you saw them from the motor car.

As the end of the car is past, you see that the lioness has risen and is standing so that you cannot see the lion clearly.

"Can't see him," you whisper. As you say it you see that the lions have seen you. He has turned away and is trotting off and she is still standing, the tail swinging wide.

"He'll be in the donga," the white hunter says.

You stand up to shoot and the lioness turns. The lion stops and looks back. You see his great head swing toward you, his mouth wide open and his mane blowing in the wind. You hold on his shoulder, start to flinch, correct, hold your breath and squeeze off. You don't hear the gun go off but you hear a crack like the sound of a policeman's club on a rioter's head and the lion is down.

"You've got him. Watch the lioness."

She has flattened down facing you so that you see her head, the ears back, the long yellow of her is flat out along the ground and her tail is now flailing straight up and down.

"I think she is going to come," the white hunter says. "If she comes, sit down to shoot."

"Should I bust her?" you say.

"No. Maybe she won't come. Wait till she starts to come."

You stand still and see her and beyond her the bulk of the big lion, on his side now, and finally she turns slowly and goes off and out of sight into the donga.

"In the old days," the white hunter said, "the rule was to shoot the lioness first. Damned sensible rule."

The two of you walk toward the lion with your guns ready. The car comes up and the gun bearers join you. One of them throws a stone at the lion. He doesn't move. You lower the guns and go up to him.

"You got him in the neck," the white hunter says. "Damned good shooting." There is blood coming from the thick hair of his mane where the camel flies are crawling. You regret the camel flies.

"It was a lucky one," you say.

You say nothing about having squeezed off from his shoulder, and then, suddenly, a strain is over and people are shaking your hand.

"Better keep an eye out for the old lady," the white hunter says. "Don't wander too far over that way."

You are looking at the dead lion; at his wide head and the dark shag of his mane, and the long, smooth, yellow sheathed body, the muscles still twitching and running minutely under the skin. He is a fine hide and all that but he was a damned wonderful looking animal when he was alive—it was a shame that he should always have had the camel flies, you think.

All right. That is the nearest to a sporting way to use a motor car after lion. Once you are on the ground and the car is gone, lion hunting is the same as it always was. If you wound the lion in any but a vital spot he will make for the shelter of the donga and you will have to go after him. At the start, if you can shoot carefully and accurately and know where to shoot, the odds are ten to one in your favor against anything untoward happening, provided you do not have to take a running shot at first. If you wound the lion and he gets into cover it is even money you will be mauled when you go in after him. A lion can still cover one hundred yards so fast toward you that there is barely time for two aimed shots before he is on you. After he has the first bullet, there is no nervous shock to further wounds, and you have to kill him stone dead or he will keep coming.

If you shoot as you should on the Serengeti, having the car drive off as you get out, the chances are that the first shot will be a moving shot, the lions will move off when they see the man on foot. That means that unless you are a good or a very lucky shot there will be a wounded lion and a possible charge. So do not let anyone tell you that lion shooting, if you hunt big maned lions, who, being super-fine trophies, will obviously have been hunted before and will be adept at saving their hides, is no longer a sporting show. It will be exactly as dangerous as you choose to make it. The only way the danger can be removed or mitigated is by your ability to shoot, and that is as it should be. You are out to kill a lion, on foot and cleanly, not to be mauled. But you will be more of a sportsman to come back from Africa without a lion than to shoot one from a motor car, or from a blind at night when the lion is blinded by a light and cannot see his assailant.

"Notes on Dangerous Game: The Third Tanganyika Letter"
Esquire, July 1934

In the ethics of dangerous game is the premise that the trouble you shoot yourself into you must be prepared to shoot yourself out of. Since a man making his first African shoot will have a white hunter, as a non-native guide is called, to counsel him and to aid him when he is after dangerous animals, and since the white hunter has the responsibility of protecting him no matter what trouble he gets into, the shooter should do exactly what the white hunter tells him to do.

If you make a fool of yourself all that you get is mauled but the white hunter who has a client wounded or killed loses, or seriously impairs, his livelihood. So when the white hunter begins to trust you and let you take chances, that is a mark of confidence and you should not abuse it. For any good man would rather take chances any day with his life than his livelihood and that is the main point about professionals that amateurs never seem to appreciate.

There are two white hunters in Africa who not only have never had a client mauled—there are many such, but these two have never been mauled themselves; and there are very few of these. It is true that Philip Percival had a buffalo die with his head in the now ample Percival lap, and that Baron von Blixen, if there were any justice for elephants, would have been trampled to death at least twice. But the point is that they do not get mauled and that their clients get record heads, record tusks, and super lions year after year. They simply happen to be super hunters and super shots. (*There are too many supers in these last two sentences. Re-write them yourselves lads and see how easy it is to do better than Papa. Thank you. Exhilarating feeling, isn't it?*)

Both mask their phenomenal skill under a pose of nervous incapacity which serves as an effective insulation and cover for their truly great pride in the reserve of deadliness that they live by. (*All right now, better that one. Getting harder what? Not too hard you say? Good. Perhaps you're right.*) Blix, who can shoot partridges flying with a .450 No. 2 Express rifle will say, "I use the hair trigger because my hand is always shaking so, what?" Or, stopping a charging rhino at ten yards, remarking apologetically to his client who happened to have his rifle already started back to camp by the gun bearer, "I could not let him come forever, what?"

(*You see, this is where Papa scores. Just as you learn to better one of those awful sentences, with too many supers or too many verys in it and you think he's gone wa-wa on you, you find that it is the thing he is writing about that is interesting. Not the way it is written. Any of you lads can go out there and write twice as good a piece, what?*)

Philip, who swears by the .450 No. 2 as the only, or at least lightest, stopper for a man to use on animals that will "come," killed all his own lions with a .256 Mannlicher when he had only his own life to look after. I have seen him, careful, cautious, as wary about procedure as Saleri, Marcial Lalanda, or any of the old masters of chance controlling, light up like a schoolboy at the approach of vacation, when all the safe and sane methods were finally exhausted or rendered impractical and there was no choice but to go after as he went after them in the old days before it was a matter of the safety of the client. (*Excuse me, Mr. P. You see I do this for a living. We all have to do a lot of things for a living. But we're still drinking their whiskey, aren't we?*)

Many people want not to shoot but to have shot dangerous game. These people, regardless of their means, usually make the African shoot only once, and their white hunter usually fires as many or more shots than his client does. A very good standard by which to judge your real effectiveness against buffalo, rhino, elephant, lion and leopard is to keep track of how many times your white hunter shot on the safari. (*You shot twice, Mr. P. Correct me if I'm wrong. Once at that leopard's mate when she broke back and you spun her over like a rabbit, and the other time when we caught the bull in the open and had two down and the third bull with four solids in him going at that same gallop, all one solid piece, the neck a part of the shoulders, dusty black and the horns blacker, the head not tossing on the gallop. You figured he would make the bush so you shot and the gallop changed into a long slide forward on his nose.*)

Philip Percival ranks leopard as more dangerous than lion for these reasons. They are nearly always met unexpectedly, usually when you are hunting impala or buck. They usually give you only a running shot which means more of a chance of wounding than killing. They will charge nine times out of ten when wounded, and they come so fast that no man can be sure of stopping them with a rifle. They use their claws, both fore and hind when mauling and make for the face so that the eyes are endangered, whereas the lion grabs with the claws and bites, usually for the arm, shoulders or thigh. The most effective stopper for a leopard is a shotgun and you should not fire until the animal is within ten yards. It does not matter what size shot is used at that range. Birdshot is even more effective than buckshot as it hangs together to blow a solid hole. (*Mr. P. took the top of the head off one once with a load of number sevens and the leopard came right on by and on for fifteen yards. Didn't know he was dead it seems. Tripped on a blade of grass or something finally.*)

Personally, so far, and it is from a very minute quantity of experience indeed—the killing of four of them—I cannot see the buffalo as comparing in dangerous possibilities to either lion or leopard. We twice saw lion catch and kill wildebeest. This is a very rare thing. Philip Percival had seen lion kill only once before in all his years of hunting. It was while he was out with Mr. Prentice Gray, who recorded the occurrence, I believe. The sight of that speed, that unbelievable smooth rush the lioness made to close the gap between herself and the fast galloping, though ungainly, antelope made me see what a charge from a slightly wounded lion could be if allowed to get under way. The buffalo, on the other hand, seemed unbelievably slow compared to a Spanish fighting bull, and I see no reason why a man who could wait for him as he came could not be sure of blowing the front of his head in if he let him get close and shot carefully with a heavy enough rifle. Certainly a tunnel in thick bush, or high reeds, or any dense cover can make the wounded buffalo dangerous, but that is a case of circumstances rather than the animal, and in the same circumstances a lion would be much more deadly. In the open a lion or leopard is a hundred times more dangerous.

The buffalo has courage, vindictiveness and an incredible ability to absorb punishment but I believe that in the bull ring he would be more like the big truck that comes charging in during intermission to water the dusty sand than like the light hoofed quick whirling, fast charging fighting bull.

Of course, he is not an animal in the open and you must take him where you find him and follow him where he goes, and he goes into bad places, but the point was to compare the inherent danger in the actual animals on an equal terrain—not in the peculiar circumstances under which he must be dealt with. (*There won't be any more asides you will be glad to hear. Am going to write to Mr. P. a letter instead. The asides were put in when I read this over on the boat. Got to missing him.*)

To me, also, and the experience it must be again stated is profoundly limited, the rhino is a joke. He may be a bad joke, too, but his atrociously poor eyesight gives the hunter an advantage over him that his bulk, his really remarkable speed and agility, and his sometimes idiotic pugnacity cannot overcome unless aided by advantage of terrain. Many times the rhino will have this advantage which will usually consist in encountering him on one of the paths or tunnels he has made through otherwise impossible tall grass and bush, and then he is as dangerous as a vindictive, horned locomotive. He is too, very fast. I believe he is faster than a buffalo. But fundamentally, to me, he seems a dangerous practical joke let loose by nature and armed with a horn which the Chinese pay high prices for to grind up and use as an aphrodisiac, and the pursuit of which by white and native hunters has made him shy and furtive in his habits and driven him from the plains to the broken hills and high mountain forests—where he can grow his horn and browse in peace, and where, incidentally, he is much better hunting.

Elephant I have never shot so I cannot write of them even to give the questionable impressions of the greenhorn. We plan to go out again to Kenya for six months next year to try to get a really good one, to hunt buffalo and rhino, and to see how far wrong first impressions of these were, and to try to get a good bull sable. Meantime, I know nothing about elephant from personal experience, and since notes on dangerous game by a man who has never hunted elephant are like campaign impressions of a bloke who has never seen a major engagement, that is the sort of notes these notes will have to be.

(*There turns out to be one more of these. One night when we were eating supper at Mombasa after fishing, A. V. and Mr. P. and I were talking about writing these letters and I suggested Alfred write one about hunting elephant with Blix before he started to write on racing. I was writing on rhino and buffalo, etc., I said. Mr. P., who was on his first deep sea fishing trip didn't say much, but the next day we got into a big school of large dolphin and caught about 15 before the lousy boat broke down. Mr. P. got so excited that his legs shook, he screwed the reel brake backwards until it stuck, he had dolphin jumping into, out of, and over the boat. Sometimes he jerked their bait out of their mouths; occasionally he let them swallow it, but always he had a dolphin jumping on his line.*

"How'd you like it, Pop?" I asked him.

"God," he said, "I haven't had so much fun since the day you shot the buffalo." Then, a little later, "I'm going to write an article on it for Esquire. *Call it Dolphin Fishing by One Who Knows."*)

Appendix IV:
Early Drafts and Deleted Passages
from *Green Hills of Africa*

The following eighteen passages are early drafts of parts of the book that were revised or are passages that were cut during Hemingway's process of revision. The passages are arranged here according to their general relationship to the final text from beginning to end.

1. Item 91, Ernest Hemingway Collection, John F. Kennedy Library and Museum, Boston. Two pages of handwritten manuscript fragments. This is an early draft of the beginning of the book.

So, now I can remember all of it.

It is still permitted to love a new country. It is a new country if there is no literature. If there is nothing old for you to take over, when there are more animals than people. It is a new country if there is still time to die in it and leave nothing to your children if other people have lost it.

We had hunted them unsuccessfully for ten days and the rains were moving steadily northward from Rhodesia.

The rains were moving steadily northward from Rhodesia and each day it took the sun longer to clear away wooly clouds that covered all the sky.

We were sitting in the blind built by Wanderobo hunters at the salt lick when we heard the truck coming. At first it was far away. Then it was stopped. Then it came slowly, agonizing, in a clank of loud irregular explosions passing close behind us to go on up the road. The tracker stood up.

"It is finished," he said.

There had been rain the night before and we had found the long, heart-shaped fresh tracks of four kudu bulls when we had come to the salt lick beside many lesser kudu tracks. There was also a rhino, who, from the fresh tracks and the kicked up mound of dung came there each night. Sitting in the blind I had seen a lesser kudu bull come out of the brush to the open edge of the sand where the salt was and stand there heavy necked, grey and handsome against the sun while I refused the shot, wanting not to frighten away the greater kudu that would surely come at sunset. M'Cola lay beside me, his bald black head bent down below the cover and the two trackers watched from either end.

2. Ernest Hemingway Papers, 1925–1966, Accession #6250, etc., Clifton Waller Barrett Library of American Literature, Albert and Shirley Small Special Collections Library, University of Virginia, Charlottesville, VA. *Green Hills of Africa* holograph manuscript in ink and pencil, pages 4–5. Early draft from the beginning of chapter 1 when they hear the broken-down truck. This passage was reworked into a shorter, more poignant one.

But before we even heard the truck the buck had heard it and run off into the trees. Probably everything else that had been coming through that open bush toward the salt had heard that clanking knock of the truck and stopped still or turned back. Anyway we were bitched for that day and it was the ~~eighth~~ ninth day straight we had been bitched on kudu.

Disappointed about the truck, tired from having been up since four thirty, but excited about the lick we had found, and confident that we would get kudu on this lick, I sat in the front of the car with Kamau the Kilingu driver and watched the headlights pick up eyes of night hawks on the sandy road. The eyes shown brightly; you did not see the brown spot of bird until the car was almost on them. Then they flew softly always missing the car.

It was nearly forty miles to camp and as we drove through the dark I drank whiskey, mixed with water from a canteen in a cup, my rifle butt on my foot, the barrel in the curve of my left arm, the flask between my knees. We passed the campfires of many people beside the road who were moving by this sandy track across the country from Handeni to Kandoa to escape from the famine that was emptying the country ahead of us and drinking whiskey and water alone in the car with the driver, Kamau, the gun bearer, M'Cola, and the two trackers I felt closer to Africa than I had yet been and further away from anything that was European. The whiskey of course was European but I was not considering that.

Then we came onto the bulk of the truck halted beside the road.

3. Ernest Hemingway Papers, 1925–1966, Accession #6250, etc., Clifton Waller Barrett Library of American Literature, Albert and Shirley Small Special Collections Library, University of Virginia, Charlottesville, VA. *Green Hills of Africa* holograph manuscript in ink and pencil, page 26. Early draft of the passage about *Huckleberry Finn* including remarks about Stein and Anderson that were cut to make a more timeless statement.

All modern American literature comes from one book by Mark Twain called Huckleberry Finn. If you read it you must stop where the nigger Jim is stolen from the boys. But it's the best book we've had. [But from that comes all that is American in a woman called Stein that you will hear of as long as she is alive, from it comes what another writer called Anderson started with and what I knew to start with. It is a great book, the best we have ever had in America.] All American writing comes from that.

4. Ernest Hemingway Papers, 1925–1966, Accession #6250, etc., Clifton Waller Barrett Library of American Literature, Albert and Shirley Small Special Collections Library, Univer-

sity of Virginia, Charlottesville, VA. *Green Hills of Africa* holograph manuscript in ink and pencil, pages 29–30. The following is an early draft with a greatly expanded version of what Ernest Hemingway enjoyed in life and what a writer's relationship to the state should be as related during his conversation with the Austrian Kandisky. In the final version, Hemingway cut everything after "Yes. Hunting kudu and many other things."

"And what do you want?"

"To write as well as I can and to learn as I go along. At the same time, I have my life which I enjoy and which is a damned good life."

"Hunting kudu?"

"Yes. Hunting kudu and many other things."

"What other things?"

"To see, to hear, to eat, to drink, to sleep, to read, to see pictures, different cities, oceans, fishes, to see fighting, to do thinking, to be in boats, to sit in saddles, to feel horses between your legs, different guns, all trees, mountains."

"Go on."

"To watch the snow come, the rain, the grass, rain on tents, the different winds, the changes of season, some ships, to talk, to come back and see your children, one woman, another woman, various women, but only one woman really, some friends, animals, cowardice, courage, pride, co-ordination, the migration of fishes, rivers, fishing, forests, fields, all good painting, the principles of revolution, the practice of revolution, the Christian theory of anarchy, the seasonal variation of the Gulf Stream, its monthly variation, the trade winds, counter currents, the Spanish bull ring, cafés, wines, the Prado, Pamplona, Santiago de Campostella, ~~Sheridan, Casper,~~ Wyoming, Michigan, Florida, Arkansas, Montana, Ontario, Illinois, France, Italy, Austria, Germany, Switzerland, Cuba, Kenya, Tanganyika."

"But Kenya and Tanganyika do not mean anything to you."

"They will."

"What do you think a writer's relation to the state should be?"

"A writer, if he is any good, should be against the state no matter what it is. There will always be plenty of bad writers who will work for the state. A good writer has something that is not for sale. That he has no right to sell or to loan. Like the standard meter that is kept in Paris. He can fight for the state, or for any employer or any organization, as a man, if he chooses, but if he writes for them he is a whore."

"What can he believe?"

"Anything he finds to be true."

"Can he put his beliefs in his writing?"

"Only if he is sure they are true. A man's beliefs, if he learns in life, change many times. What do you say if we talk about something else?"

"It is interesting what you say. Naturally, I do not agree with many things."

"Naturally."

"It's awfully very profound before lunch."

Pop said, "What about a gimlet, comrades?"

"Let's all have a gimlet."

Pop never drank before lunch except as a mistake and I knew he was trying to help me out.

"Let's all have a gimlet," I said.

"I never drink," Kandisky said.

5. Ernest Hemingway Papers, 1925–1966, Accession #6250, etc., Clifton Waller Barrett Library of American Literature, Albert and Shirley Small Special Collections Library, University of Virginia, Charlottesville, VA. *Green Hills of Africa* holograph manuscript in ink and pencil, "Insert p. 29." A second draft of the previous passage, which Hemingway also cut.

"To see, to hear, to eat, ~~almost never too much,~~ to drink, to sleep, to read, to see pictures, to know differ-

ent cities, different oceans, different countries, ~~and dif-~~
~~ferent continents,~~ to stay in places and to leave, to trust,
to distrust, to no longer believe and to believe again, to
care about fishes, the different winds, the changes of the
seasons, to see what happens, to be out in boats, to sit
in a saddle, to watch the snow come, to watch it go, to
hear the rain on a tent, to know where to find what I
want."

"You know that?"

"Yes."

"And you know what you want."

"Yes."

6. Ernest Hemingway Papers, 1925–1966, Accession #6250,
etc., Clifton Waller Barrett Library of American Literature, Albert and Shirley Small Special Collections Library,
University of Virginia, Charlottesville, VA. *Green Hills of
Africa* holograph manuscript in ink and pencil, "Page 29
4th page insert." Hemingway cut the following line about
painting and writing from his discussion with Kandisky
about literature just before he talks about the fourth and
fifth dimension in writing.

"To get the thing in writing that all the line of great
painting has."

7. Ernest Hemingway Papers, 1925–1966, Accession #6250,
etc., Clifton Waller Barrett Library of American Literature, Albert and Shirley Small Special Collections Library,
University of Virginia, Charlottesville, VA. *Green Hills of
Africa* holograph manuscript in ink and pencil, "Page 29
5th page insert." Hemingway cut the following lines from
the discussion about the importance of prose.

"Especially all those who tell him that this work is of
no importance. Besides he must be intelligent since that is
the first demand of prose and he must last for it is a lifetime's work."

8. Ernest Hemingway Papers, 1925–1966, Accession #6250, etc., Clifton Waller Barrett Library of American Literature, Albert and Shirley Small Special Collections Library, University of Virginia, Charlottesville, VA. *Green Hills of Africa* holograph manuscript in ink and pencil, pages 34–35. Hemingway cut the qualifying comment from his response to the tribal dance that Kandisky performed for them.

Undoubtedly it was very fine but it was like modern painting looks to someone who has not looked at it before and has seen other painting so the eyes look for something else.

9. Ernest Hemingway Papers, 1925–1966, Accession #6250, etc., Clifton Waller Barrett Library of American Literature, Albert and Shirley Small Special Collections Library, University of Virginia, Charlottesville, VA. *Green Hills of Africa* holograph manuscript in ink and pencil, pages 85–88. Early draft of the end of chapter three, which was completely reworked.

"Yes but I'm dignified with him. Don't you think he is wonderful?"

"Yes," I said. "Really, I believe he's the best I've ever known."

"You're wonderful too. But why do you always feel pleased when you're brave."

"Pop's pleased when he's brave too. Only he doesn't tell you."

"But there's nothing extraordinary about being brave. You're both brave."

"Of course we are. But it's always a pleasure."

"But what is there extraordinary about it?"

"Nothing. Only you've never known any yellow bastards."

"What are they like?"

"You're never comfortable with them."

"Who is yellow?"

I told her two who were.

"Are they really?"

"Of course," I said and told her about two different times for each. That's why you're always uncomfortable with them. Because they are uncomfortable with themselves."

"But Karl is brave."

"As brave as anybody ever could be."

"He's like Hamlet."

"Yes, he really is and Archie thinks he is. Archie's not like Hamlet. He's like a man who's studied Hamlet. He's studied such a lot of things."

"But why are you always so pleased when you're brave?"

"I don't know. I'm just always pleased."

"It's nice but it's sort of silly."

"Listen. The things that please me are very simple things. Most of them seem to have to do with natural reflexes and co-ordination. Like things that happen so quickly in trout fishing, correcting from a cast already started in the hundredth part of a second in the air. When I was a kid every time I would do that I would be pleased. Now shooting and all the things that are made up of so many things to do and think at once are all surrounding one central necessity please me."

"Go on. But that's not about being scared."

"I'm never proud of acting properly. That's nothing. I'm happy and pleased at being happy in action instead of worried."

"But you always are. You always were. So is Mr. J. P."

"Yes but he doesn't have to read books written by some bitch he's tried to help get published who says he's yellow."

"She's just malicious. She knew that would make you angry."

"I'll say it did. She's skillful when she's malicious with

all that talent gone to malice and nonsense and self praise. Well she's cashing now. Anybody can whenever they want."

~~Hommes des lettres. Woman of letters. Salon woman. What a lousy stinking life."~~

"We have fun though don't we?"

"God damn it if we don't. I've had a better time every year since I can remember. And we have a better time together all the time and it always was good."

"Africa has been the best."

"Yes. You couldn't make anyone see how fine it is."

"I know about your bragging about it when you're brave. I was just teasing you. You're a Gascon. You're just as brave as you say you are and you shoot better than you can brag ever. But you're awfully noisy sometimes."

"I'm one of the noisiest bastards that ever lived. But by Jesus I can certainly shoot."

"There you go. You mustn't brag so, Papa. Really. But isn't Mr. J. P. wonderful really?"

10. Ernest Hemingway Papers, 1925–1966, Accession #6250, etc., Clifton Waller Barrett Library of American Literature, Albert and Shirley Small Special Collections Library, University of Virginia, Charlottesville, VA. *Green Hills of Africa* holograph manuscript in ink and pencil, "Page 91 insert." Hemingway cut the following sentences about the value of having been to war from the passage where he is reading Tolstoy's *Sevastopol*.

about how it [war] was the thing you paid the most for in some ways but learned the most from. You saw things in a week that it would take a lifetime to see or learn.

11. Ernest Hemingway Papers, 1925–1966, Accession #6250, etc., Clifton Waller Barrett Library of American Literature, Albert and Shirley Small Special Collections Library, University of Virginia, Charlottesville, VA. *Green Hills of*

Africa holograph manuscript in ink and pencil, page 98. Hemingway cut the following greenhorn comment from when he first sees a rhino trotting at high speed.

He was red colored and I could not believe such a big animal could go so fast.

12. Ernest Hemingway Papers, 1925–1966, Accession #6250, etc., Clifton Waller Barrett Library of American Literature, Albert and Shirley Small Special Collections Library, University of Virginia, Charlottesville, VA. *Green Hills of Africa* holograph manuscript in ink and pencil, on the back of "Insert page 127" [the first part of chapter five, which contains the beautiful passage that begins: "We stood now in the shade of trees with great smooth trunks, circled at their base with the line of roots that showed in rounded ridges up the trunks like arteries; the trunks the yellow-green of a French forest on a day in winter after rain . . ."] was written the following statement.

"And if you fail you may simply write good prose and that is worth doing."

13. Ernest Hemingway Papers, 1925–1966, Accession #6250, etc., Clifton Waller Barrett Library of American Literature, Albert and Shirley Small Special Collections Library, University of Virginia, Charlottesville, VA. *Green Hills of Africa* holograph manuscript in ink and pencil, page 222. This is an early draft of the passage at the beginning of chapter eight where Hemingway is ill with dysentery and imagines what it is like to be a hunted animal from the time it is shot until its death.

At least I knew what I was doing. I did nothing that had not been done to me. I had been shot and I had been crippled and gotten away. I expected, always, to be killed by one thing or another and I, truly, did not mind that any more, death is a thirst you only slake once and the rules for drinking are quite clear, but since I still loved to hunt I resolved that I would only shoot as long as I could kill cleanly and as soon as I lost that ability I would stop.

14. Ernest Hemingway Papers, 1925–1966, Accession #6250, etc., Clifton Waller Barrett Library of American Literature, Albert and Shirley Small Special Collections Library, University of Virginia, Charlottesville, VA. *Green Hills of Africa* holograph manuscript in ink and pencil, page 241. In the middle of chapter eight when the characters are talking and drinking around the campfire was included the following sentence, which Hemingway later cut.

"Now, he's drunk, we get the truth." I said. In this nightly formula of dull, repetitious, affectionate and hallowed insults was concealed all the fondness and respect three people could feel for each other.

15. Ernest Hemingway Papers, 1925–1966, Accession #6250, etc., Clifton Waller Barrett Library of American Literature, Albert and Shirley Small Special Collections Library, University of Virginia, Charlottesville, VA. *Green Hills of Africa* holograph manuscript in ink and pencil, pages 309–11. This is an early draft of the scene in chapter ten in which Ernest, Pauline, and Philip Percival are sitting around the campfire and talking about revolutions, which Hemingway later slightly revised.

"Been in France lately?"

"Didn't like it. Gloomy as hell. Been a bad show there just now."

"By God," said Pop, "it must have been if you can believe the papers."

"When they riot they really riot. Hell, they've got a tradition."

"Were you in Spain for the revolution?"

"Yes."

"How was it?"

"Good. But the real one's coming."

"Did you see the revolution in Cuba?"

"From the start."

"How was it?"

"Beautiful."

"Stop it," P.O.M. said. "I know about those things. I was crouched down behind a marble-topped table which they were shooting in Havana. They came by in cars shooting at everybody they saw. I took my drink with me and I was proud not to have spilled it or forgotten it. The children said, 'Mother, can we go out in the afternoon to see the shooting?' They got so worked up about revolution we had to stop mentioning it. Bumby got so blood thirsty about Mr. M. He had terrible dreams."

"Extraordinary."

"Don't make fun of me. I don't want to just hear about revolutions. All we see or hear is revolutions. I'm sick of them."

"The old man must like them."

"He's crazy about them. But I'm sick of them."

"You know, I've never seen one." Pop said.

"They're beautiful. Really. For quite a while. Then they go bad."

"They're very exciting. But I'm sick of them. Really I don't care anything about them."

"I've been studying them."

"What did you find out?" Pop asked.

"A hell of a lot of things, really. I've seen five big ones now. They were all very different but there were a lot of things you could co-ordinate. I'm going to write a study of them."

16. Item 697, Ernest Hemingway Collection, John F. Kennedy Library and Museum, Boston. Three-page handwritten manuscript fragment with an unused passage from the book. This scene is an alternate version of the opening of chapter eleven.

The sky is very high there and branches come between, from under which, beyond a tent, you step out to see too many stars. The moon gone down, the breeze not risen you urinate uplooking at the uncross-like blur of Southern Cross and thus each morning in the profundity of initial urination reflect upon the publicity of constellations, and not awake you listen to the night move highly past you. Then walk to where Pop sits before the fire, pipe comforted, his feet perched, loving the time before daylight and the windless burning of dead branches he says, "How are you, governor?"

"No worse than you."

"How's the old malady?"

"No trace."

"Did you sleep well?"

"I can't remember going to bed."

"I'll tell him to bring breakfast."

Under the lantern in the dining tent you eat the cool easy-slipping fruit, the warm, brown-crisped and squintfully egg-topped hash, well catchup-ed against the time of day, and sitting, happy, with the third mug of coffee see M'Cola's waiting face, and know that you are late.

"The Kilingozis are waiting."

These Kilingozis, who are waiting, we acquired five days ago. They were brought by an old man, a white-headed, very old man, a farmer of the village, and they have written testimonials of their worth.

"The bearer is one of the best boys in the district. He knows the game well and is a good tracker."

It is signed by someone who described himself as a professional hunter of Tanga.

One of these guides is an actor and a businessman and cannot track at all. Neither can he keep quiet on a train and his brain flutters like a fairy's. He also loves to give orders. He is a good looking nigger and until we showed we were not amused he would have liked to wear a black and white ostrich plumed head-dress to hunt in.

The other is short and quiet and can track. His name is Abdullah.

Now they are waiting in the dark beside the car. M'Cola brings the two guns, the water bottle, the field glasses, and the camera slung across his back. You get in the front beside Kamau, a good driver, small, neat, possessor of a marvelous tweed coat with soap carried in the breast pocket. You sit beside him holding the rifle in the crook of your arm to protect the foresight, the sight protector long since lost, the butt resting on your foot. The others, M'Cola and the two Kilingozis, are in back.

"Today may be the day," Pop says.

"We'll blast them," you tell him.

But neither of you are confident, the luck has been out too long and at noon you are back and it is still out.

17. Item 698, Ernest Hemingway Collection, John F. Kennedy Library and Museum, Boston. Three-page handwritten manuscript fragment containing another version of the opening of chapter eleven that pontificates on the reasons for drinking alcohol on safari.

~~In the morning when I woke it was still dark. Standing clear of the tent the~~

~~I was dressed and it was still dark with Pop sitting in his chair before the open fire smoking a pipe and as I walked a little way from camp.~~

There was a lantern in the dining tent

The sky is very high there, and branches come between in the early morning, from under which, beyond a tent, you step out to see too many stars. The uncross-like blur of ~~the~~ Southern Cross you urinate below each morning in that high sky, too light now, the moon gone down, the breeze not risen, and not awake you listen to the night move highly past you. Then walk to where Pop sits before the fire, pipe-comforted, loving the ~~early~~ time before daylight and the windless burning of dead branches he says, "How are you, governor?"

"No worse than you."

"Why do we do it each night?"

~~"It's fun. Or isn't it?"~~

"God knows," I say.

For every night, tired from behind your ears, down through your back, out forward down those long ones that have twitched in fatigue after the climb back through those others that ache down to between your toes you sit gently becoming drunk. Taking in alcohol we exude martial memories and modestly constructed tales of our prowess and the things we've seen in which though always frightened we behave extremely well. We know this is ridiculous and we do it because it pleases us to do it. We have earned the right to be drunk through doing sober what you could not do with liquor. We have earned the right to lie if we choose because we know the truth. We obey certain laws because it suits our ultimate convenience. We obey other laws because we believe in them. We are not like you are, nor like you are. We could make our living anywhere and in any country because we have one thing to sell which is always saleable. Ah yes are we becoming drunk?

18. Ernest Hemingway Papers, 1925–1966, Accession #6250, etc., Clifton Waller Barrett Library of American Literature, Albert and Shirley Small Special Collections Library, University of Virginia, Charlottesville, VA. *Green Hills of Africa* holograph manuscript in ink and pencil, pages 464, 464 insert, 465, and 466. The following description of Hemingway's friend Edward Dorman Smith, mentioned in the latter part of chapter thirteen, and the times they spent together, along with a long consideration of cowardice, Hemingway later cut entirely from the text.

Captain Edward Dorman-Smith M.C. of His Majesty's Fifth Fuseliers. Now one of the bright young men of the war office and if he were there we would discuss how to describe this deer park country and whether deer park was enough to call it. A major he was when we first met in Milan. When the war was over we thought our occupation gone. We'd never known civil life nor what was fun to do, nor when you did it. I wanted to write and nobody ever wrote worse. If you think it's bad now you should have read it then. Chink went back to Ireland and I went home and then to Canada and then back in Europe on all his leaves we went to all the places we had wanted to go in the war, mostly on foot, enjoying every time we set our boots down on the ground, through forest, or steep slopes, hard roads, or meadows, or the crests of hills, and all the meals in all the inns, hungry all the time, when I would fish a stream he would go somewhere and climb a range of hills and then we'd meet somewhere and drink, and we made some fine trips. Old Chink coming down through that breaking crust in the dark that night up at the top of the Saint Bernard to carry the packs up when I was floundering through to the waist and we saw the monks come shooting down on skis. I knew we had to make the monastery but it was very hard that night and I was plenty sick and the next morning we were in Italy when we came down out of the snow and it was Spring. Then coming down that southern slope, having to cut slits in Hadley's shoes. Old Chink. I'd had good friends and the best life any bastard ever lived. I'd always had a good life. Nothing hurt me at anytime except the things that happened to other people. The funny thing was how my own life kept on being good. Africa now was the best of all. I had had the best time here that I had ever had. M'Cola was as good a skate as I had ever known and Pop the best man I had ever met. The best, no doubt about it. He and Chink were a lot alike. Pop was older and more tolerant for his years and just as good company. I was learning under Pop while Chink and I had discovered a big part of the world together and then our ways had gone a long way apart. Of the others that I saw the most of since, ~~Archie~~ [MacLeish] ~~had the most charm and we had had good times together. But he was really a coward so you were never completely comfort-~~

able with him. Dos was a damned fine guy but right now he was perhaps a little over-married. That would pass or get worse I thought. except for Dos there was something wrong with all of them. The charming ones were cowards and so you were never really comfortable with them and they were never really comfortable with themselves. The oldest friends I had were the best ones. Chink, Hickok and Mike Ward. Except Karl [Charles Thompson]. Karl was a damned good guy. He could be better than anyone. I wondered what he'd done down there. He was no coward. But Dos was a very fine good friend, and as brave as a damn buffalo. Hickok was the most intelligent and one of the best. Scott was a coward of great charm. I wondered why the cowards all had so much charm. Maybe Archie wasn't a coward. Maybe it was just caution. What the hell was a coward anyway? A coward was a man who was afraid when there was nothing, as yet, to be afraid of. We're all afraid. Plenty afraid. But if you with so much to fear legitimately you feared things before they got bad. Oh what the hell. That definition did not hold. A really brave man feared nothing for himself. It was a question of dignity. A brave man had a certain pride. A coward said this pride was of no importance. Perhaps it wasn't but it was of great importance to whoever had it. It made things so bloody much easier. A man without inner dignity is an embarrassment. The cowards had the charm though. Not all of the charming ones were cowards though. Look at Tunney. There was a very brave man and he had great charm. Charm is of two kinds, I thought. Either a trick, or it comes from modesty. My father was a coward. He shot himself without necessity. At least I thought so. I had gone through it myself until I figured it in my head. I knew what it was to be a coward and what it was to cease being a coward. How, truly, in actual danger I felt a clean feeling as in a shower. That was Of course it was easy now because I no longer cared what happened. I knew it was better to live it so that if you died you had done everything that you could do about your work and your enjoyment of life up to that minute, reconciling the two, which is very difficult, so that you had no ~~responsibility~~ outstanding debts so that you were paid up to that time. That's all you could do and you were all right. Take that damned sable bull. I should have killed him but it was a running shot . . .

Acknowledgments

To Patrick Hemingway, I extend my deepest appreciation for his guidance and for sharing his knowledge of Africa, hunting, literature, Ernest Hemingway, and my grandmother, Pauline Pfeiffer Hemingway. His participation in this project was essential to its fruitful conclusion. I am grateful to Michael Katakis for his enthusiasm, vision, and support. Sincere thanks to Susan Moldow and my editors at Simon & Schuster—Nan Graham, Brant Rumble, and Liese Mayer—as well as their colleagues Jeff Wilson, Brian Belfiglio, and John Glynn. I am especially grateful to Tom Putnam, director of the John F. Kennedy Library and Museum in Boston, and to Susan Wrynn, curator of the Ernest Hemingway Collection at the Kennedy Library, as well as their colleagues Laurie Austin of the Audiovisual Archives and Stacey Chandler of the Textual Archives for their unfailing professionalism and steadfast support; without them, this work could not have been accomplished. For permission to publish my grandfather's letter in the United States I am grateful to the Ernest Hemingway Foundation and to Professor Kirk Curnutt for his kind assistance. For assistance with my grandmother's African safari journal, I am thankful to the staff of the Stanford University Library Special Collections, especially Tim Noakes and Mattie Taormina. For permission to publish selected manuscript pages and for assistance with my grandfather's handwritten first draft of *Green Hills of Africa*, I thank the University of Virginia Library, especially Christina M. Deane and Heather M. Riser of its Digitization Services Department. For research assistance at the Lilly Library of Indiana University in Bloomington, Indiana, I am grateful to the library staff. I would also like to acknowledge the following individuals: Nick Aslin, Joseph and Patricia Czapski, Brian A. Gaisford, Pam Guhrs-Carr, Vic Guhrs, Angela Hemingway, Carol Hemingway, Valerie Hemingway,

Huw Jones, Liisa Kissel, John-Michael Maas, Sandra Spanier, my dear neighbor Kenneth Wallin, my daughter, Anouk Anji Hemingway, and Chloe, too. I am particularly grateful to my wife, Colette C. Hemingway, who remembers listening to mating lions at night on the Maasai Mara, and who did the lioness's share of work for this edition. Hey la Mama!

Notes to the Introduction

1. Patrick Hemingway, "Introduction," in Ernest Hemingway, *Green Hills of Africa* (Norwalk, CT: Easton Press, 1990), 1.
2. On the history of the African safari, see Bartle Bull, *Safari: A Chronicle of Adventure* (New York: Viking Penguin Inc., 1988).
3. Miriam B. Mandel, "Introduction," in M. B. Mandel, ed., *Hemingway and Africa* (Rochester, NY: Camden House, 2011), 15–16. On the costs, see Silvio Calabi, "Ernest Hemingway on Safari: The Game and the Guns," in Mandel, ed., *Hemingway and Africa*, 88–89.
4. See Ernest Hemingway to Jane Mason, letter, August 10, 1933, aboard the *Reina del Pacifico*, Ernest Hemingway Collection, John F. Kennedy Library and Museum, Boston.
5. Michael Reynolds, *Hemingway. An Annotated Chronology* (Detroit: Omnigraphics, Inc., 1991), 73.
6. For reference to the hunting boots and the partridge and boar hunt, see Ernest Hemingway to Pauline Hemingway, letter, ca. October 1933, Ernest Hemingway Collection, John F. Kennedy Library and Museum, Boston.
7. Carlos Baker, *Ernest Hemingway: A Life Story* (New York: Charles Scribner's Sons, 1969), 247.
8. Ernest Hemingway Personal Papers, Ernest Hemingway Collection, John F. Kennedy Library and Museum, Boston.
9. For more about the guns that were used on the safari, see Silvio Calabi, Steve Helsley, and Roger Sanger, *Hemingway's Guns: The Sporting Arms of Ernest Hemingway* (Bangor, ME: Down East Books, 2010).
10. See Carlos Baker, ed., *Ernest Hemingway: Selected Letters 1917–1961* (New York: Charles Scribner's Sons, 1981), 402.
11. Hemingway's Palace Hotel bill, December 9, 1933, Ernest Hemingway Collection, John F. Kennedy Library and Museum, Boston.
12. George Eastman's memoir of his 1926 safari with "Phil" Percival, *Chronicles of an African Trip* (Rochester, NY: John P. Smith and Company, 1927) was printed privately for the author and contains many excellent photographs. Hemingway met Alfred Vanderbilt (1912–1999), who was hunting with Percival's partner, Baron von Blixen, and Vanderbilt joined the Hemingway party for deep-sea fishing off the coast of Mombasa afterward, which Hemingway describes in his third Tanganyika Letter, included in Appendix III of this edition.
13. See Patrick Hemingway, "Introduction," in Chris Johns, *Valley of Life: Africa's Great Rift* (Shrewsbury, England: Swan Hill Press, 1991), 19–31.
14. For the bigger picture, see Elizabeth Kolbert, *The Sixth Extinction: An Unnatural History* (New York: Henry Holt and Company, 2014).
15. Philip H. Percival, *Hunting, Settling and Remembering* (Agoura, CA: Trophy Room Books, 1997), 120.
16. Hemingway wrote Jane Mason on October 16, 1933, from Madrid that he and Charles would hunt for two months while Pauline would join

them for one month (Ernest Hemingway Collection, John F. Kennedy Library and Museum, Boston).

17. In some notes that Hemingway made on his second safari (included in Appendix II of this edition), he remembered that at the height of his dysentery he had as many as 150 bowel movements a day.

18. See Tim Belknap, "Who was Fatty Pearson? A World War II British foot soldier's best friend in the air, and the man who rescued Ernest Hemingway," *Air & Space Magazine* (November 2012).

19. Michael S. Reynolds, *Hemingway: The 1930s* (New York: W. W. Norton & Company, 1997), 161; Ruth A. Hawkins, *Unbelievable Happiness and Final Sorrow: The Hemingway-Pfeiffer Marriage* (Fayetteville: University of Arkansas Press, 2012), 162–64.

20. Pauline Pfeiffer Hemingway to Mrs. Clarence E. Hemingway, letter, January 1934, from Nairobi, Lilly Library collection, Indiana University, Bloomington, IN.

21. His weight had shot up to 207 pounds by October 16, which he told Jane Mason in a letter written from Madrid was because he had switched the Gulf Stream for the café (Ernest Hemingway Collection, John F. Kennedy Library and Museum, Boston).

22. Ernest Hemingway to Maxwell Perkins, letter, January 17, 1933, in Matthew J. Bruccoli, ed., *The Only Thing That Counts: The Ernest Hemingway–Maxwell Perkins Correspondence 1925–1947* (Columbia: University of South Carolina Press, 1996), 206.

23. See Gregory Hemingway's remarks in Christene C. Meyers, "Hemingway's Son remembers Papa," *Billings Gazette*, June 13, 1976.

24. See Brian Herne, *White Hunters: The Golden Age of African Safaris* (New York: Henry Holt & Co., 1999), 204–5.

25. Guy Hickock, "Sitting Down Is the Best Way to Shoot a Lion; Take it From Ernest Hemingway, Who Knows," *Brooklyn Daily Eagle*, April 25, 1934.

26. Baker, *Ernest Hemingway: A Life Story*, 259. Ernest Hemingway to Maxwell Perkins, letter, April 30, 1934, in Bruccoli, *The Only Thing That Counts*, 210.

27. See Ernest Hemingway to Waldo Peirce, letter, May 1934. Hemingway states he has 100 pages done in a letter to Mr. and Mrs. George Grant Mason, Jr. written on June 10, 1934. For the reference to 137 pages completed, see Ernest Hemingway to Pauline Pfeiffer Hemingway, letter, June 19, 1934, Ernest Hemingway Collection, John F. Kennedy Library and Museum, Boston.

28. Ernest Hemingway to mother of Pauline Pfeiffer Hemingway, letter, August 14, 1934, Ernest Hemingway Collection, John F. Kennedy Library and Museum, Boston.

29. Hans Koritschoner (1888–1962) was from a musical family of Jewish heritage in Vienna. He came to East African just before World War I to fight with the German army under Paul Emil von Lettöw-Vorbeck, was wounded, and spent time in a prisoner-of-war camp in Palestine. He returned to East Africa after the war to work as a sisal farmer in Tanganyika. Koritschoner wrote to Ernest Hemingway on December 22, 1938, and told Hemingway of his new career as an anthropologist, which began soon after their chance encounter in 1934. The letter is preserved in the Ernest Hemingway Collection in the John F. Kennedy Library and Museum, Boston. After World War II, Koritschoner remained in Tanganyika but changed his name to Hans Cory. His papers are in the collec-

tion of the University College Library in Dar es Salaam. See Norman N. Miller, "Tanzania: Documentation in Political Anthropology—The Hans Cory Collection," *African Studies Bulletin* 11, no. 2 (1968), 195–213.

30. Hans Koritschoner mentions the significance of his tribal art collection in his letter to Ernest Hemingway of December 22, 1938, in the Ernest Hemingway Collection at the John F. Kennedy Library and Museum, Boston.

31. See Hans Koritschoner to Ernest Hemingway, letter, December 22, 1938, Ernest Hemingway Collection, John F. Kennedy Library and Museum, Boston. See also Hans Cory (Koritschoner), *Our Family Chronicles*, chapter 22, 1956, available at http://wwii-server.history .fsu.edu/scripts/as_web6.exe?Command=Bookmark&File=Hine-Letters .ask&Name=5546%20%20%20%20%20.

32. Remarkably, Hemingway gave the first draft manuscript of *Green Hills of Africa* to Jane Armstrong as compensation for her services. Her daughter later sold it to the University of Virginia Library, along with a copy of Armstrong's typescript and a letter of authentication written by Ernest Hemingway, in late June 1947. The first brief but thoughtful study of the holograph manuscript is Barbara Lounsberry, "The Holograph Manuscript of *Green Hills of Africa*," *The Hemingway Review* 12, no. 2 (1993), 36–45. Aside from the first draft, most of the existing manuscripts of *Green Hills of Africa* are preserved in the Hemingway Collection of the John F. Kennedy Library and Museum, Boston. Part of the setting copy (pages 180–224), with Hemingway's handwritten edits, is preserved in the Ernest Hemingway Collection of the Special Collections Archives at the University of Maryland.

33. Maxwell Perkins to Ernest Hemingway, letter, November 28, 1934, in Bruccoli, *The Only Thing That Counts*, 217.

34. See Maxwell Perkins to Ernest Hemingway, letter, August 30, 1935, in Bruccoli, *The Only Thing That Counts*, 224–25. On the serialization in *Scribner's Magazine*, see Robert W. Trogdon, *The Lousy Racket: Hemingway, Scribners, and the Business of Literature* (Kent, OH: Kent State University Press, 2007), 147–54.

35. Ernest Hemingway remarked on the perils of illustrating novels in an introduction to the illustrated edition of *A Farewell to Arms*, published in 1948. See Ernest Hemingway, *A Farewell to Arms: The Hemingway Library Edition* (New York: Scribner, 2012), viii.

36. Ernest Hemingway to Maxwell Perkins, letter, November 20, 1934, in Bruccoli, *The Only Thing That Counts*, 216.

37. For a representative selection of reviews of the book when it was first published in America and England, see Robert W. Trogdon, ed., *Ernest Hemingway: A Literary Reference* (New York: Carroll & Graf, 1999), 179–83. See also Robert W. Trogdon, " 'Forms of Combat': Hemingway, the Critics, and *Green Hills of Africa*," *The Hemingway Review* 15, no. 2 (1996), 1–14.

38. On the book's initial sales, see Trogdon, *The Lousy Racket*, 164–66.

39. A monographic study devoted to *Green Hills of Africa* was published in 1990. See Axel Carl Bredahl and Susan Lynn Drake, *Hemingway's "Green Hills of Africa" as Evolutionary Narrative: Helix and Scimitar* (Lewiston, NY: Edwin Mellen Press, 1990). A multiauthor volume on Hemingway and Africa also appeared in 2011; see Mandel, ed., *Hemingway and Africa*. Also of interest is Christopher Ondaatje, *Hemingway in Africa: The Last Safari* (Toronto: Harper Collins, 2003).

Ernest Hemingway was born in Oak Park, Illinois, in 1899, and began his writing career with *The Kansas City Star* in 1917. During the First World War he volunteered as an ambulance driver on the Italian front but was invalided home, having been seriously wounded while serving with the Red Cross. In 1921 Hemingway settled in Paris, where he became part of the expatriate circle of Gertrude Stein, F. Scott Fitzgerald, Ezra Pound, and Ford Madox Ford. His first book, *Three Stories and Ten Poems,* was published in Paris in 1923 and was followed by the short story collection *In Our Time,* which marked his American debut in 1925. With the appearance of *The Sun Also Rises* in 1926, Hemingway became not only the voice of the "lost generation" but the preeminent writer of his time. This was followed by *Men Without Women* in 1927, when Hemingway returned to the United States, and his novel of the Italian front, *A Farewell to Arms* (1929). In the 1930s, Hemingway settled in Key West, and later in Cuba, but he traveled widely— to Spain, Italy, and Africa—and wrote about his experiences in *Death in the Afternoon* (1932), his classic treatise on bullfighting, and *Green Hills of Africa* (1935), an account of big-game hunting in Africa. Later he reported on the Spanish Civil War, which became the background for his brilliant war novel, *For Whom the Bell Tolls* (1940), hunted U-boats in the Caribbean, and covered the European front during the Second World War. Hemingway's most popular work, *The Old Man and the Sea* (1952), was awarded the Pulitzer Prize in 1953, and in 1954 Hemingway won the Nobel Prize in Literature "for his powerful, style-forming mastery of the art of narration." One of the most important influences on the development of the short story and novel in American fiction, Hemingway has seized the imagination of the American public like no other twentieth-century author. He died in Ketchum, Idaho, in 1961. His other works include *The Torrents of Spring* (1926), *Winner Take Nothing* (1933), *To Have and Have Not* (1937), *The Fifth Column and the First Forty-nine Stories* (1938), *Across the River and into the Trees* (1950), and posthumously, *A Moveable Feast* (1964), *Islands in the Stream* (1970), *The Dangerous Summer* (1985), and *The Garden of Eden* (1986), and *True at First Light* (1999).

and back one word.

"Mama!" Woll shouted. Then anot[her]
[s]ay stream. Then "Mama! Mama!"

Through the dark came all the por[ters?]
[th]e cook, the skinner, the boys and the head[man?]
[Ki]mba. "Mama!" Ncola shouted. "Mama p[i?]

The boys came dancing, crawling an[d]
eating time and chanting something from down in the
libe "Hey la Mama! Hey la Mama! H[ey]
[Mam]a!"

The rolling eyed skinner pulled Poll[y] up[?]
back the others, the big cook and, all t[he]
[oth]ers pressing to touch some part to c[ut?]
if not to left to touch and held
[th]ey danced and sang through the da[rk]
[a]round the fire and to